THE SELECTED ESSAYS OF
T. Harry Williams

THE SELECTED ESSAYS OF

T. Harry Williams

WITH A BIOGRAPHICAL INTRODUCTION BY ESTELLE WILLIAMS

Louisiana State University Press

BATON ROUGE AND LONDON

Copyright © 1983 by Louisiana State University Press
All rights reserved
Manufactured in the United States of America
DESIGNER: Joanna Hill
TYPEFACE: Linotron Trump Medieval
TYPESETTER: G & S Typesetters, Inc.
PRINTER: Thomson-Shore
BINDER: John Dekker & Sons

Library of Congress Cataloging in Publication Data

Williams, T. Harry (Thomas Harry), 1909–
  The selected essays of T. Harry Williams.
    1. United States—History—Civil War, 1861–
1865—Addresses, essays, lectures.   2. Reconstruction—Addresses, essays, lectures.   3. United
States—History, Military—20th century—Addresses,
essays, lectures.   4. Southern States—History—
1865– —Biography—Addresses, essays, lectures.
5. Southern States—Biography—Addresses, essays,
lectures.   6. Williams, T. Harry (Thomas Harry),
1909– . I. Title.
E650.W53   1983   973.7   82-18646
ISBN 0-8071-1095-7

Contents

THE SELECTED ESSAYS OF
T. Harry Williams

A Biographical Introduction by Estelle Williams

T. Harry Williams came to the South from the Midwest. He brought
with him an impressive degree of integrity, intellect, courage, determination, and talent. He even brought a tolerable (human) degree of
selfishness. But most important, with him this young man who
came south brought along a vision: he wanted to teach, and he
wanted to write books. Over a long and distinguished career he
achieved both of those goals.

Born May 19, 1909, in Vinegar Hill, Illinois, Harry always said
that his birthplace was "an axe handle and a twist of tobacco" from
Galena, the home of Ulysses S. Grant. His mother died before he
was two years old from what was then diagnosed as consumption.
His father moved to Hazel Green, Wisconsin, where he left the rear-
ing of his son to his parents. Harry's grandfather, fearing the child
might have contracted the disease that killed his mother, slept with
him on a screened porch for several years whenever the weather permitted. He took a great interest in the child, who learned to read
long before he started to school and had read every book in the local
library by the time he was fourteen.

In his youth Harry had both religious and irreligious influences.
His grandmother insisted that he attend Bible instruction. The Bible
instructor, though, was often horrified by his young student's challenges, especially after Harry had read Ingersoll's lectures. Harry's
father, a well-read sheep farmer who enjoyed reading aloud from By-

ron and Burns, was a rather outspoken atheist. In Hazel Green "a literally classless, unbigoted environment," there was little else for a
boy to do but read and people-watch. Besides his father and grandmother there were many fascinating characters to watch and learn
from. Harry had a wealth of stories to tell about them; his first published story, "Old 666," was about one of Hazel Green's most ardent
anti-Catholics.

After high school graduation in 1927, Harry enrolled in Platteville
State Teachers College and received his degree four years later. Finding himself unable to secure a teaching position, he entered graduate
school at the University of Wisconsin, where he received a master's
degree two years later. Again unable to find a position he returned to
graduate school, this time to pursue a Ph.D., specializing in his
newly discovered interest—the Civil War. He had come by this new
interest quite by accident. When Harry left Platteville, one of his
instructors advised him to try to get Professor Carl Russell Fish as
his major professor. Professor Fish's field was the Civil War. When
Fish died, Harry fell under the tutelage of W. B. Hesseltine, who
was Fish's replacement. Hesseltine was only a few years older than
Harry, and they immediately formed a close friendship that lasted
the rest of their lives.

In the fall of 1936, Harry began teaching history in the Extension
Department of the University of Wisconsin. He traveled each week
to two or three towns in northern Wisconsin. After two years in that
position, Harry went to the University of Omaha for three years. In
1941 he came to Louisiana State University. There he remained until his retirement in May, 1979.

He did not hesitate to come to Louisiana State University. The sal-
ary of $2,900 a year was more than he had been making at the Uni-
versity of Omaha. LSU was in its heyday—not just on the football
field, but also in scholastic achievements. The university boasted
not only of the LSU Press, whose Southern Biography Series Harry
would ultimately serve as editor, but also of the *Southern Review*,
which was fast building a national reputation. Some of the colleges
of the university had nationally known scholars, and T. Harry Williams aimed one day to join their ranks.

When the money for the *Southern Review* was cut off and a fear of censorship developed at LSU, many of the young scholars left. Some left the South entirely. But Harry stayed on. At national conventions during this period he was often asked: "Why do you stay in the South?" His answer was always that he liked the South. He wanted to be a part of the South. He became a part of it, even at times speaking for the South; and the South, particularly Louisiana, rewarded him. Toward the end of his life he knew he had not made a mistake by staying.

Although he loved the South, Harry could see its shortcomings. He had the advantage of an outsider's view of the region. But because he lived in the state through its transition from the Old South to the New South, he could look with pride and admiration upon the progress made by his adopted region, particularly on the racial question. Harry didn't believe in segregation, of course; yet he had some understanding for the fact that native Louisianians were accustomed to it—saw it as part of their heritage. "I could understand their viewpoint," he said, "without agreeing with it. What did bother me though was the shutting off of discussion of the question." He felt that no problem, no question, should be taboo for open and frank discussion. When he first came to Louisiana, he found most southerners willing to discuss the racial issue in private though not in public. But all that changed as the New South gradually joined the mainstream of American life.

Even though the South needed to adapt in many ways to the rest of the country, Harry did not want to see the United States homogenized. He thought regional differences were good. He wanted some of the southern characteristics preserved—its "sense of manners, its civility." He wanted the South to keep those mystical qualities that had always puzzled historians, economists, poets—the qualities that had lured the young midwesterner to seek fulfillment of his vision in its midst.

He had wanted to teach and he wanted to write books. Having adopted the South, Louisiana, as his home, he proceeded to do both. And he did both exceedingly well. Because he believed that a knowledge of history was vital to one's humanity, Harry was always interested in and excited about his subjects. As one colleague described him: "With an encyclopedic command of the facts, an unexcelled vividness of expression, and an almost matchless sense of both pathos and humor, he made his courses into high theater. He was the chorus evoking the mood, introducing and describing the characters, and interpreting the action."

A dynamic and vivid classroom lecturer, he was popular with all the students and loved by many of them. Although he lectured in a large auditorium, he did not use a microphone. He did not want his movements hampered. He was rarely still when he lectured, his arms thrashing the air back and forth, his forefinger and thumb joined together as he drew a point to focus. Then too he did not want to become entangled in wires when he rowed across the platform to impress on the student Washington's crossing the Delaware, or when he fought a duel taking the part of either Andrew Jackson or his victim, or when he struck his famous September-morn pose with his arms crossed to cup his bosom and one leg slightly raised over the other. Harry believed in visual aids—an authentic Springfield rifle, a Civil War side piece, a chamber pot with Ben Butler's picture in the bottom, which he artfully produced from a brown paper bag as he explained the reaction of the women of New Orleans to one of Butler's orders.

Soon after Harry came to LSU some of the students in one of his classes presented him with a heavy woolen, dark blue jacket that had belonged to a Union cavalryman. He was asked—since he was a Yankee—to put it on, which he did that one time, thus starting the myth that he taught his classes wearing a Yankee uniform or a Confederate uniform and using Grant's memoirs as a textbook. But as he fell more and more into the role of a southerner and to prove he was bipartisan he often wore a Rebel tie to class.

These were light touches—moments of relief from the serious lecture, thoughtfully prepared and up-to-date on the most recent of his own and his fellow historians' research. He believed in bringing history to life, presenting it to the student through the men who made or represented the period of history under study. This was what he called personalizing history. His classroom performance easily proved that scholarship and dullness are not necessarily synonymous.

Harry's presentations were powerful. He was once said to be more eloquent than a Baptist preacher. Students often left the classroom in tears after his moving lecture on the surrender at Appomattox. "A good teacher," he once said, "has to know his subject matter. But he also should think, and have some ideas about the subject, so his teaching will not be a mere rendering of facts. You have to develop a skill in presentation, and you have to be enthusiastic about what you are doing. If you are not excited, it's pretty hard for students to be excited. I try to put across the human interest, because you have to realize that history deals with people—human beings."

For the final course of his teaching career at LSU he announced that enrollment in his Civil War course would be unlimited. "It will be the class I favor the most," he said. "I've been teaching here since 1941 and have taught many thousands of students. I've taught parents and I've taught their children. But I haven't taught their grandchildren yet. I guess it's time to quit before I do."

The grandchildren were not there, but they will not be denied. LSU videotaped Harry's last semester lectures, and in the words of Mary Champagne, a local reporter and former student, "On video tape at the library General U. S. Grant, William Tecumseh Sherman, and John A. McCernand will again besiege and take Vicksburg. General Robert E. Lee will continue to outfox for a time the Federals in Virginia. The South will again invade Gettysburg." He taught his last class on December 5, 1979. In an auditorium filled to capacity—students, faculty members, visitors—this great, much-loved teacher, after describing the last incident of the war he had spent most of his life studying, said in the hush that was audible: "That's it. Thank you very much."

Harry's excellence in teaching carried over to the other half of his vision, his research and writing. He never chose a subject to work on just out of the blue. If he became interested in a topic or a man, he began his search for material. He was a thorough researcher and only when all major sources had been exhausted did he begin to write. He was, in his own words, a "narrative historian." He wrote as he lectured, for the general reader and listener. In explaining his approach to writing, he once remarked, "Instead of saying the United States acted unilaterally, I write that the U.S. decided to go it alone. It all means the same thing."

Success in his writing career came early. His first book, *Lincoln and the Radicals*, was published by the University of Wisconsin Press in 1941. It was chosen by Lincoln scholar Paul Angle as one of the fifty-eight best works on the Civil War president from a complete Lincoln shelf of 2,300 volumes. It remains in print and still sells steadily.

Because of his training under Professors Fish and Hesseltine, by the time he came to LSU Harry had determined that his field of research would be the Lincoln era. Although he had a great admiration for Ulysses S. Grant and longed one day to write a book about him, Harry felt that his next book should be a biography of a Confederate general. Upon discovering a wealth of material in the LSU library on General P. G. T. Beauregard, he made the obvious choice—to write about that "glamorous, colorful" Creole. Just as the research on Beauregard was completed, Harry was asked by an editor at Alfred A. Knopf's to write a book on Lincoln and his generals.

The Beauregard research was put aside as Harry signed a contract with Knopf in February of 1948 to write the Lincoln book. After completing his research, he began writing in the summer of 1950. Since there was no air conditioning in his home, he wrote on a card table out under the trees. He completed the manuscript and submitted it to Knopf in May of 1951. The manuscript moved quickly through the publication process, and on November 14, 1951, Alfred Knopf informed Harry that the book had been selected by the Book of the Month Club.

The first news releases saw nothing strange about a history professor who could write a book. What was strange was that a history professor could write a book that more than 160,000 people would buy during its first year—a history professor who was a Yankee, who lived in the South, loved the region, and expected to stay there. The book appeared officially on February 25—a few days earlier in Louisiana. On February 23 Harry's picture was on the cover of *Saturday Review*; on February 24 he made the front page of the *New York Times Book Review*. He thought he was "probably the happiest author in the country." In the weeks that followed, *Lincoln and His Generals* was favorably reviewed by most of the major newspapers in the country.

When the excitement of *Lincoln and His Generals* began to die down, Harry again set up the card table and took out his research notes—this time in his new air-conditioned house. It was time to get back to General Beauregard—the summer of 1953. He had written only the first page sometime during the summer of 1952. But that first page had captured the secret of that picturesque personality as he moved upon the great stage where he was to act out his life—with all the drama of the dashing Confederate general at Charleston, First Manassas, Shiloh; of the successful New Orleans businessman; and of the champion of the Louisiana Lottery. *P. G. T. Beauregard* was published in 1955. It too was widely reviewed, but there was no mention this time of the "Yankee" author. In the local newspapers the spotlight now focused on "one of the city's own."

By the summer of 1955 it had become evident that the card table and the dining-room table and Harry's small office at LSU were not going to be adequate for a prolific researcher and writer. He would have to have a better place to work, a more convenient place, a place with atmosphere.

In the late forties Harry had bought a small house located on two and a half acres. When a larger house was built this small house was connected to one side of the carport, but left unused. The time had now come to put it to use. The walls in its main room were lined with bookshelves, the floor carpeted, an overhead florescent light installed. Harry's books were moved from his office on the campus. All of the necessary equipment for a working library was bought: an unabridged dictionary and stand, file cabinets, a six-foot door set up on legs to serve as a desk. What had been the kitchen became the typist's room, equipped with an electric typewriter and a sturdy desk. As the need arose for more book space, shelves were built in two other small rooms, even in the bathroom.

Harry's "free-standing" house had come into being. It was alternately called his "library," his "studio," and even "Harry's little out-house." By whatever name, Harry loved it and spent almost all his time there. It was a great place to work, or to hide, or to read without being disturbed. The books then flowed in rapid succession. *With Beauregard in Mexico—Reminiscences of P. G. T. Beauregard* (1956), *Abraham Lincoln: Selected Speeches, Messages, and Letters* (1957), *A History of the United States* with R. N. Current and Frank

Freidel (1959), *Americans at War* (1960), *Romance and Realism in Southern Politics* (1961), *Military Memoirs of a Confederate by E. Porter Alexander* (1962), *McClellan, Sherman and Grant* (1962), *The Union Sundered* (1963), *The Union Restored* (1963), *Hayes: The Diary of a President* (1964), *Hayes of the Twenty-third* (1965), and *Huey Long* (1969).

Harry's principal books illustrate his philosophy of biography and history, which he defined as a modified version of the "great man" theory: "I believe that some men, men of power, can influence the course of history. They appear in response to conditions; many give a new direction to history. In the process, they may do great good or evil or both, but whatever the case they leave a different kind of world behind." This was the kind of man Harry liked to write about—the great leader who moves in a dynamic way. He thought that the biographer, though drawn to the man whose life he recorded in minute detail, must be objective, must not sit in judgment. His job was to record why his subject did what he did and how he saw the world around him. These were the compelling issues.

And this was the philosophy he followed when he wrote his biography of Huey Long. He was certainly drawn to Huey. He had first become interested in him while a student at the University of Wisconsin in the early 1930s. Harry and his fellow graduate students would gather in the Wisconsin Union building and listen when Huey made his famous national broadcasts. "He seized our imagination. . . . We were excited by him. . . . He seemed to hold out hope." Among the speeches Harry remembered best was the one Huey gave at the Democratic national convention in 1932, "the most remarkable performance I had ever heard."

When he started the research for the Long book, Harry used all of the conventional methods, but to these he added the then new technique of oral history. He found most valuable the information he got from the interviews he conducted with people who had known Huey Long: members of his family, politicians who held high places in his organization, politicians who opposed him, and businessmen, educators, musicians, football coaches and players, other individuals, many of them obscure but all having something significant to contribute to the Long story. He interviewed a total of 295 individuals.

By the summer of 1964 Harry had acquired a summer retreat in Wisconsin, and there in the quiet of a redwood cottage, perched on a rock near a small lake, he began to write. Using the wealth of material from newspapers, handbills, pamphlets, books, thousands of Long letters, stacks of official documents, and transcripts of his own interviews, Harry began his picture of the Kingfish.

The completed manuscript was turned over to his editor at Knopf's in September, 1968. Since there would be nothing else to do on this manuscript until the galleys came from the publisher, Harry turned to his next project—a history of U.S. wars. Through the years, as his interest in military history was developing, he had done research on this project. It is hard to say just when he started to write, but he certainly spent the latter part of 1968 and early 1969 getting ready. When all of the proofreading and indexing for the Long book was completed in June, 1969, he was into the first chapter of this latest project.

But that project was put aside in September of 1969, when the *Huey Long* books arrived in the bookstores in Louisiana. For the next several months Harry traveled around the state and made a few trips to other states attending autographing parties. Each day's mail brought stacks of reviews from various newspapers over the country. The New York *Times* sent a reporter to Baton Rouge to interview the author. He wrote a delightful article entitled "T. Harry Williams, at Home Down South." Harry had been on the first page of the *New York Times Book Review* when *Lincoln and His Generals* was published; now he had the first three pages—Tom Wicker's review of the book on the first and third pages and Walter Clemons' story on the second. Then came the reviews from the journals, in which Harry's colleagues gave their opinion of the book and of oral history as a research technique.

The excitement began to die down, but flared up again on February 13, 1970. Harry's book had been nominated for the National Book Award. On March 2, the winner was announced: *Huey Long*. A call came from New York: Could Professor Williams appear in person to receive the prize at the annual banquet? No. He had just left the hospital. He had another two weeks in bed—recuperating from pneumonia.

That disappointment was soon forgotten, though. On May 4 in the late afternoon, Harry learned that *Huey Long* had won the Pulitzer Prize. He had waited all day hoping for that news, but at three o'clock—four o'clock New York time—when he had heard nothing, he went to keep an appointment with his doctor. By five o'clock when he left the doctor's office, everybody in Louisiana—even one of his granddaughters who was sunbathing in Plain Dealing, Louisiana—knew he had won the coveted award. He learned of it only when he stopped by his office on his way home. He immediately phoned the drugstore where I had gone to pick up a prescription. He was so excited he just said: "Tell her I got it. She'll know what it means." Harry was tremendously gratified by the award and by the praise and prestige that followed it. Years later, when asked what the award had meant to him, he replied: "The Pulitzer Prize—it's a kind of magical thing."

When all of this excitement died down, Harry returned to writing his war book. But he rarely had only one project going at a time. He was always doing research on one subject while he was writing on another. He had become interested in Lyndon Baines Johnson. When he was president of the Organization of American Historians in 1972–73 his April 12, 1973, presidential address was entitled "Huey, Lyndon, and Southern Radicalism." In this he said: "It is not possible as yet to arrive at a measured evaluation of Johnson. But surely it is time to take a new look at him, to attempt to see him as he really was, this tormented man from his tormented region who had such large visions of what his country might become. Until the evaluation is made, we can accept one that he himself made in a subdued moment. He said that he was not sure what the historians would say about the achievement of his administration. 'But I do believe—in fact, I know—that they will all say we tried.'" What the historians would say! By the time this address was delivered, historian Williams knew what his next project would be. He had done some research on Johnson but had touched only the surface: now he would take Johnson's full measure. At the time of his death neither of these last two projects was completed. He was writing the chapters on World War II and had brought the Johnson research into the presidential years.

On April 27 and 28, 1979, the History Department of Louisiana State University celebrated Harry's retirement. The event was marked by a banquet attended by hundreds; a symposium of four noted speakers: Frank E. Vandiver, Don E. Fehrenbacher, Senator Russell B. Long, and Harry McPherson; the creation of a T. Harry Williams Scholarship Fund, begun by Harry's graduate students but added to by his many friends and admirers; and the establishment of a T. Harry Williams Chair in American History, which according to Chancellor Paul Murrill "would recognize the intellectual leadership, prestige, and honor which Williams has brought to the campus."

On April 29, 1979, Harry entered the hospital, suffering from a severe respiratory infection. He died on July 6. The midwesterner who had come south with a vision of becoming a teacher and a writer left behind him a legacy that will not be lost. Those who seek to understand the Civil War, the South, and southern leaders will always be intellectual heirs to his sparking tradition of scholarship and writings. Through his scholarship, his teaching, his literary accomplishments, the force of his mind and spirit, Harry left behind a measure of the same greatness that so appealed to him in his work. He was a rare and exciting human being, a dear man, a true gentleman—one might even say, southern gentleman—as well as a fine historian. He had realized his dream, and students of the South will for many generations remain the beneficiaries of that realization.

PART I

Civil War and Reconstruction

The Committee on the Conduct of the War: An Experiment in Civilian Control

Senator James W. Grimes of Iowa arrived in Washington, November 5, 1861, for the second session of the thirty-seventh Congress, wearied with the long journey and convinced by conferences with other leaders of the "Radical Republican" faction that the administration of Abraham Lincoln was fast carrying the country and the party to destruction. "If the other Northwestern members feel as I do," he wrote his wife, "there will be something more during the coming session than growling and showing our teeth. And from what I hear, they do feel excited and incensed."[1]

The irate Iowa Senator expressed the disturbed feelings of the "Radical Republican" group. This segment of the party was more fiercely opposed to slavery than the other factions of the Republican coalition, and its chieftains saw in the outbreak of war a golden opportunity to destroy the institution. They proposed to accomplish this destruction by any method that promised success; but if a majority in Congress could be commanded, they preferred a drastic confiscation act. While laboring to achieve this necessary control of Congress, the Radicals supported a piecemeal system of emancipa-

From the Bobbs-Merrill Reprint Series in History. Originally in *Journal of the American Military Institute*, now *Military Affairs*, III, No. 3 (Fall, 1939), 139–56, and reprinted herein with permission. Copyright 1939 by the American Military Institute. No additional copies may be made without the express permission of the editor of *Military Affairs*.

tion to be effected by proclamations of freedom issued by generals in command of departments. Finally they hoped to force the President to issue a general edict freeing all slaves in the border states. Almost immediately the forces of Radicalism came into conflict with Lincoln, who was striving to hold together a coalition on the sole issue of preservation of the Union. The President stubbornly ignored the angry exhortations of the Radicals to formulate a policy which would guide the army in its treatment of fugitive slaves.[2] Early in December he aroused a storm of Radical denunciation by deleting from Secretary of War Simon Cameron's report a section that recommended the arming of slaves.[3] His message to Congress deprecated hasty, radical action and almost ignored the subject of emancipation.[4] Equally exasperating to the Radical cabal was Lincoln's administration of the army. The important commands, the major and brigadier generalships, were overwhelmingly held by known opponents of the anti-slavery movement. Generals George B. McClellan, Henry W. Halleck, Don Carlos Buell, and many others had expressed dissent with the aims of abolitionism. Such officers, complained the Radicals, would never use the army as an instrument to effect the freedom of the slaves.[5] The Radicals assailed them because they usually assisted slaveholders to recover fugitives who had escaped into the Union lines.[6] Lincoln had given only one important appointment to an officer with Radical antecedents: General John C. Frémont, erstwhile commander of the department of the West. But he overruled Frémont when the latter proclaimed the slaves in his department free, and later removed the general in what seemed to the Radicals an act of supreme injustice.[7] The Radicals believed that McClellan and his coterie of subordinates were in sympathy with the slaveholding South and hopeful that a compromise would make a resort to battle unnecessary. Thus they explained the inactivity of the Union armies. Visions of McClellan in the rôle of Cromwell, purging Congress of Republican members and restoring the Union at the point of the bayonet, haunted the Radical mind.[8] During the summer and autumn months of 1861 the Radical faction had relied on the inadequate weapon of public protest in its battle to force the administration into an anti-slavery position. But as the politicians gathered in Washington for the opening of Congress, the leaders were convinced that mere "growling and showing of teeth" must be abandoned. They sought to establish some Congressional agency which could delve into the recesses of army secrets and guide the party in the formulation of a war policy.

The obvious device was an investigative committee "to probe the sore spots to the bottom."[9] On December 5, Senator Zachariah Chandler, one of the leaders of western radicalism, moved the creation of a committee to determine the causes of the Union disasters at Bull Run and Ball's Bluff.[10] Immediately several Senators offered amendments to include other defeats. James H. Lane and Grimes wanted an investigation of Wilson's Creek to determine whether Frémont or the administration was responsible for the failure to reinforce Nathaniel Lyon at that battle. Grimes suggested a joint committee of both houses to inquire into the causes of all Union disasters yet sustained.[11] The discussion continued next day with Grimes defending his proposition that the proposed committee be general in scope rather than restricted to specific battles. William P. Fessenden saw an even more important function for it to fulfil, "to keep an anxious, watchful eye over all the executive agents who are carrying on the war at the direction of the people. . . . We are not under the command of the military of this country. They are under ours as a Congress." It would be futile, asserted John Sherman, to create an agency merely to investigate lost battles; let the committee probe into the "general conduct of the war," past, present, and future. Grimes altered his amendment to fit this proposal, and as finally passed it established a committee "to inquire into the conduct of the present war," with "power to send for persons and papers." Senator Henry Wilson was eminently satisfied with this change from the original resolution. He predicted the importance of the newly-born agency would derive not from its revelations of past mistakes but from its influence upon the future determination of war policies. "We should teach men in civil and military authority that the people expect that they will not make mistakes, and we shall not be easy with their errors."[12]

The personnel of the Committee on the Conduct of the War, named by the Vice-president and the Speaker after conferences with the Radical leaders,[13] was preponderantly Radical. Senators Benjamin F. Wade, the chairman, and Chandler were leaders of the faction in the Senate. Three of the House members, George W. Julian of Indiana, John Covode of Pennsylvania, and Daniel Gooch of Massachusetts, belonged to the same faith. The Democratic Senate member was Andrew Johnson, perhaps the leading war Democrat in the country. Moses F. Odell of New York, the Democratic representative from the House, was also a zealous supporter of the war and an enemy of the peace Democracy. Wade, Chandler, Julian, Gooch, and Odell remained on the Committee for the full period of its three and one-half years' existence. Johnson, who took a prominent part in the work of the Committee, resigned early in 1862 to become military governor of Tennessee, and his three Democratic successors rarely attended a Committee meeting. Covode left Congress in 1864, and Benjamin F. Loan, a Missouri Radical, took his place on the Committee.[14]

When the Committee held its first meeting on December 20, an important experiment in the relations between the legislature and the executive, the civil and military authorities of a democracy at war, began. The guiding spirits of the Committee intended that it should be more than a mere fact-finding body. Chairman Wade envisioned it as a Congressional agency whose function was to insure the legislative branch of the government a voice in the conduct of the war and the determination of war policies. "We have gone forth in the spirit of the resolution that created us a committee," he said later, "to inquire into the manner in which this war has been conducted; to ascertain . . . wherein there was anything in which we could aid the administration in the prosecution of this war, and wherever there was a delinquency that we might ferret it out, apprise the administration of it, and demand a remedy."[15] Congress, he asserted, expected the Committee to obtain such facts as would be useful in determining the causes of military failure, "in order to apply any remedy that may be necessary."[16] This concept of its functions drew the Committee into frequent intercourse with the President and his administrative officers. As the inquisitors ascertained "the existence of malpractices, short-comings, and things inconsistent with the proper and beneficial conduct of the war," they sought interviews with Lincoln, the Secretary of War, and the Cabinet, disclosed their testimony, and "endeavored to work out a redress."[17] In the first days of the Committee's existence, this contact with the executive was fairly harmonious. But when Lincoln persisted in retaining McClellan in command over the protests of Wade and Chandler, the situation became more strained. By the summer of 1862 cordial cooperation had virtually ceased.[18]

With one member of the Cabinet, however, the Committee maintained continuous, confidential relations. This man was Edwin M. Stanton, who became Secretary of War in the first month of 1862 with the enthusiastic blessing and support of all the Radical leaders.[19] On the day that Stanton took office, the Committee tendered its services, "either individually or as a body." During the next few days the members and the new Secretary worked over the testimony which the Committee had gathered.[20] These cordial relations continued through the remainder of the war. Each member possessed a card admitting him to Stanton's office "at all times," and Wade and Chandler appeared there every morning. After taking important testimony, the Committee frequently adjourned to the White House, sent for Stanton, and read the evidence to him and the President. The Secretary and Wade would then unite in urging a particular recommendation upon Lincoln.[21] The Committee Radicals and Stanton were as one on the subject of emancipation, and the Secretary, with his knowledge of Cabinet decisions and his far-flung powers over the army, was an invaluable ally.

Although not a single member possessed either military experience or education, the Committee did not consider that this should preclude it from investigating army affairs or rendering judgments on the capabilities of military men.[22] Wade and Chandler, in common with many civilians of the 'sixties, felt a profound contempt for any claims that military science was a specialized, technical subject, mysterious to anyone not educated at West Point.[23] The former asserted that the average American could easily make himself a master of military science in a short time.[24] Convinced that their opinions on military questions deserved as much consideration as those of any general, the members never hesitated to overrule the military men.[25] This was especially true when the Committee attempted to impose its concepts of correct military strategy upon the generals and the administration. The leading members had very positive ideas regarding the conduct of operations and continually urged the adoption of their plans upon the commanding officers. They believed that wars were won by fighting; their idea of action was perpetual attack. "In military movements delay is generally bad—indecision is almost always fatal," was the Committee's maxim.[26] If the enemy would not give battle on disadvantageous ground, Wade told Mc-Clellan, "push on the expedition until he would fight."[27] The Committee continually censured officers for taking precautionary measures to insure a safe retreat. The members feared that this indicated a lack of resolve to win battles and would result in hesitant, unsuccessful movements.[28]

The majority of the witnesses who testified before the Committee were necessarily officers of the army. The Committee realized that such men, engaged in active operations afield, could not hurry to Washington on receiving a summons. Consequently they permitted the men to fix their own time of attendance.[29] Many of these witnesses, products of West Point and the regular army, viewed the Committee as a meddlesome civilian agency and objected to supplying it with information of a purely military nature. This was most marked when the Committee sought to induce generals to disclose their future plans, to lift the veil of military secrecy.[30] When the investigators failed to get this information from the commanding generals, they endeavored to secure it from subordinate officers. The army, insisted Wade, had no right to withhold secrets from Congress.[31] The military recoiled from such questions. Not only did the soldier deem it dangerous to reveal proposed movements to a wide number of persons, but his training inhibited him from discussing the plans of his superior with a civilian body. Generals Fitz-John Porter and Charles Stone refused to do so on the ground that they would be violating army regulations.[32] The Committee met the same reaction when it asked military witnesses to discuss and criticize the actions and decisions of other officers. Since the members were determined to probe the secrets of army administration, it seemed perfectly natural to them that they should collect the opinions of all army witnesses, regardless of rank. Consequently they encouraged subordinates to speak freely of the actions of their superiors, to give opinions about battles they had not seen, and to say what they would have done had they been present on a certain field.[33] For a subordinate to criticize his superior was heresy to the military creed and dangerous for the subordinate; hence many refused to answer. Such actions always disgusted the civilians of the Committee who could not see that an "independent opinion" was destructive of military discipline.[34]

The officers who refused to furnish the Committee with the desired testimony were younger men closely associated with General McClellan. They owed their high place in the army to McClellan, opposed emancipation as a war policy, and heartily disliked the Committee. Other regular army officers—Keys, Heintzelman, Hooker, Barnard—leaned toward the Committee in politics and believed resentfully that McClellan and his conservative successors had purposely slighted them in the matter of promotions. This faction maintained close relations with the Committee, furnished opinions freely in testimony and private letters, and were highly critical of their superiors.[35] Officers who had entered the army from civilian life, such as Butler, Wallace, and Frémont, found that their philosophy coincided perfectly with that of the Committee; these men readily supplied any testimony the inquisitors wanted.[36] Because of its power over promotions, shrewd witnesses, whatever their background, gave the Committee the evidence it was after and played up to its radicalism. The Committee kept a check-list of the political opinions of officers,[37] and men who had spoken out against emancipation found the powerful influence of Wade and Chandler holding back Senate confirmation of an advanced commission.[38]

Certain rules of the Committee's procedure and its incessant attempts to secure the removal or subordination of officers opposed to the Radical war policies caused contemporary and later critics to label it a Court of Star Chamber, an Aulic Council, an Inquisition conducting military trials.[39] At the first meeting the Committee decided that all hearings would be secret, and the members swore not to reveal any information given by witnesses.[40] Enemies of the agency charged that it habitually violated its own restriction,[41] but Wade indignantly repelled such insinuations.[42] Nevertheless, the Committee's secret information often and purposely reached the desired audience. In the course of an investigation designed to rehabilitate the military reputation of General Frémont, Wade revealed the results of the investigation to the general's foremost journalistic champion, Charles A. Dana of the New York *Tribune,* and urged the editor to work for Frémont's restoration.[43] Again in July, 1862, the Committee amended its rule by permitting members to present its testimony in Congressional speeches. This was to enable Chandler to deliver a philippic against McClellan, defeated in the Peninsula and on the verge of removal.[44] The secrecy regulation invested the Committee with features unlike those of other investigative bodies. A witness appeared alone in the Committee room. He did not know whether previous witnesses had impugned his conduct or what charges the Committee might bring against him in a report to Lincoln. Thus the results of an inquiry in 1862 convinced the Committee that General Stone, a McClellan intimate, was guilty of treasonable relations with the enemy. But when Stone testified, Wade refused to acquaint him with the nature of the indictments against him, and the officer was forced to make a general and inadequate defense.[45] On another occasion the Committee collected a mass of evidence to prove that General Meade was not responsible for the victory at Gettysburg. Meade himself finally appeared as a witness and found only Wade awaiting him.[46] The chairman lulled the suspicious general by telling him that the Committee was compiling a history of the war and wanted his contribution.[47] As a result Meade was unable to make any specific refutations of previous criticisms.

The Committee, despite the secret hearing and the sinister epithets of its assailants, was not a court. It possessed no judicial powers and could not pass a sentence. Rather it was a grand jury. The Committee, Wade said, rendered no final judgments on military men. "We only state what in our opinion tends to impeach them . . . and then leave it to better judges to decide."[48] When the Committee decided to seek the downfall of a particular officer, because of his suspected sympathy for slavery or a failure to achieve victories, the members began to collect evidence to accomplish their purpose. This labor completed, they would submit their findings to Lincoln and demand that the offending general be dismissed. If the President demurred, they threatened to arouse Congress and public opinion against him, to make their testimony public, "with," as Wade said on one occasion, "such comments as the circumstances of the case seemed to require."[49] If the pressure of the Committee failed to move Lincoln, as was sometimes the case, the members strove to weaken the forces of the intended victim and waited for the publication of their report ultimately to blast his reputation and usefulness. The same procedure, with certain necessary variations, was followed when the Committee was attempting to secure the advancement or prevent the removal of an officer who believed in the Radical war aims. In the famous case of General Stone, whom the Committee suspected of treason, the investigation resulted in a military arrest. Wade gave Stanton the damaging testimony and privately told him the general should be arrested. Stanton was eager to pull down a McClellan favorite, Lincoln was afraid to oppose the Committee, and the unfortunate Stone went to Fort Lafayette.[50]

The Committee, with a concept of itself as a policy-forming agency and a determination to control the military machine for the furtherance of Radical principles, began its career profoundly impressed that a dangerous crisis threatened the nation and believing that the outcome depended largely on the success of its activities.[51] The members turned their attention at once to the inactive Army of the Potomac. They summoned numerous generals, and questioned them as to McClellan's plans, his secrecy of counsel, and his reason for not fighting.[52] The generals were told that Congress and the country wanted the army to undertake an offensive movement.[53] The Committee became convinced that McClellan was trying to protract the war until a wearied nation recalled the Democratic party to effect reunion,[54] and the leading spirits resolved on an appeal to Lincoln. On January 6, 1862, the Committee met the President and his Cabinet in a long, stormy interview. Wade demanded that Lincoln order McClellan to advance and fight, but the Cabinet, with the exception of Salmon P. Chase, condemned this proposal. The chairman bitterly condemned McClellan's generalship and urged Lincoln to conduct the war on "radical" principles.[55] A week later McClellan met the Committee in an off-the-record conference, and Wade and Chandler vainly exhorted him to strike a blow at the Confederates.[56] Balked in its effort to prod the army into action, the

Committee enlisted the aid of Stanton. A series of conferences, during which the Committee disclosed much of its testimony,[57] resulted in a united effort of the Secretary and the Committee upon Lincoln. The latter yielded and issued his three orders of January 27 calling for a general advance of the armies on Washington's birthday.[58] McClellan so protested the order, however, that it was never carried into execution. This resulted in renewed pressure of the Committee and Stanton upon the general,[59] and finally the former bluntly informed Lincoln that unless the army moved it would offer a resolution in Congress directing Lincoln to instruct McClellan to advance.[60] The President promised to hurry McClellan on and at the same time yielded to another Committee demand by organizing the Army of the Potomac into corps. This was a bold attempt to weaken McClellan's authority. The generals commanding divisions fell into two groups: the senior officers who did not owe their position to McClellan and who tended to agree with the Committee politically, and the younger, conservative generals who owed their place to McClellan's favor.[61] If the twelve divisions were arranged in corps, the senior, radical officers would receive the new rank of corps commanders, and McClellan's authority would be divided among a council of his enemies.[62] For a month the Committee pressed Lincoln to take this step, and on the eve of McClellan's spring campaign the President issued the order.[63]

After this victory the Committee rested until McClellan took his army to the Peninsula to attack Richmond from the east. Lincoln had always feared this procedure would leave Washington open to capture, and after the general's departure the Radicals dinned into his ears that McClellan had purposely left the capital defenseless. On April 2, General Wadsworth, the commander of the Washington defenses, appeared at the War Department and asserted that the forces under his command were inadequate to defend the city.[64] Stanton, following what seems a course of action concerted with Wade, dispatched Wadsworth's report to the Committee. Wadsworth met the Committee the next day, repeated his charges, and indulged in a general excoriation of McClellan's generalship.[65] The Committee, Stanton, and Wadsworth then descended upon Lincoln and convinced him that the city lay helpless before the Confederates. They demanded that he detach a corps from McClellan's army to augment the defending forces, and the alarmed President ordered McDowell, then embarking his troops for the Peninsula, to remain in front of Washington.[66] The Radicals themselves were under no delusion that a "Rebel" force might suddenly capture Washington.[67] Rather it was their hope that while McClellan was engaged in the Peninsula, McDowell, a Radical officer, could achieve the honor of capturing Richmond.[68] Neither officer was destined to achieve this objective. McClellan's weakened army met defeat in the Virginia swamps, and McDowell remained near the capital.

When the news of McClellan's failure reached Washington, the Committee sprang into action. General John Pope, destined to succeed McClellan with the aid of the Radicals, appeared before the agency, denounced McClellan's conduct of the campaign, proposed a counter plan of his own, and delighted the members with his obvious radicalism.[69] A few days later the Republicans of the Committee, in a meeting unknown to the Democratic members, lifted the secrecy injunction in order to let Chandler use the records for a Senate attack on McClellan. The Michigan senator's speech, a blistering review of the general's command of the army, was a Radical manifesto.[70] The President, moved by impatience with McClellan and by the Radical pressure, ordered the bulk of the general's army transferred to Pope's command. The jubilation of the Committee at this victory was short-lived. Pope suffered a crushing defeat at Manassas, caused, said Chandler, by McClellan's treasonable refusal to offer him proper support.[71] To the great disgust of the Radicals, Lincoln again gave the command to McClellan, but the general's dilatory pursuit of Lee after Antietam moved the President to retire him from active duty. The Committee was pleased with his removal and could claim that its pressure and protests had contributed largely to his downfall.

The President, however, dashed the Radical hopes of controlling the army by giving the command of the eastern army to McClellan's trusted friend, Ambrose Burnside. In December, 1862, the new commander hurled his troops against those of Lee at Fredericksburg and recoiled with terrific slaughter. Immediately a Senate resolution directed the Committee to inquire into the causes of the disaster and to verify rumors that Burnside's subordinates had conspired to effect his defeat.[72] Four of the leading members repaired to the camp of the army at Falmouth, where they remained for two days gathering testimony. Burnside, on whom the wrath of the Committee might have been expected to fall, won its support by reversing his political beliefs. He told the gratified members that slavery should be destroyed and that he had labored to inspire other officers with a hatred of the institution.[73] The Committee then singled out William B. Franklin, commander of the left wing at the recent battle, as the scapegoat. Wade and Chandler indicated by their questions to witnesses that they intended to fix the onus upon this supporter of McClellan.[74] Upon returning to Washington, the Committee submitted the testimony to the Senate with no comments, but the Radical press used it to whitewash Burnside.[75] Burnside resigned shortly afterwards, disgusted by the intrigues of subordinates to secure his place, and the Committee enlarged its investigation of his direction of the army.[76] In its report it censured Franklin for not attacking in full force at Fredericksburg and blamed him for the defeat.[77]

As Burnside's successor Lincoln appointed the radical Joseph Hooker, considered by the Committee to be the ablest man in the army.[78] This pleased the Committee, although the Radical spirits felt that there were still too many conservative officers in the army.[79] When Hooker was defeated at Chancellorsville, the Committee refused to follow its usual course of making an investigation. Wade and Chandler came down to the camp at Falmouth to conduct an unofficial inquiry. On their return they loudly proclaimed that the army was in fine condition and waiting to be led to victory by Hooker.[80] The latter, however, faced by intrigues among his corps commanders similar to those he had once instigated against Burnside, soon asked to be relieved from command. The Committee investigated his tenure of command and concluded that his conservative subordinates had distrusted him because of his affiliation with the Radical faction and his support of an emancipation policy.[81] In its report the Committee censured the administration for not giving Hooker proper support at Chancellorsville.[82]

In choosing a general to take the place of Hooker, Lincoln decided on George G. Meade, a conservative McClellan officer.[83] The new commander's victory at Gettysburg saved him from a Committee attack, although the Radical leaders sneered at him as another McClellan, slow and dilatory.[84] In Washington the Committee worked to restore Hooker, waiting for Meade to commit a blunder.[85] The Radicals felt, however, that they could ignore Meade temporarily with the elevation of Ulysses S. Grant to the position of lieutenant general and supreme commander of the Union armies. Grant had previously encountered the hostility of the Committee and the Radicals because of his suspected Democratic opinions,[86] but he subsequently won their favor by indorsing emancipation and the use of Negro soldiers.[87] The Committee hoped, therefore, that he would purge the eastern army of its conservative officers, and Chandler presented him with a list of generals suspected of "McClellanism" with a recommendation for their removal.[88] However, when Grant permitted Meade to continue in command of the Army of the Potomac, the Committee decided to take action itself. It launched an investigation and summoned witnesses, the majority of whom were officers associated with the Radical faction. It learned that Meade and his corps commanders had no heart in prosecuting a war against slavery, that subordinates were responsible for the victory at Gettysburg, and that Meade, had he wished, could have destroyed Lee's army after the battle.[89] Armed with this testimony, Wade and Chandler called on Lincoln to "demand the removal of General Meade, and the appointment of someone more competent to command." They suggested Hooker and threatened to make their testimony public unless the President acceded.[90] Lincoln felt strong enough to refuse the Committee, but the latter bided its time for another lunge at Meade. Grant had given the members no aid in the attempt to oust Meade and their suspicions turned against him. Wade thought his Wilderness campaign a terrible blunder and urged Lincoln to dismiss him.[91]

The Committee made another unsuccessful attempt to secure Meade's downfall when it investigated the causes of the slaughter of Union troops in the Petersburg mine crater and ascribed the blame to Meade's refusal to render proper support to the attacking force.[92]

Grant supported Meade strongly during the inquiry, and the Committee sought for an issue on which they could oppose the popular general. The members found it when Grant removed one of their favorite officers, Benjamin F. Butler, from command after his failure to capture Fort Fisher. Immediately the Radicals rallied to Butler's defense with a Senate resolution instructing the Committee to investigate the Fort Fisher expedition.[93] When Butler testified, the Committee permitted him to place a history of his whole war career on the record in addition to his account of the recent battle.[94] The Committee obviously intended to vindicate Butler completely,[95] but the war ended before it could complete the investigation, although Wade issued a belated report upholding Butler in every respect and criticizing Grant severely.[96] With the Fort Fisher episode the Committee closed its investigations of army affairs, and the conclusion of peace witnessed the end of its labors. However, the Radical cabal had seen the value of such an agency in a struggle with a hostile executive, and when the Radical machine clashed with Andrew Johnson over the issues of reconstruction, the Congressional leaders prepared for the battle by creating the joint committee on reconstruction.

Space forbids any detailed consideration of all the other inquiries carried on by the Committee on the Conduct of the War. It also investigated many expeditions and battles of minor importance, the use of iron-clad ships, alleged Confederate atrocities, convalescent camps, trade with the enemy, paymasters and chaplains, types of heavy ordnance, contracts to furnish ice for the army, the treatment of Union prisoners in the South, and the prevalence of scurvy in the army. The importance of the Committee, however is in the thorny problem of the degree of control which the legislature, or any representative of the civilian branch of the government, should exercise over the military organization during wartime. In no other of our wars had Congress made such a determined attempt to control military operations or to dictate the personnel of the army. The experiment of the Committee was essentially a product of the times, and the people of the times expressed a contempt for technical education and a preference for amateurism in war. Again the Committee, with its political criteria for measuring the abilities of generals, was but reflecting the spirit of the period. The nation was engaged in a civil war which was the culmination of decades of controversy over the slavery question. Political parties and individuals differed fiercely on the disputed issue. The Civil War generals, many of whom had been in civilian occupations before the outbreak of the struggle, possessed pronounced and clashing opinions on the subject. Inevitably their views carried over after the war began. Then the slavery issue became a part of the conduct of the war. One political party demanded the abolition of slavery as a measure of military necessity; the other denounced this as a subterfuge to achieve a political objective. Because this question had military implications, the generals, whether they would or no, had to take sides. Thus they were dragged into the political maelstrom, and partisan rather than military standards determined their fortunes.

The experiment of the Committee reveals valuable knowledge as to the motives which actuate such an agency and the influence it exerts upon the army. The Committee, in addition to its insistence that generals of the right political faith command the army, tended to favor officers who recommended dashing charges and constant forward movements. The members had no patience with generals who spoke about the necessity of drill, careful preparation, siege, machinery, and precautionary measures. Hence every officer about to undertake a movement felt the pressure of achieving a rapid, smashing victory. Yet he knew that if he failed as a result of these tactics the Committee would demand his removal. Perhaps this accounts for the uncertain movements of many generals during the war. The Committee was usually able to grasp the broad concepts of strategy as related to the whole theater of the war, but the details of battlefield tactics remained a mystery to the members. Over and over in the committee rooms, the members quarreled with soldiers in discussing the latter subject. Reading the testimony at a later date, one is struck by the seeming inability of what might be called civilian and military minds to meet on common ground. The Committee, if divorced from its unfortunate political bias, might have performed a very real service. No other body in the country had its unique opportunity to gather information from all fields of the war.

This information, presented in objective form to the army, would have been of great value. One student of the Civil War has suggested to the author that the Committee, had it so chosen, could have come closer to fulfilling the functions of a General Staff than any agency of the war period.

That Strange Sad War

The heat of July hung heavily over the trenches at Petersburg when General George Pickett went to ask General Lee for a pass to Richmond. Pickett thought he had a reason to be absent that could not be refused. "My son was born this morning," he said. But looking at Pickett with that air of grave rebuke that only he could mount, Marse Robert replied, "Your country was born almost a hundred years ago." Almost a century before 1864 would have been on the eve of the Revolution, and when Lee said "your country" he was certainly not referring to the Confederate States of America. It is probable that he was not thinking of the United States of America either, but talking to Pickett, who would understand, he must have had in mind the Commonwealth of Virginia. This was the Lee who in 1861 had written, "I wish for no other flag than the 'Star spangled banner' and no other air than 'Hail Columbia'" and who had undergone the deepest anguish before deciding to go with his native state. And this was the Pickett who in 1861 had mourned, "I do believe . . . that the measure of American greatness can be achieved only under one flag" and who later in the war would exclaim, "Oh, this is all a weary, long mistake. May the merciful and true God . . . end it ere another day passes."

This speech, which Williams called his "bread and butter speech," appeared in *Colorado Quarterly*, X (Winter, 1962), 265–75. Reprinted here by permission.

The Virginia generals of the Confederacy—they are an interesting
and perplexing and in some ways a tragic lot. Hardly a one of them
but had contemplated the possibility of fraternal war without horror.
Like Lee, many of them had followed Virginia into the Confederacy
only after a severe trial. Perhaps they did not, as Mrs. Lee said of her
husband, weep "tears of blood," but they searched their souls. And
some, like Pickett, expressed during the war sentiments that indicated regret and perhaps even revulsion at the situation into which
others had forced them. Thus General Richard Ewell wrote to his
niece that the conflict had been precipitated by "a set of fanatical
abolitionists and unprincipled politicians backed by women in pet-
ticoats and pants," and Ewell made it plain that his register of
villains comprised people from both sections and that his list of
women encompassed the belles of Dixie, including his niece. They
fought for the Confederacy, these Virginia generals, but one wonders
about them. Did they fight with much conviction or joy—or did
they act from stern and reluctant devotion? One can wonder about
many things in this conflict that we call the American Civil War,
that "strange sad war," as Whitman called it, and this perpetual
sense of wonderment, this impression of always finding something
new or unusual to marvel at is perhaps its greatest fascination.

Unusualness and uniqueness aside, the Civil War is in mundane
fact a big, commanding, and transforming event, significant for
American and world history alike. We say that it was the first modern war, the first war of materiel, the first war in modern times to
approach totality and the first to be directed against civilians, and all
these labels are accurate. It was not as expansive or as expensive as
the great conflicts of our own century, although by the standards
of its own century it was overwhelmingly huge. But in terms of human costs it was a frightful struggle by any measurement, the most
terrible war we have known. The total service deaths aggregated
618,000: 360,000 from the North and 258,000 from the South, and
when we say that this total exceeds the service deaths in all our
other wars combined, an estimated 600,000, we have made an impressive statement. But the casualty figure, appalling as it is, does
not in itself convey the full import of the loss. To realize that, we
must relate the Civil War data to a war of our time. In World War II

the American service deaths were 384,000 out of a total population of 135,000,000. If the World War II deaths had equaled the Northern ratio of service casualties to population, they would have reached 2,500,000; and if they had equaled the Southern ratio, they would have climbed to almost 5,000,000! The overall results of the war, its impact on concepts of government and the future course of the nation, are too well known to require delineation. But it is worth noting that these results were largely accepted as permanent, even by the defeated. Not many civil wars have had effects as enduring as ours.

These are aspects of the war that endow it with high interest and importance, but they do not arouse in us that feeling of wonder, that discernment that here is something unique in the American and possibly in the human experience. They are not the elements that make it that strange war. To catch this face of the war, we have to look at some rapidly shifting and seemingly unrelated scenes.

It was a modern war, grim and destructive, and featuring such new devices as railroads, the telegraph, armored ships, improved small arms and artillery, breech-loading and repeating rifles, balloons, precursors of the machine gun, submarines, trenches, and flame throwers. But it was also a storybook war, fought in the style of older conflicts when men charged in long, straight lines on the foe. This is the picture of the battles we get in the contemporary illustrations, those colorful depictions which are both accurate and inaccurate. The forces of technology were altering the nature of war, and nowhere do we see the meaning of this change demonstrated as dramatically as on the third day at Gettysburg in the famous Confederate attack on Cemetery Ridge. The scene has caught the imagination of every writer who has described it. Bruce Catton sees it like this: "The smoke lifted like a rising curtain, and all of the great ampitheater lay open at last, and the Yankee soldiers could look west all the way to the belt of trees on Seminary Ridge. They were old soldiers and had been in many battles, but what they saw then took their breath away, and whether they had ten minutes or seventy-five years yet to live, they remembered it until they died. There it was, for the last time in this war, perhaps for the last time anywhere, the grand pageantry of war in the old style, beautiful and majestic and terrible: fighting men lined up for a mile and a half from flank to flank, slashed red flags overhead, soldiers marching forward elbow to elbow, officers with drawn swords, sunlight gleaming from thousands of musket barrels, lines dressed as if for parade." And Fairfax Downey thus relates the Confederate charge: "On they came and on. . . . It was as if the Union gunners were caught in a trance, fascinated by that splendid display of martial pageantry—the last great charge in the old tradition. Men would not look upon its like again. Shoulder to shoulder marched the ordered ranks. So had men charged since organized warfare began. . . . Upright, aligned, close-ranked, they marched on."

The spectacle witnessed at Gettysburg was repeated on many a field and throughout the war; right up to the end generals were flinging their men forward in these headlong charges. And nearly always they failed. Rarely did a frontal assault succeed against a determined foe in a strong position. The explanation of what happened at Gettysburg and in other battles lay in technology or science. By 1860 the firepower of armies had been increased to a point where the defense was superior to the offense. Although breech-loading and repeating rifles were introduced in the war, they were used sparingly. The basic weapon of the infantry soldier was the Springfield rifle, a single-shot, muzzle-loading gun, but substantially superior in range and rate of fire to anything in previous wars. The basic artillery weapon was the brass Napoleon—although some rifled pieces were employed—a single-shot, muzzle-loading smoothbore, but also superior in range to earlier guns. Because of these weapons Civil War armies could kill at a greater distance than had been possible before, could spray an area with greater firepower. Whereas in the Napoleonic wars 20,000 troops to the mile were considered necessary to hold a defensive position, in the first years of the Civil War 12,000 to the mile were found sufficient, and eventually 5,000 were regarded as enough.

Why then all these practically doomed frontal attacks? Were the generals just stupid? No, the generals were not more inept than generals usually are, and even the very best of them, such as Grant and Lee, indulged in the line advance. What we have here is a not un-

familiar phenomenon in war, a lag in weapons and military thinking, or specifically a lag in technology and tactics. The new firepower called for new tactical arrangements, a wider deployment, a
looser formation, but the generals continued to think in terms of the
limited firepower of earlier wars against which the double line of
battle had been effective. It is true that some commanders did develop new methods of deployment, often because the nature of a particular field forbade the customary arrangement. Sherman in the
West would advance half a regiment as skirmishers, thus giving the
skirmish line a combat mission, and Longstreet did the same thing
in the Wilderness campaign. But these anticipations of the extended
order of later wars were the exception. Most battles were fought
pretty much in the line formation shown in the drawings of the day,
or at least the generals directing them tried to fight them that way.

It was the tactical practices that caused the terrific casualty rates
that often astonish modern students, rates that in some engage-
ments ran from sixty to eighty percent killed and wounded for many
units. And it is precisely these methods of conducting battles that
invest the war with one of its peculiar fascinations, in this case the
fascination of paradox. It is not just that the generals do not adjust
their tactics to the weapons, but something more. Here is an apparently modern war that was in large part fought in an unmodern manner. Actually, the Civil War was two wars. It had many of the attributes of twentieth-century conflict—it was big, mechanical, and
mechanistic. But it was also like wars earlier in the century and even
before, partly in fact but more in men's minds—the strategic notions of the generals, for example, were straight out of the eighteenth century. The Civil War was, then, a transitional conflict, the
last of the older and the first of the modern wars, and having features
of both it is doubly interesting. Despite its semblance of modernity,
it was an intensely personal war. When we gaze on the battle scenes,
we may reflect that this was not the way to do it, but we never think
that we are dealing with machines or nameless aggregations. Always
we are conscious that this was a war waged by human beings whom
we can know. And whatever war has become today, we feel we can
always look back and see it as it once was, in all its "grand pageantry
. . . beautiful and majestic and terrible." We may wish to look back

for varying reasons, for instruction or for entertainment or even for escape, but assuredly we will continue to look. For this war, whatever the reasons, has sunk deeply into the national consciousness. If the man on the streets were asked to name the outstanding commanders of World War II, he would probably stop with Eisenhower, MacArthur, and Patton. But there are thousands who can rattle off the names of army commanders of the Civil War and of corps, division, and brigade generals as well. It may not be our best-conducted war, but with all its omissions, indeed, perhaps because of them, it is and it promises to remain our best known and our best cherished war.

It was, and here again we see its modern nature, a war of ideas. This was no eighteenth century type of conflict, with limited or dynastic objectives. It was an all-out struggle. The North had to restore the Union by force; the South had to establish its independence by force. To achieve its objective, the North had to win a total or near total victory. To attain its objective, the South did not have to win a total victory. It had only to convince the North it could not be conquered; but the South could not compromise its objective of independence. Thus the purposes of the contestants were total, and they had to fight until one or the other triumphed. Such a war was bound to be, or more accurately, was certain to become a rough and lethal affair. Before the shooting had ever started, proponents of both sections had stated the case that the North and the South represented diverse civilizations, with one or the other, depending on the origin of the teller, being greatly superior to the other. Thus a Georgia editor exclaimed of the North: "Free Society! We sicken at the name. What is it but a conglomeration of greasy mechanics, filthy operatives, small-fisted farmers, and moon-struck theorists? All the North . . . are devoid of society fitted for well-bred gentlemen. . . . The prevailing class one meets with . . . are hardly fit for association with a Southern gentleman's body-servant." On the other side, a Northern editor contrasted the "intelligent, educated, and civilized" people of the North with their "ignorant, illiterate, and barbarian companions" to the South. And as the war began, northern spokesmen warned that the nation faced a foe whose lower culture rested on

"anarchy, fraud, and treason" and a people "to whose natural ugli-
ness of disposition is added the ferocity of exasperated wild beasts."

It is conjectural how many people on both sides believed all this
gasconade before or even after the war started. Probably most dis-
counted much of it as the mouthings of such articulate types as politicians and intellectuals. Yet each section went to war certain of the
righteousness of its cause and convinced that the other could not
fight well or long. As the war settled into the long haul, inevitably
real animosities and finally hatreds developed. These emotions were
in part a natural outgrowth of the conditions created by the war, its
shortages, sacrifices, and losses. Civilians and especially those in the
South, which suffered more painfully the impact of the war, came to
cherish feelings of abhorrence for the enemy. A Georgia girl confided
to her diary: "Yankee, Yankee, is the one detestable word always
ringing in Southern ears. If all the words of hatred in every language
under heaven were lumped together into one huge epithet of detesta-
tion, they could not tell how I hate Yankees." And a Virginia girl exulted at the news of Lee's invasion of Pennsylvania: "I wish I could
be there to witness the entrance of our troops in some of these
Union towns. . . . I am sometimes astonished at the force of my feelings against the Yankees, but when I remember what we have suffered and lost, when I think of all the horrors they have inflicted
upon our people, and of the shameful display of barbarity and un-
civilized warfare they have always displayed, I cannot wonder at the
strength of such feelings."

Northern civilians did not experience as directly the ruth of the
war, but they too endured privations. Moreover, they were more influenced than Southerners by the medium of propaganda. Both the
United States and Confederate States governments resorted to the
medium of propaganda to demonstrate to their people that the enemy was cruel and barbarous and must be resisted to the last. Here
again, in the dissemination of official propaganda, we see a man-
ifestation of the modernity of this war, although neither government, as would be the case today, established a special agency to produce propaganda but relied on existing agencies to do the job. But
the Northern government, possessing numerous and excellent facilities in such areas as printing and illustrating, was much more active

than its rival in manufacturing and disseminating its material. The effect of this propaganda cannot be accurately evaluated, but it would seem to have been great. Intensifying already existing attitudes, it persuaded the Northern people, as the events of the war persuaded the Southern people, that they were fighting an enemy lower in the scale of civilization than themselves. Thus an editor wrote after perusing a piece of official propaganda: "It is not surprising, however, for no one who has thoughtfully read the many records of the aspects and characteristics of a society based upon slavery was unconscious of its essential and necessary barbarism. Their civilization is a mermaid—lovely and languid above but ending in bestial deformity."

It was, then, a war of ideas and ideals and of emotions and passions. But again we have to note a paradox. Whatever feelings animated the civilian masses of both societies, the men in the armies conducted their conflict with almost knightly courtesy and consideration. If this manner of making war was not universal, it was at least common enough to fill many pages of diaries and reminiscences by participants. Nor is it to be explained by saying that the soldiers had some peculiar sense of amity not felt by civilians, although the armies did finally come to have a kind of *mystique* that they shared a great experience that in some fashion united them. Witness the admission of a Union officer of his reactions at Appomattox when the Confederates came forward to stack their arms: at this last meeting of the armies the men in gray approached "with eyes looking level into ours, waking memories that bound us together as no other bond." But this was a bond that merely marked the respect of one aggregation of fighting men for another, and in any case it was a phenomenon of the later stages of the war. The manifestations we are talking about appeared at an early date and were of an entirely different character. They were expressed in the almost constant fraternization engaged in by the officers and the enlisted men of the opposing forces and in the chivalric code of behavior observed by the contestants in this hard-fought struggle.

The reasons for these demonstrations are fairly obvious. Men fraternized because they had something to communicate to each other. Originally and only recently they had been members of the same political and social organism. They had the same cultural and historical heritage, they responded to many situations in the same way, and they had common reactions that they wanted to share with each other. Most important, it was possible for them to communicate because there was no language barrier between them as might have existed between the armies of two nations. In some cases individuals knew each other from before the war. This was particularly true of the ranking officers, who had contracted friendship at West Point or at army posts and who maintained their relations under the stress of conflict. The enlisted men had, of course, not known one another, but during the war they got acquainted by the thousands, especially those on picket or outpost duty between the armies. These men, stationed at a particular point for long periods, usually separated by only a stream of water, invariably found that they had something to talk about with the pickets across the way, and they talked and out of their talk enduring and protective friendships developed. Men observed a chivalric code because they conceived of war as an exercise to be conducted by set rules, as something resembling a tournament. Winston Churchill has called the Civil War the last great war fought by gentlemen. Perhaps it would be more accurate to say that it was the last romantic war, the last conflict in which men could afford to think about war romantically, a luxury that we of today know is impossible. The fraternizing and the chivalry may not have been unique to the Civil War, but certainly there was more of both than in any other of our wars and possibly more than in any war in history. They give the Civil War a character and a flavor all its own: they are another reason we call it that strange war. Again we may see this aspect of the conflict in a series of episodes or scenes.

In the late spring of 1862 General Pickett writes in a letter that his friend of prewar days, General George B. McClellan, commander of the Federal Army of the Potomac, is ill: "I have heard that my dear old friend, McClellan, is lying ill about ten miles from here. May some loving, soothing hand minister to him. He was, he is, and he will always be, even were his pistol pointed at my heart, my dear, loved friend. May God bless him and spare his life." One can hardly imagine Patton writing a letter like this about, say, Rommel.

The pickets along a stream in Virginia have formed a friendship common to their kind. As related by a fascinated Federal observer, they have devised a workable truce. If an officer came down to the banks, the pickets on the other side would shout, "Go back or we'll shoot." Once when the Confederates were directed to open fire they called out, "Get into your holes, Yanks, we are ordered to fire." On July 4 a Northern band struck up "Hail Columbia," and suddenly a North Carolina regiment on the opposite side rose as one man and cheered. Identical scenes occurred on hundreds of rivers between thousands of pickets. Often the large Northern bands would play concerts near a stream. Thousands from both armies would congregate and call for their favorite pieces. After obligingly playing the airs of both sides, the band would cap the affair by rendering one dear to the hearts of all, "Home Sweet Home."

At the battle of Cedar Mountain in 1862 Captain Blackford of the Confederate army is stationed at a particular spot to direct troops. Suddenly the Federals attack here and break the gray line. A Yankee officer with his sword broken almost to the hilt comes up to where Blackford sits on his horse. Then a Confederate general rides out from the woods, seizes a standard from a soldier, and organizes a counterattack that restores the break. While this is happening, the Northern officer stands staring in open admiration of the Confederate general, utterly overcome by this display of personal magnetism. Turning to Blackford, he inquires the identity of the Confederate, and with great pride Blackford replies, "That is Stonewall Jackson." Carried away with enthusiasm, the Yankee waves his stump of a sword and cries, "Hurrah for General Jackson. Follow your general, boys." And Blackford, overcome by the sentiment of the whole scene, leans down and instructs the Federal officer to take a back path and return safely to his own army. This is not an isolated episode. Once in the Western theater General Nathan Bedford Forrest saw the Federals signaling to each other with flags from behind their fortifications. Thinking the flags indicated a desire to surrender, he spurred his horse toward the Federal line. A Yankee officer, seeing that Forrest misunderstood and was riding to death or capture, at great risk to his own life jumped up on the parapet and warned the Confederate to go back.

It is May of 1863, and General G. K. Warren of the Federal army is writing his report of the battle of Chancellorsville, that engagement where the contending armies fought fiercely in the tangled region known as the Wilderness. As Warren contemplates the terrain, the idea comes to him that the fighting in all the Virginia theater is of such a nature as to reflect great credit on both the Northern and the Southern armies. Glowing with pride, he takes his pen and writes a tribute, not just to his own troops but to his opponents as well: "A proper understanding of the country, too, will help to relieve the Americans from the charge frequently made at home and abroad of want of generalship in handling troops in battle—battles that had to be fought out hand to hand in forests, where artillery and cavalry could play no part; where the troops could not be seen by those controlling their movements; where the echoes and reverberations of sound from tree to tree were enough to appall the stoutest hearts engaged, and yet the noise would often scarcely be heard beyond the immediate scene of strife. Thus the generals on either side, shut out from sight or from hearing, had to trust to the unyielding bravery of their men until couriers . . . brought word which way the conflict was resulting before sending the needed support. We should not wonder that such battles often terminated from the natural exhaustion of both contending forces, but rather that in all these struggles of Americans against Americans no panic on either side gave victory to the other like that which the French, under Moreau, gained over the Austrians in the Black Forest." Even in the midst of war Warren could write as an American to praise other Americans, could think of the Confederates in no other way than as his countrymen.

These episodes are colorful and entertaining, and they seem so characteristic of this strange war that we may overlook their real significance. There is a terrible pathos in them that reminds us of something we should never forget, even during the glitter of the centennial commemorations—the Civil War was a tragedy, the only one in our history, an incredibly sad war. The pathos comes from our realization that two peoples so much alike were fighting each other. Perhaps the strangeness of the war can explain the sadness, can tell us why they fought. Historians have argued for generations the issue of whether the Civil War was an irrepressible conflict. Perhaps it was. There may have been no other way to remove the evil of slavery than by a collision of the sections. There are seemingly some situations in the affairs of men that can be resolved only by tragedy, and this may have been one. But still we must think the war might have been averted by some compromise before it started. Admittedly a compromise would only have bought time, but time can be vital in the settling of disputes. The episodes we have been describing demonstrate the deepness of the bonds of union between the northern and the southern people, bonds that survived even in the strain of war. Maybe if by some miracle the masses of the people could have been brought together face to face, they would have devised a compromise that would have preserved the Union. Maybe if by another miracle the armies could have been brought together, they would have framed an agreement that would have restored the Union. At least some competent observers thought the armies would, if they could, fraternize and make peace. These are things we can never know. All we can say is that in the midst of division there was still a strange sad unity in a strange sad war. Maybe when General Lee said "your country" to Pickett, he was thinking of the United States after all.

Lincoln and the Radicals: An Essay in Civil War History and Historiography

The politicians were drifting into Washington for the opening of the second session of the thirty-seventh Congress, and Joshua F. Speed, Lincoln's friend, watching and weighing what he saw and heard in those early winter days of 1861, was apprehensive for the President and for what Speed conceived to be the President's policy. "I can see that Lincoln is going to have trouble with the fiery element of his own party," Speed advised a man who was, like himself, a border-state Unionist. Shortly Speed had more exact and more ominous information for his colleague: "I am fully persuaded that there is mischief brewing here; a large and powerful party of the ultra men is being formed to make war upon the President and upon his conservative policy."[1] The ultra men were, indeed, incensed at Lincoln, and they did organize for action against him. They called themselves the Radicals, and history knows them by that name, or as the Radical Republicans. They may or may not have made war on Lincoln—historians, who are marvelously talented at giving different meanings to the same phrase, differ on this issue—but at the very least they made him deep and constant trouble in the years ahead. In 1864 many of them were prepared, as Lincoln well knew, to prevent his renomination as the Republican standard-bearer. "He is fully apprehensive of the schemes of the Radical leaders," recorded Attorney General Edward Bates in his diary. "He is also fully aware that they would strike him at once, if they durst; but they fear that the blow would be ineffectual, and so, they would fall under his power, as beaten enemies."[2]

Men like Speed and Bates considered themselves to be Conservative Republicans, and if they sometimes thought that Abraham Lincoln was not always as conservative as he should be they nevertheless counted him on their side. So also did the Radicals rank him, and they were certain that they knew what conservatism was and they were contemptuous of both its practices and its practitioners, whether they were Lincoln or lesser men. Speaking of Senator William P. Fessenden, who moved among the Radicals without being completely one of them, Thaddeus Stevens sneered: "He has too much of the vile ingredient, called conservatism, which is worse than secessionism."[3] A Radical newspaper derided the leadership of its own party as "this albino administration, and its diluted spawn of pink eyed patriots—this limp result of the feeble embrace of half-furnished conservatives and limited emancipators."[4] The Radicals were also certain that they would defeat the Conservatives, and they knew why they would win—it was because they comprehended the right doctrine, because they realized the divine purpose, because they were the appointed instruments to eradicate evil. In 1865, at the moment of victory, Senator "Bluff Ben" Wade exultingly described for the Senate how belief in principle had enabled the Radicals to lay conservatism in the dust. Wade, who considered Lincoln or anybody to the right of himself as a conservative, explained that the Conservatives, once so powerful, had lost out because they were without principle, and being such, they made the fatal error of opposing the destruction of the slavery monster. "But where are you now," he asked, "ye conservatives, that then stood with your heads so high? The radicals have their feet upon your necks, and they are determined that their feet shall rest on the neck of the monster until he breathes his last."[5]

There were, then, in the Republican party during the Civil War men and factions that called themselves Radicals and Conservatives, and they spoke of their beliefs as entities that could be identified and segregated one from the other. Their sense or system of dichotomy has passed into the historical writing about the war. The conflict between the Radicals and the Conservatives, revolving around the wartime disposal to be made of slavery, looms large in all the books, and has been until recently a staple article in all analyses of Northern and Republican politics. But now it has been challenged by some scholars and most notably by Professor David Donald, whose original insights have done so much to illumine our understanding of the broader nature of the war. In a stimulating essay, "The Radicals and Lincoln,"[6] Professor Donald suggests that we discard altogether the Radical-Conservative polarism. His argument, if I do it justice, runs as follows. Historians have made the Radicals the villains of an illusory struggle. Any president is bound to disappoint most of the people who voted for him, even as many as nine-tenths of them; so Lincoln disappointed his followers, most of whom, regardless of their factional persuasion, viewed him as incompetent or imperfect; Lincoln, like every president, was the center of a tug for power between various groups in his party; he worked with these factions, including the Radicals, and not against them; and in the final analysis Lincoln has no serious differences with the Radicals, who were not a cohesive faction during the war and did not become one until Reconstruction. In short, Mr. Donald seems to be telling us that what we have supposed was an important and unique conflict was only an expression of the normal workings of American politics and that such contests characterize all administrations. Having disposed of the Civil War Radicals, Mr. Donald apparently is content to rest, but others want to push his thesis toward new frontiers. Professor Eric McKitrick, in a recent study of Reconstruction, states that the Radicals were not a particularly cohesive or effective faction even in the years after the war and that they did not control the process of reconstruction.[7] Obviously we are moving toward a new interpretation of the whole Civil War era which will run thus: There were no Radicals and besides they weren't very radical.

This latest view of the Radicals, this revision of revisionism, we may say, reflects in part one of the most settled convictions of historians—that they know more about what the people of a particular time were up to than the people concerned. But in larger measure it is the expression of something more important, of a new style or

doctrine in historical thought. In recent years we have been subjected in the literature to what has been called the history of consensus and consent. Influenced by both the insecurities and the conservatism of our age, historians have sought for security and unity in
the American past. They have depicted an America which has never
been beset by serious differences or divisions, one in which all parties and factions have worked toward essentially the same objectives. The interpretive thrust of the new persuasion is seen most
plainly in works treating the Revolutionary period and the Populist
movement, but it has affected viewpoints in all areas of our history.
It speaks in the Civil War era in the voices of Professors Donald,
McKitrick, and others, and here it promises, Civil War historians
being notoriously eager and able to bay after a fresh scent, to wax
louder in the years ahead. There are, however, signs of a reaction
against the whole concept of consensus history, and we may be
about to experience one of those examinations of contrasting views
that impel introspection and clarify the meaning of history. At this
budding point in Civil War historiography, when new interpretations
that have not entirely crystallized meet old ones that may need
modification, it would seem essential to reconsider the issue most
in dispute. The question at hand might be phrased: Shall we keep
the Radicals?

At the very beginning it is proper to say that whether Professor
Donald is right or wrong in his analysis of Northern politics he has
performed a needed service by clearing away some confusing under-
brush. Previous historians have exaggerated the congruity of the
Radicals and the sharpness of their differences with the Conservatives. And he supplies a helpful corrective to the accepted picture
with his reminder that a degree of conflict is inherent in the operation of any of our parties. But he errs, it seems to me, on a number of
points. For one, he attempts to write off differences of opinion as in-
consequential by citing friendly surface manifestations between
Lincoln and certain Radicals, notably Charles Sumner, although it is
a familiar fact in politics that men with divergent opinions will
nearly always keep up some kind of personal relationship; and for
another, he conveys a wrong impression by stating that as many

Conservatives as Radicals opposed Lincoln, giving as his examples men like Horatio Seymour, Reverdy Johnson, and O. H. Browning, who were really Democrats or political mavericks. The most serious flaw in his case, however, and it would seem a fatal one, is the assumption that the years between 1861 and 1865 represent a normal political situation marked by normal political reactions. It was not a normal situation because a war, a civil and a modern war, was being fought, and great wars have a way of overriding normality. It was not a normal condition because the paramount divisive issue of the war, as of the decade before, was slavery, an abnormal issue, the only issue in our history that defied the usual methods of political settlement, the only one that eventuated in a resort to force. Slavery was the kind of question that excited violent controversy even among people who were in general agreement as to its ultimate disposal. Finally, Professor Donald neglects, as have all of us who have written on the subject, to define who and what the Radicals were. We very much need a structure or pattern of Radicalism. This paper will attempt some tentative suggestions as to what that structure might be.

Any analysis of the Radicals must, of course, begin with some consideration of the Republican party, for the Radicals have to be related to other elements in the organization and to the organization as a whole. The Republican party was, perhaps because of its youth, a remarkably homogeneous and tenacious assemblage. Agglomerate in make-up, like all our major parties, it nevertheless displayed a fairly consistent purpose in moving toward its economic and political objectives. Its cohesiveness and cunning in the economic area have been exaggerated by historians, but still it was in substantial accord on vital legislation; certainly it was not rent by any serious economic differences, and those that arose were susceptible of ready adjustment. Like all parties, it had a strong institutional urge to survive, to grasp and hold the power and patronage that meant survival, and this quality has perhaps not been sufficiently noted by historians. Because it was new to the ways of office, it was especially avid to retain the rewards of office, and this desire invested it with a rare capacity to sustain internal differences and absorb them. The Republican factions could dispute constantly and violently among themselves until a crisis, like the election of 1864, threatened displacement. Then they quickly closed ranks—until the crisis had passed.

Only one serious divisive issue agitated the party, but this issue, because of its unique nature and because it tended to pull other issues into its orbit, was of overruling importance. The question was, of course, slavery, or more accurately, the policy to be adopted toward slavery during the war. All factions of the party were in one degree or another opposed to the peculiar institution and committed to its extinction. But they differed as to when and how it should be extinguished. To borrow European terms, on the slavery problem there was a right, a center, and a left faction. The right was made up mainly of border-state Unionists, such as Speed, Bates, and Montgomery Blair, who were antislavery more in theory than in fact, who were more content to talk against slavery than to act against it, and who hoped its ultimate extinction would come by state action and would be fairly ultimate. The center included the men whom we call, and who called themselves, the Conservative Republicans. Before the war they had advocated some plan to bring about the eventual and gradual disappearance of slavery, their favorite device being to prevent it from expanding to the territories and thus causing it to wither on the vine and die. Once the war started they were willing to hasten its demise; they thought that a plan should be devised during the war to accomplish the destruction of slavery *after* the war, preferably by a scheme of compensated emancipation. It was "the calm, deliberate opinion of that great conservative class," said Senator James Dixon, that slavery must go, but it should go out with order and proper ritual. The mood of the conservative approach was suggested by one journalist: "Slavery has been the cause of enormous wrongs, but it must not, therefore, be stricken in passionate revenge."[8] The left comprised the Radicals, who became during the war the dominant faction. The Radicals were more committed to the destruction of slavery than any of the other factions, and they were determined to use the war as an opportunity to strike it down. Put simply and baldly, their program was to destroy slavery as part of the war process, to destroy it suddenly and, if necessary, violently, to destroy it, if not in revenge, with passion.

All factions of the Republican party were united, then, on certain objectives. They were for the Union, they were for the war to preserve it, and they were antislavery. Only on the issue of how to proceed against slavery during the war did they divide seriously and significantly, and this division appeared, as Joshua Speed and others saw it would, almost immediately after the conflict began. Lincoln too saw the issue emerging, and he knew what it portended. As if sensing the program the Radicals would soon develop, the President, in his message to Congress of December, 1861, delineated what measures against slavery should not be executed. "In considering the policy to be adopted for suppressing the insurrection," he said, "I have been anxious and careful that the inevitable conflict for this purpose shall not degenerate into a violent and remorseless revolutionary struggle. . . . We should not be in haste to determine that radical and extreme measures, which may reach the loyal as well as the disloyal, are indispensable." Interestingly enough, when toward the end of the war George W. Julian described how the Radicals had wrenched control from the administration and imposed their own policy toward slavery, he used almost exactly Lincoln's own words to characterize the Radical procedure. From the beginning of the war the Radicals had, Julian explained, "persistently urged a vigorous policy, suited to remorseless and revolutionary violence, till the Government felt constrained to embrace it."[9] Politicians often indulge in an exaggerated and extreme rhetoric that makes them seem more agitated than they really are. But even allowing for this habit, it is evident that Lincoln and Julian, both of whom, incidentally, were more precise in language than most of their type, were talking about something that was very real and very vital to them. "Remorseless and revolutionary violence"—these are not the kind of terms customarily employed by politicians to characterize the program of other politicians, especially those of the same party; and these are not the kind of labels that American politicians ordinarily accept, let alone boast of wearing. We are dealing here, it is emphasized again, with something decidedly out of the ordinary in politics. The Civil War is the only episode in our history, or the only important episode, when men have insisted on the total or absolute solution to a problem, and in the North the Radicals were the men with the final solution. The divisive issue in the Republican party was, therefore, veritable, concrete, substantial, and, above all, abnormal to the political process.

In attempting to structure the Radicals, it is necessary at the start to discard any modern concepts of radicalism, notably those related to an economic basis. The Radicals and other Republicans may have had their differences on particular issues, but essentially their economic beliefs were fairly conventional.[10] Nor were the Radicals radical in the European sense of wanting to make over all at once all of society. But they were radical, as they realized and, indeed, proudly proclaimed, in one area of thought and action and on one issue. The area might be narrow but it contained most of the social tensions then occupying the American people, and the issue might be solitary but at the time it overrode all others. The Radicals were real radicals in that they wanted to accomplish a great change in society, or in one part of it, namely, to destroy slavery and to punish those who supported slavery. They proposed to effect this change suddenly and without much regard for the opinions of those who opposed them, and without much thought of the problems that such a change might bring, especially to the people most concerned, those in the South. They were, then, radical and even revolutionary in attitude and temperament; and if not all Radicals subscribed in toto to every aspect of the attitude or recognized every action required by it, they are still identifiable as a faction. If they were not radical in the accepted or European sense, they are yet the closest approach to a real radical group we have had in this country.

The broadest characterization to be made of the Radicals, the one that encompasses practically all their qualities, is that they were doctrinaire and dogmatic. They possessed truth and justice and they had the total solution; they were men of principle and they were prepared to enforce their principles. "The radical men are the men of principle," Ben Wade boasted; "they are the men who feel what they contend for. They are not your slippery politicians who can jigger this way or that, or construe a thing any way to suit the present occasion. They are the men who go deeply down for principle and are not to be detached by any of your higgling. The sternness of their principle has revolutionized this whole continent."[11] In short, the Radicals were not pragmatic or empiric; and not being so, they were not typical or normal American politicians. They could not conceive that sometimes the imposition of right principles produces bad results, they could not credit that sometimes the removal of an evil may cause greater evils; they were so sure of their motives that they did not have to consider results. The rightness of their cause is not at stake, is not perhaps the kind of subject on which the historian should pronounce. Whatever the case, few would deny that the anti-slavery crusade had about it elements that were grandly righteous. But it was the kind of righteousness that reckoned little of consequence, especially the consequence to others.

Essentially the conflict in the Republican ranks was over how the problem of slavery should be approached, on a basis of principle or pragmatism. This is not to say that all Conservatives were pragmatic. Some were, in their own way, quite as doctrinaire as were most Radicals, but many were not; and the great Conservative and the great opponent of radicalism was the supreme pragmatist in our history. And it was precisely because he was what he was that the Radicals scorned and despised Abraham Lincoln. Professor Donald makes the point that many Republicans, Radicals and Conservatives alike, considered Lincoln to be indecisive and incompetent and said so, and he further observes that such personal denunciations of a president are heard in every administration. There is perception in this and also a lack of it. Historians will, of course, give different readings to the same documents, but it would seem that the personal criticism of Lincoln emanating from the Radicals was of a different order from that coming from other Republicans, being particularly savage and venomous. At any rate, we know that Lincoln was deeply pained by the tone of the Radical blasts, notably by the Wade-Davis Manifesto, and that he once spoke sadly of the "petulant and vicious fretfulness" displayed by most Radicals.[12]

But the Radicals went beyond mere evaluations of Lincoln as an executive or administrator. In their lexicon the theme was that the President was a man without principle or doctrine. He had no anti-slavery instincts, no crusading zeal to eradicate evil, no blueprint for reform, no grasp of immutable truth. Wendell Phillips, on the eve of the election of 1864, expressed exactly the Radical summation of

Lincoln. The note struck by Phillips was not that Lincoln was incompetent or even bad but that being without dogma he was simply nothing. The administration had tried "many times," Phillips observed, to resist "the Revolution" embodied in radicalism but had been overborne by it. And if Lincoln was re-elected the administration would continue to resist; at the least, Lincoln, because he could not realize the importance of principle, would do nothing to assist the Revolution. The Radicals did indeed think that Lincoln was deficient, but not so much as a political operator as a moral leader, and it was primarily for this reason that they wanted to discard him in 1864. James A. Garfield stated revealingly the objections of the Radicals to a further tenure for Lincoln: "I hope we may not be compelled to push him four years more."[13] Running all through the Radical literature on Lincoln is a suggestion of condescension, the condescension of the ideologue for the pragmatist, of the generalist for the particularist. Because the President had no firmly based beliefs, charged Joshua R. Giddings, the party had been forced to abandon its fundamental beliefs. "We are to go into the next Presidential election without doctrines, principles, or character," Giddings wailed, and added contemptuously: "But to make the union and the support of the administration the test questions." Casting up at the end of war the reasons for the triumph of the Union, L. Maria Child recalled the "want of moral grandeur" in the government during the first years of the war and the consequent failure of Northern arms. But then Radical counsels had come to prevail and immediately things changed: great ideas and great principles were installed and victory had naturally followed. Simple Lincoln had not understood that victory depended on the right doctrine, but he had gone along with the men who did. How fortunate it was after all, Miss Child patronized, that he had been a man who was willing to grow.[14]

The ardent feminine Radical was certain that the hearts of the soldiers had been sad and cold until the correct dogma had been instituted, whereupon they had become irresistible. But in the early stages of the war many Radicals, while they hoped the men in uniform would think right, did not wish them to become too victorious too soon. Rather, they were willing that the armies should fight on indefinitely, until the voters at home were persuaded to the Radical program; and if reverses in the field were necessary to effect this conversion the Radicals were quite content to have the soldiers suffer the reverses. This is not to say that the Radicals wanted the armies or the war to fail. But certainly many of them, in their devotion to doctrine, were prepared to prolong the struggle until their objectives were accomplished. "If it continues thirty years and bankrupts the whole nation," cried Ben Wade, "I hope to God there will be no peace until we can say there is not a slave in this land."[15] The speeches and writings of Radicals of all sizes are crammed with affirmations that defeat will be good for the popular soul, that penance and punishment must precede redemption. Wendell Phillips intoned: "God grant us so many reverses that the government may learn its duty; God grant us the war may never end till it leaves us on the solid granite of impartial liberty and justice."[16] And from that most doctrinaire of all Radicals, Charles Sumner, came this: "We are too victorious; I fear more from our victories than from our defeats. . . . The God of battles seems latterly to smile upon us. I am content that he should not smile too much. . . . There must be more delay and more suffering,—yet another 'plague' before all will agree to 'let my people go': and the war cannot, must not, end till then."[17] It is contended that such statements do not represent the normal sentiments of politicians discussing normal political issues. They are not oratory but theology. Whatever they reflect of the sincerity and sense of justice of the speakers, they reveal that determination in radicalism and abolitionism to remove evil regardless of who suffered, the sinners in the South and even the drafted instruments who were, at the right time, to crush the sinners. These are the implacable declarations of men who had the absolute solution and who would insist on that solution regardless of consequence. The pragmatist in the White House could not have spoken in such a spirit, nor would he, if he could help it, accept the solution.

As a part of the solution, the Radicals proposed to make over the social structure of the South, to make it over to accord with the dictates of moral theory. This determination is one of the most significant manifestations of their doctrinaire zeal. "The whole social system of the Gulf States is to be taken to pieces," exulted Phillips;

"every bit of it." Thaddeus Stevens hoped for the same result, but he was skeptical that it could be achieved. "Whether we shall find anybody with a sufficient grasp of mind and sufficient moral courage, to treat this as a radical revolution, and remodel our institutions, I doubt," Stevens wrote. "It would involve the desolation of the South as well as emancipation; and a repeopling of half the continent. This ought to be done but it startles most men."[18] Not only would the Radicals reconstruct the society of a part of the country, but in the process of removing an evil that could not be abided they would punish the people responsible for the evil, punish them not reluctantly or with stern love but with a kind of ecstasy that went with the joy of doing God's will, with a zeal that became men charged with constituting a society that glorified their Creator. The punishment of slaveholders is an element that bulks large in Radical thought. It deserves more attention than it has received from historians as another key to the Radical psychology and as an indicator of the sweep of the Radical program. The Radicals proposed penalties that were not only stringent but remarkably durable.

From the Radical chorus on what should be done to the South a few voices are extracted. Owen Lovejoy: "If there is no other way to quell this rebellion, we will make a solitude, and call it peace." Zachariah Chandler: "A rebel has sacrificed all his rights. He has no right to life, liberty, property, or the pursuit of happiness. Everything you give him, even life itself, is a boon which he has forfeited."[19] Thaddeus Stevens: "Abolition—yes! abolish everything on the face of the earth but this Union; free every slave—slay every traitor—burn every Rebel mansion, if these things be necessary to preserve this temple of freedom to the world and to our posterity." Henry Wilson: "Sir, it seems to me that our duty is as clear as the track of the sun across the heavens, and that duty is before the adjournment of this Congress to lay low in the dust under our feet, so that iron heels will rest upon it, this great rebel, this giant criminal, this guilty murderer, that is warring upon the existence of this country."[20]

Again it is submitted that statements such as these are more than the rhetorical mouthings common to politicians, more than the customary commentaries on normal political issues. These are the expressions of abstract reformers who were so certain of their motives that they did not have to consider the results of their course, who were so convinced of their righteousness that they wanted to punish the sinners as well as the sin. One may readily concede that the anti-slavery cause was a noble endeavor and yet at the same time note, as Lincoln noted, that it had its darker and socially mischievous side. For the Radicals came and, being what they were, came soon to demand the very policy Lincoln had warned against when he begged his party not to resort to a "violent and remorseless revolutionary struggle." Historians have talked much about the deep-laid plans of the Radicals to solidify and expand their dominance in the years after the war. The recent revisionists have questioned this thesis, doubting that the Radicals saw that far ahead, and they are in part right. Indeed, on one count the opposite of the conventional view would seem to be true—that in their terrible certainty and zeal the Radicals did not look far enough into the future. Intent on removing a sin, they did not consider, as did the pragmatic Lincoln, that the sinners would have to be lived with after the war. They were for the Union but in it they would make no viable place for the defeated side. Perhaps the real criticism of the Radicals should be not that they planned too well but too little.

The Radicals not only spoke a revolutionary vocabulary, they employed on occasion revolutionary techniques. Somewhere along the line, probably in the long frustrating struggle against slavery, many of them had acquired revolutionary temperaments. To achieve their objectives or just to snap the unbearable tension of being unable to lay hands on evil, that is, slavery, they were willing to use short cuts, to skirt around the edges, to play loosely with accepted procedures; they talked openly of the end justifying the means; they were ruthlessly determined to accomplish their end because it was both theirs and right. We see one aspect of this psychology, and again the constant commitment to doctrine, in the insistent Radical demand that the management of the war, in its civilian and military branches, be entrusted exclusively to Radical antislavery men, to men who, in Radical terminology, had their hearts in the struggle. It may be said by some that the Radicals were only trying in the normal fashion of politicians to get their hands on some patronage. But surely any reading of the documents will demonstrate that this was more than just a grab for jobs. These dedicated doctrinaires intended if they could to proscribe from the government and the armies every individual who did not agree with them completely. The expressions of Radical opinion on this goal are too plentiful and too plain to admit of much doubt. Over and over they say that the President who did not know doctrine must be surrounded in his cabinet by men of doctrine, that the armies must be led by "generals of ideas" who were swayed by "the great invisible forces," that the imposition of a Radical policy on the administration would be barren unless it was administered by Radical men.[21]

The Radicals displayed their revolutionary spirit on many occasions and in several areas of government and politics. One of the most sensational manifestations was their attempt in 1864, first, to prevent Lincoln's renomination by the Republicans, and after that failed, to force his withdrawal as the party's candidate. The episode is a rare case of political behaviorism. In our system the party in power almost has to go into a presidential election with the man who has been president. If he wants the nomination, the party is constrained to give it to him, for to repudiate the man is to repudiate the party's record, and this is a party confession of failure. The business is so risky that it has rarely been tried. This rule of politics was not as well established in the nineteenth century as it later became but it was apparent then and should have been apparent to the Radicals in a wartime election. The most unique feature of the affair was the effort of some Radical leaders to force Lincoln off the ticket in the late summer and substitute for him a candidate named by the Republican National Committee.

In 1864 the Radicals wanted to deny Lincoln the nomination, partly because they thought he did not appreciate principle, partly because, in Garfield's words, they did not want to have to push him four years more, and partly because they felt they could not trust him to deal with the emerging problem of reconstruction. "He is hardly the man to handle the country, while its heart is overgenerous with reconstituted peace, so that due guarantees may be exacted from its enemies," observed a Radical editor.[22] As it turned out, the Radicals could not effect either of their objectives. They were unable to prevent Lincoln's nomination and they were unable to force him to yield up the nomination after he had won it. The reasons for their discomfiture were many and complex. Lincoln's popularity with the people and the politicians was too great to be disregarded. Many Republican leaders, including some Radicals, feared a disrupting fight in the party that might lead to a Democratic victory. And as bad as Lincoln was, he was infinitely better than any Democrat.[23]

It is true, as Professor Donald has reminded us, that many Republicans of all stripes were dubious about Lincoln's candidacy. But the Radicals were the core of the opposition to him, the men who organized to act against him, and whereas other Republicans diverged from Lincoln for reasons of expediency the Radicals were the only ones who opposed him on grounds of doctrine. It is also true, as Professor Donald has again told us, that the Radicals fell in behind Lincoln at the last and worked for his re-election. But they fell in with sullen acquiescence and only because they had no other alternative. As the canny observer who edited the New York *Herald* noted, all the Republican elements had to support Lincoln in the hope of getting something from him:

> Whatever they say now, we venture to predict that Wade and his tail; and Bryant and his tail; and Wendell Phillips and his tail; and Weed, Barney, Chase and their tails; and Winter Davis, Raymond, Opdyke and Forney who have no tails; will all make tracks for Old Abe's plantation, and will soon be found crowing and blowing, and vowing and writhing, and swearing and stumping . . . , declaring that he and he alone, is the hope of the nation, the bugaboo of Jeff Davis, the first of Conservatives, the best of Abolitionists, the purest of patriots, the most gullible of mankind, the easiest President to manage, and the person especially predestined and foreordained by Providence to carry on the war, free the niggers, and give all the faithful a fair share of the spoils.[24]

The election of 1864 illustrates many things, among them the wonderful diversity of American parties and the paradox that the Republicans could be at once divided by an abnormal issue and united by the normal requirements of politics.

The most instructive demonstration of the revolutionary temperament of the Radicals, certainly for the historian, is their endeavor to establish the primacy of Congress in the governmental system. Here, as with other areas of war politics, it is necessary to lay down some initial qualifications. Some Conservatives advocated a larger role for Congress in the management of the war, and the Radical push in this direction represented in part the normal reaction of the legislative branch against the executive in a time of crisis. But the Radical leaders proposed to go beyond a defense against executive expansion or even an enlargement of legislative influence. Essentially they wanted to set up a kind of Congressional dictatorship. They would do this formally—some Radicals favored the installation of the English cabinet system[25]—or, preferably, informally, by overshadowing the executive with the power of Congress. The latter course was exemplified notably in the creation and the career of the Committee on the Conduct of the War, a unique agency in our history and undeniably a Radical-dominated body. Ostensibly an investigative mechanism, it attempted to be also and with substantial success a policy-forming institution. The Committee's work cannot be adequately treated here, but in summary it is accurate to say that in no other of our conflicts did Congress attain such a dominant voice in the direction of military affairs.[26]

The lines on the legislature versus the executive issue were drawn early. Just a few months after the war started, Senator Jacob Collamer, speaking for the administration, warned his Radical colleagues: "War is not a business Congress can engineer. It is properly *Executive* business, and the moment Congress passes beyond the line of providing for the wants of the Government, and [decides] the purposes of the war, to say how it shall be conducted, the whole thing will prove a failure."[27] The Radical answer to this thesis came from many sources and most succinctly from Ben Wade: "The President cannot lay down and fix the principles upon which a war shall be conducted. . . . It is for Congress to lay down the rules and regulations by which the Executive shall be governed in conducting a war."[28] Examples of the conflict arising from these opposed concepts are many. The most interesting and revealing one is the December, 1862, attempt of the Republican senators to force Lincoln to reform his cabinet by removing Secretary of State William H. Seward.

The Radicals objected to Seward almost from the day he went into the cabinet. Their criticism of him was simple and typical: he had no principles, or the wrong ones, and, ergo, his presence in the government conducted to a listless prosecution of the war and to eventual defeat. This was, of course, the same kind of denunciation thrown by the Radicals at all their opponents, civil and military. Only men of right doctrine should direct the war because men of wrong doctrine would lose it; generals lost battles not because of a lack of generalship but because of a lack of principle. This notion of a relation between principle and military success, this determination to eliminate men without principle fascinated European observers and led them to liken the Radicals to the faction of the Mountain in the French Revolution.[29] In December of 1862 the Radicals had abundant reason to question the absence of victory. The armies seemed stalled on all fronts and the bloody defeat of Fredericksburg had shocked the country. At this moment all the frustration and ire of the Radicals fell upon Seward, who was supposed to have a malign and pervasive influence on the President and who in some mysterious way was responsible for the failure of the armies. Three days after Fredericksburg the Republican senators, at the summons of Radical members, met in a secret caucus. The result of this meeting and another on the next day was a decision to send a delegation to Lincoln to urge on him a reconstitution of the cabinet and changes in the military list. In the words of a paper agreed to by the participants, the "theory" of the American system was that the cabinet should be a unit in "political principles"; and it was "unwise and unsafe" to entrust the direction of important operations or separate commands to generals who did not believe in a vigorous prosecution of the war, or, as Wade put it, to officers who had no sympathy with the cause. The committee, composed of seven Radicals and two Conservatives, met with Lincoln in two stormy sessions. What occurred at these gatherings and Lincoln's adroit handling of the situation and his ultimate triumph are too well known to be detailed.[30] The broader meaning of the episode does, however, require notice.

Not even Professor Donald contends that this affair represents the normal workings of American politics. But he does argue that it cannot be viewed as a Radical project or plot, pointing out that the Conservatives participated in the meeting and that all the senators agreed on the sentiments in the paper to be presented to Lincoln. This is, like his thesis on a whole, partially right and partially the opposite; it clarifies our understanding of the episode and at the same time obscures it. The motives of the senators were several and complex. Some of both factions wanted Seward out because they disliked him personally or politically or because they thought he did exert a bad influence on Lincoln. Others, and again of both factions, honestly thought, and with some reason, that Lincoln did not make sufficient use of his cabinet and that an alteration in it might force him to change his procedure. But in the last analysis the December offensive has still to be viewed as a Radical maneuver. It is evident, from Senator Fessenden's account of the event, from Senator Browning's diary, and from other sources,[31] that the Radicals instigated and influenced the caucus and that the Conservatives went along, if for no other reason, because they had to. They hoped to avoid a factional fight and to soften the resolutions presented to the President; thus whereas the Radicals proposed to demand of Lincoln that he reform the cabinet, the Conservatives persuaded the caucus to approve a request for reform. Moreover, in the meetings with Lincoln the Radicals took the lead in denouncing Seward and conservative dominance in the government and the army; and, most significant, they were the only ones who contended, either to the caucus or to the President, that doctrine should be the basis for removing or retaining either civil or military officials. And while many of the senators showed a certain fuzziness about the nature of the governmental system, it was the Radicals who boldly admitted that the Senate was stepping outside its proper sphere. Fessenden told the caucus that the time had arrived when the Senate could no longer "content itself with the discharge of its constitutional duties," and after the affair was over he characterized it as "a new point in history . . . a new proceeding—one probably unknown to the government of the country."[32]

In the constitutional sense the December crisis was in large part an attempt by Congress to extend its control to the appointing and removing power of the executive. In the political sense it was, as Washington observers well realized, a scheme to force Lincoln to reconstitute his cabinet on a Radical basis, with Secretary of the Treasury Salmon P. Chase emerging as the dominating figure. It could have become something entirely different. At the height of the affair, when it seemed that the cabinet might break up, both Radicals and Conservatives descended on Lincoln with proposed slates for his new group of advisers. It has escaped the notice of all commentators that the Conservatives may have supported the original movement because they too had a motive to dissolve the cabinet. Just as the Radicals considered Lincoln to be too close to the Conservatives, so the latter thought him to be too cozy with the Radicals. The more ultra Conservatives thought that if they could surround him with men of their stamp they could control him. But Lincoln had no intention of falling under the dominance of either faction. He would have neither a completely Radical nor a completely Conservative cabinet. It is highly significant that when he rejected Browning's suggested list of Conservative members he said such a cabinet would "be in his way on the negro question." He meant that in dealing with slavery he would be bound by neither extreme, that he would go neither too fast nor too slow.

Both of the Republican factions were puzzled at times as to which side Lincoln espoused, and so also were more objective observers. "The conservative Republicans think him too much in the hands of the radicals," one reporter noted, "while the radical Republicans think him too slow, yielding, and half-hearted."[33] A Democratic journalist, trying to analyze the conflict in the Republican party, came closer than he perhaps realized to the truth, to the paradox that the Republicans were at once concurrent and contrary. Lincoln was in his beliefs, thought this man, as one with the Radicals. But he was not accepted by them as a leader because he had not done "everything in their particular way, and at their designated moment."[34] Congressman Owen Lovejoy, a Radical without the personal dislike of Lincoln manifested by many Radicals, propounded an identical analysis in more striking language. The President was like a man trying to handle two horses, Lovejoy conjectured. The superb Radical horse wanted to clear all barriers at once, while the poor Conservative horse held back. Lovejoy criticized Lincoln for checking the forward steed but then added: "If he does not drive as fast as I would, he is on the same road, and it is a question of time."[35] These last two comments embody the essence of the paradox and the essence of the Republican division. Lincoln and the Radicals *were* in agreement on the ultimate goal, the extinction of slavery. On the great end there was no fundamental difference between them. But they *were* divided on the method and the timing, on how fast and in what manner they should move toward the goal. Both were committed to bringing about a wrenching social change. One would do it with the experimental caution of the pragmatist, the other with the headlong rush of the doctrinaire. And this matter of method on this particular issue was a fundamental difference. If a question of semantics arises concerning the use of *fundamental*, it can at least be said that the difference was deeper and darker than the fissures normally separating American political groups. It should not be exaggerated. But it cannot be exorcised.

Lincoln was on the slavery question, as he was on most matters, a conservative. Unlike the ultra Radicals, he could tolerate evil, especially when he feared that to uproot it would produce greater evils. But he was not the kind of conservative who refused to move at all against evil, who let his pragmatism fade into expediency, who blindly rejected change when it could not be denied. Yet there were just such men among the ultra Conservatives of his party, and Lincoln opposed them as he did the ultra Radicals. He knew that he was not completely with them, and, as he told Browning, he would not let the Conservatives control the slavery issue. He knew too that he was against the Radicals and also with them. Speaking of the Missouri Radicals but doubtless having the whole genre in mind, he said: "They are utterly lawless—the unhandiest devils in the world to deal with—but after all their faces are set Zionwards."[36] He did work with the Radicals but he also resisted them. He used them—as he did the Conservatives—to effect a great social change with the smallest possible social dislocation. It would indeed be an error, as we are in Professor Donald's debt for telling us, to make too much out of the conflict in the Republican party over slavery. It would be a greater error to dismiss this unique episode and its unique issue as something normal or average and to treat it on the level of ordinary politics. There is little about the Civil War that is ordinary.

Abraham Lincoln: Pragmatic Democrat

When President Lincoln in May of 1862 revoked General Hunter's order freeing slaves in his department, Wendell Phillips exploded with frustrated wrath. "The President is a very slow man; an honest man, but a slow moving machine," cried the Boston abolitionist. "I think if we can nudge him a little, it will be of great advantage." But as the war continued, Phillips came to despair that the man in the White House could be nudged—fast enough or far enough. "Mr. Lincoln is not a leader," Phillips lamented. "His theory of Democracy is that he is the servant of the people, not the leader. . . . We pay dear today for having as President a man so cautious as to be timid. . . . As long as you keep the present turtle at the head of affairs, you make a pit with one hand and fill it with the other. I know Mr. Lincoln. . . . He is a mere convenience and is waiting like any other broomstick to be used." Most abolitionists subscribed to Phillips' evaluation of Lincoln, and they retained their opinion even after the President threw his support behind emancipation. In 1865, near the end of the war, L. Maria Child, reminiscing about the final victory of the antislavery cause, observed, "I think we have reason to thank God for Abraham Lincoln." Despite all his deficiencies, she con-

Reprinted by permission of the University of Illinois Press, from Norman A. Graebner (ed.), *The Enduring Lincoln*, © 1959 by the Board of Trustees of the University of Illinois.

cluded with that condescension peculiar to intellectuals, he had
been a man "who was willing to grow."

I

There was more in the abolitionist attitude than merely a feeling
that Lincoln was a good but not particularly bright man who had to
be guided along the right path. To such abolitionists as Phillips and
such dedicated Radical Republican leaders as George W. Julian,
Abraham Lincoln was a politician without principle. These men can
be accurately classified under a term popular in modern thought as
"ideologues." They had a definite and detailed ideology or philosophy, and they had a precise blueprint for social reform based on a
preconceived abstract theory. They were prepared to put their design
into effect without much regard for the opinions of those who opposed them and without much thought of the problems that abrupt
change might create. In describing their methods and goals they
used such phrases as "remorseless and revolutionary violence."
Their motto was that of intellectual radicals in all ages: Let there be
justice even though the heavens crumble down. To such men—
grim, certain, doctrinaire—Abraham Lincoln seemed theoretically
backward. So also must Andrew Jackson have seemed to the professional expositors of Jacksonian Democracy, Theodore Roosevelt to
the advanced pundits of Progressivism, and Franklin D. Roosevelt to
the social welfare philosophers of the New Deal. None of the great
American political leaders has been a systematic thinker or an advocate of change for the sake of theory.

Lincoln believed deeply in certain fundamental political principles, but he never assumed to elevate his beliefs into a doctrine. And
his opinions or ideas bore little if any resemblance to what is called
ideology today. Lincoln would be patiently amused at the attempts
of moderns to classify his thinking into some neat niche under some
convenient label. We are familiar with and tolerantly scornful of the
efforts of politicians and special interests to annex him for their own
ends. He has been claimed by Republicans and Democrats, by parties from the far right to the distant left. He has been put forward as
the spokesman of unbridled individualism—and of unrestrained

statism. But the ax-grinders have not been the only classifiers. The academic scholars, perhaps influenced more than any other group in contemporary society by the concept of ideology and always convinced that a man's ideas can be arranged in a logical pattern, have tried their hand at pinning tidy thought tags on Father Abraham. Characteristically, they have come up with contradictory conclusions.

Some historians, noting Lincoln's tributes to equality of opportunity and the virtues of hard work, and his obvious caution in the face of change, have depicted him as the personification of the economic conservative. Other writers, impressed by the same evidence but giving it an opposite twist, have decided that Lincoln knew little about the economic trends of his times, that he was, in fact, almost an economic simpleton and possibly a folksy front for the industrial capitalism then rising to power. But most historians, responding to the intellectual climate of our day and reflecting their own beliefs, have made Lincoln a liberal, which by their definition means a modern Democrat. Citing his statements that human rights were above property rights, and his friendly words for labor, they have presented him as an early New Dealer, as a pre-Fort Sumter Franklin D. Roosevelt.

All these attempts to categorize Lincoln's thinking fall wide of the mark. Indeed, it is doubtful if easy, explanatory labels can be affixed to any of the American political leaders. The nature of our political system is so complex that no facile polarism can be imposed upon it, especially when the polarism employs such terms as conservative and liberal drawn from European usage. Lincoln, like Jefferson, Jackson, and the two Roosevelts, was a pragmatist. In his approach to social problems he represented the best tradition of British and American politics. The spirit of American pragmatic reform, Frederick Lewis Allen has suggested, may be illustrated by comparing society or the nation to a machine. If something goes wrong with the machine, what should one do? The reactionary might say, "Don't fool with it, you will ruin it." The radical might say, "It's no good, get rid of it and find a new one." But the pragmatist would try to fix the machine up, to remove the defective part and add a new one. Translated into political language, his attitude would be to make a needed change at the right time. American pragmatism has stressed the necessity for continuous, co-operative experimental reform—but it has also insisted, above all, that while changes are being made the machine must be kept running. A proposed change may be moral or theoretically right, but it has also to be demonstrably sound in the light of past experience and present realities.

Lincoln's political beliefs, or what might be termed his inner opinions, were based firmly on principle. His public or outer opinions were always restrained by his strong pragmatic sense, by his fine feeling for what, given the fact of human limitations, was politically possible. One of the keys to his thinking is his statement that few things in this world were wholly good or wholly evil. Instinctively Lincoln distrusted doctrinaire thinkers like the abolitionists who claimed to know what was good and evil, and who were prepared to act upon their opinions. He distrusted the abolitionists because they were blueprint people, because they proposed to make a change based on theory, because they would force this change over all resistance and without regard for social consequences. Lincoln was as much opposed to slavery as the abolitionists. "If slavery is not wrong," he said, "nothing is wrong." But he did not consider that he had the right, even as President, to translate his opinion into action and impose it on others. "I am naturally anti-slavery," he said in 1864. "And yet I have never understood that the Presidency conferred upon me an unrestricted right to act officially upon this judgment and feeling."

By temperament Lincoln was tolerant, patient, noncensorious. By nature he was practical, moderate, gradual. Being what he was, he preferred to see changes come slowly and after due deliberation and with the consent of all affected groups. Almost instinctively Lincoln inclined to a middle-of-the-road position on issues. "Stand WITH anybody that stands RIGHT," he advised the Whigs in 1854. "Stand with him while he is right and PART with him when he goes wrong. Stand WITH the abolitionist in restoring the Missouri Compromise; and stand AGAINST him when he attempts to repeal the fugitive slave law. In the latter case you stand with the Southern disunionist. What of that? . . . In both cases you are right. In both cases you expose the dangerous extremes. In both cases you stand on middle ground and hold the ship level and steady." A man who thought like this was definitely not the kind of leader desired by ideologues like Phillips—a leader who was ready to do what God would do if God had possession of all the facts.

II

The historians of intellectual life have emphasized that four primary principles formed the basis of American political philosophy in the middle years of the nineteenth century when Lincoln was growing into mental maturity. Americans might quarrel about the application of these principles to specific current issues, but to an extraordinary degree they were accepted as common beliefs, so much so that some writers have referred to them as articles of the national faith. The four ideas may be conveniently summarized:

(1) A supernatural power, God or a Guiding Providence or nature, exercised a controlling influence over the affairs of men. God had created a divine or higher law for the guidance of humans, and men could apprehend this law and should seek to approximate their own statutes to it.

(2) Man was not just another creature on the planet, but a being with a higher nature; or, as some put it, he had within him a spark of the divine. He had a mind, and hence could reason, and he had a conscience, and hence could distinguish right from wrong. This being true, he could govern himself through democratic forms and could achieve, if not perfectibility, a high degree of political maturity and a fair measure of happiness.

(3) The best economic system was one based on private ownership of property and one in which most people were property owners. The right to acquire property was a natural right, and all men should strive to secure property. Under the workings of the system, some would get more than others but no great inequities would result as long as equal opportunity existed. And no class or group should enjoy special privileges that gave it an artificial advantage over others.

(4) The American Union was a unique and precious experiment in government. As the most successful example of popular government in a big country, the United States was the supreme demonstration

of democracy and the hope of world democracy. It made men free in America, and eventually by the sheer force of its example would make them free everywhere. Americans were profoundly conscious of the Union's value to themselves and of its universal mission. This consciousness was one of the strongest forces sustaining American nationalism.

Lincoln took over all four of the common beliefs of his time and made them a part of his own thought. This is not to say that he borrowed them blindly or adopted them without analysis. Such a procedure would have been foreign to Lincoln's nature. Every idea he ever held was the result of long and tough thinking, of introspective brooding during which he turned a proposition over and over in his mind. When he finally arrived at the formulation of a fundamental principle, it usually became a permanent part of his mental make-up. Nevertheless, Lincoln must be classified as a derivative rather than a seminal thinker, as an expresser—in superb words—rather than an originator of ideas. He did, however, give a significant extension to one of the four principles, the exaltation of the American Union.

Statements attesting Lincoln's belief that a supernatural force controlled human activities are sprinkled throughout his public and private papers, and they appear in practically every phase of his political career. Even in his early years he was intrigued by the concept of this compelling force, which he sometimes called history. As he grew older he came to call it God. For most Americans, the notion of a Guiding Providence meant only that a benign deity exercised a general influence over the affairs of men and that within the divine framework men had some freedom to work out their destinies. History was not a haphazard process tending to nowhere in particular, but a progressive movement that was being guided toward a definite and high goal.

But Lincoln, with a deep mystic strain in his nature and with a constant sense of fatalism, both public and personal, pushed this idea farther than most. It is no exaggeration to say that during the Civil War he developed a mechanistic interpretation of history. The great event with which his name is associated, the destruction of slavery, was, he believed, an act of divine power of which he was but the instrument. In a remarkable letter written in 1864 he reviewed the course of wartime emancipation, and then he added, "I claim not to have controlled events, but confess plainly that events have controlled me." In 1861 nobody had "devised, or expected" that the war would end slavery but now the institution was approaching extinction. "God alone can claim it. Whither it is tending seems plain. If God now wills the removal of a great wrong, and wills also that we of the North as well as you of the South, should pay fairly for our complicity in that wrong, impartial history will find therein new cause to attest and revere the justice and goodness of God." Lincoln stressed this theme again in the Second Inaugural Address when he said that the war was God's way of removing the evil of slavery as a punishment to both the North and the South for having condoned it. He realized that his ascription of inexorability would offend some people. "Men are not flattered by being shown that there has been a difference between the Almighty and them," he told Thurlow Weed. "To deny it, however, in this case, is to deny that there is a God governing the world."

The corollary to the principle of a supernatural power, the existence of a supernatural law, also formed a part of Lincoln's thought, but in his application of the principle to current issues he parted company with some of his fellow workers in the antislavery movement. From a reading of his papers, it is obvious that Lincoln believed there was a moral or higher law. "I hold," he said in the First Inaugural Address, "that in contemplation of universal law, and of the Constitution, the Union of these States is perpetual." It is just as obvious that he thought the Constitution approximated the spirit of divine law and embodied the best experience of man in government. He saw, or as Carl Sandburg has said, he sensed, that in a democracy there must be a balance between freedom and responsibility. The great merit of the American federal system was that it provided a balance between the government and the individual and between the nation and the states. Lincoln addressed himself to one of the fundamental problems of political science when, with his own government in mind, he asked: "Must a government, of necessity, be too strong for the liberties of its own people, or too weak to maintain its own existence?" The American system of divided powers, he thought, provided the only answer: "A majority, held in restraint by constitutional checks, and limitations, and always changing easily, with deliberate changes of popular opinions and sentiments, is the only true sovereign of a free people. Whoever rejects it, does of necessity, fly to anarchy or to despotism."

Lincoln accepted the principle of a higher law, but he refused to give it the logical extension, logical in theory, that some opponents of slavery gave it. If the supernatural law was perfect, it followed that human statutes that contravened it were illegal and must be changed. And if they could not be changed, they should not be obeyed. Some of the antislavery people persuaded themselves that the divine law concept justified the violation of any law protecting slavery. This was what William H. Seward meant when, in hurling defiance at the Fugitive Slave Act, he said, "There is a higher law than the Constitution." Lincoln also disliked the fugitive slave measure, but he could never have agreed to the idea that individuals could flout it, or any other law, merely because it conflicted with their interpretation of higher law. In some countries it might be necessary for men to defy the law, but in the United States, where change was easy and deliberate, such action was unnecessary and irresponsible. It constituted a flying to anarchy.

Lincoln's confidence in the competence of men to govern themselves, in the democratic experiment, is apparent in his every political act from the Illinois legislature to the White House. Nowhere in his writing is expressed any doubt of majority rule or any fear of the tyranny of numbers. "Why should there not be a patient confidence in the ultimate justice of the people?" he asked in the First Inaugural Address. "Is there any better, or equal hope, in the world?" At the same time it is evident that Lincoln did not accept completely the roseate diagnosis of human nature that was so popular in the nineteenth century. This principle of the democratic faith was taken by some to mean that man, good, intelligent, and possessing a higher nature, was capable of approaching perfectibility and of achieving a perfect society. Such an optimistic prognosis was too much for Lincoln to swallow; it ran counter to his observation of reality. We don't have to read the Bible to find out that men are bad, he is supposed to have said, we can tell that by looking around us.

Rather than believing in the perfectibility of man, Lincoln thought that man was imperfect but was, nevertheless, the best instrument with which to accomplish the divine purpose. Rejecting the dream of unlimited social progress, Lincoln still believed that man was capable of improving himself and of increasing his political competence. His analysis was closer to the practical ideas of the Founding Fathers than to the romantic ideals of the thinkers of his own time. Lincoln readily grasped that the Fathers had not tried to establish a system of government based on human perfectibility but instead had created one that would enable men to raise progressively the level of their political maturity. In one of those "Fragments" in which he was wont to record his thinking, Lincoln wrote: "*Most governments* have been based, practically, on the denial of equal rights of men . . . ; *ours* began, by *affirming* those rights. They said, some men are too *ignorant*, and *vicious*, to share in government. Possibly so, said we; and, by your system, you would always keep them ignorant and vicious. We proposed to give *all* a chance; and we expected the weak to grow stronger, the ignorant wiser; and all better, and happier together. . . ."

It is Lincoln's economic thought that has provoked the widest differences of opinion among students of his life. The confusion derives from an attempt to apply labels, liberal and conservative, that have little applicability to the American scene, at least to the nineteenth century, and to a tendency of authors to project their own ideas and their images of the economic institutions of their day backward into time. Actually, Lincoln's economic views cannot be called either liberal or conservative in our sense of the words. Economics-wise he belongs to no party or group today, certainly not to the Republican and positively not to the New Deal. His economic concepts were completely the product of the economic system that he knew, and that system bears little resemblance to our own.

Lincoln grew to maturity during the preindustrial age of America's history; he became President when the nation stood at the threshold of the era of big business. Industrial combinations in the form that developed in the years after Appomattox did not exist. It is true that there were substantial aggregations of capital, especially in the Northeast, but these organizations and their future economic implication did not impress Lincoln and most Americans. (The opinion of some writers that Lincoln had only a very general understanding of economic matters is probably correct.) In the system that Lincoln saw about him—and this was particularly true of his own section, the Northwest—a large number of people owned property, in the shape of farms, factories, and shops, and made their living from the operation of their holdings. Unlike the present system, relatively few people worked for other people for wages or salaries. Many owners of property were also laborers in the sense that they worked in their own establishments. In short, this was a capitalistic economy that contained a lot of capitalists.

Lincoln's economic ideas were those of the average small capitalist of his time. It might be said that Lincoln and most Americans were "men on the make." That is, they wanted to raise their material standing by exercising the virtue of acquisitiveness. They saw nothing wrong with the drive to acquire property; indeed, they tended to glorify the property-getting process as a social good. In Lincoln's opinion the great merit of the American economic system was that it offered an equal opportunity to all men to secure property. And in his view equal opportunity would result in a system in which most men owned property. Lincoln respected labor, and he attested his respect in notable words on a number of occasions. Thus in his annual message to Congress in December, 1861, he said: "Labor is prior to, and independent of, capital. Capital is only the fruit of labor, and could never have existed if labor had not first existed. Labor is the superior of capital, and deserves much the higher consideration." But Lincoln's tributes to labor are usually misunderstood and misapplied today. They were not delivered to labor as a rival power to capital but to labor as a means of creating capital. Through his labor a man could become an owner or an employer. Lincoln always vehemently denied that American society was divided into two rigid classes of employers and employees. Most men, he argued, neither worked for others nor hired others to work for them; rather, they worked for themselves and were both capitalists and laborers. "There is no permanent class of hired laborers amongst us . . . ," Lincoln contended. "The hired laborer of yesterday labors on his own account to-day; and will hire others to labor for him to-morrow.

Advancement—improvement in condition—is the order of things in a society of equals."

No great inequalities would result from the free competition for property, Lincoln thought, as long as the opportunities to compete were equal to all. In a speech at New Haven in 1860 he gave perhaps the fullest expression of his economic views. "What is the true condition of the laborer?" he asked. "I take it that it is best for all to leave each man free to acquire property as fast as he can. Some will get wealthy. I don't believe in a law to prevent a man from getting rich; it would do more harm than good. When one starts poor, as most do in the race of life, free society is such that he knows he can better his condition; he knows that there is no fixed condition of labor, for his whole life." Lincoln's optimistic vision of economic progress may seem naïve to later liberals, and it probably has only a limited validity for the problems of our day. But for his time it was valid enough. By much the same process that he described, Lincoln himself had risen from laborer to capitalist.

III

Of the four principles comprising the current creed of his time, the one that aroused Lincoln's deepest devotion was the exaltation of the American Union. This idea, or this image, of nationalism elicited the most frequent and the most eloquent passages in his writings, and to it he gave a significant extension that constitutes his only original contribution to political theory. It may be added that as a political actor Lincoln's chief concern was with nationality. When we say that as President he saved the Union, we are also saying that he preserved the nation—as both an abstraction and a physical reality. Perhaps Lincoln's truest title is not the Great Emancipator but the Great Nationalist. Three ideas stand out in Lincoln's concept of the nature and the significance of the Union. They, too, may be conveniently presented in itemized form:

(1) The nation was an organic whole, an entity that could never be artificially separated by men. The realities of geography—rivers, mountains, ocean boundaries—demanded that the United States remain united. Where, he asked the South in 1861, could a satisfactory

line of division be drawn between two American nations? "Physically speaking, we cannot separate. We cannot remove our respec-
tive sections from each other, nor build an impassible wall between
them." In his message to Congress in December, 1862, he gave a
moving and also an exceedingly realistic description of the oneness
of the United States, of what he called the "national homestead."
The outstanding American geographical fact, he emphasized, was
the great interior heartland of the Mississippi Valley dominating the
whole nation. Did anyone really believe, he asked, that the Mississippi River could be permanently divided by a man-made line?
The present strife between the North and the South had not sprung
from any natural division between the sections, he insisted, but
from differences among people, "the passing generations of men."
The land, the national homestead, "in all its adaptations and apti-
tudes . . . demands unity, and abhors separation. In fact, it would, ere
long, force reunion, however much of blood and treasure the separation might have cost."

(2) The American nation was uniquely different from all others in
the cementing bond that held it together. Some nations were united
by race, some by culture, some by tradition. But the United States,
said Lincoln in his most original piece of thinking, was bound by an
idea, the principle of equal opportunity for all that was pledged in
the Declaration of Independence and embedded in the national consciousness. In a speech at Independence Hall in Philadelphia while
on his way to Washington in 1861 to be inaugurated President, Lincoln tried to express what he thought was America's great idea. "I
have often inquired of myself, what great principle or idea it was that
kept this Confederacy so long together," he said. "It was not the
mere matter of separation from the motherland, but that sentiment
in the Declaration of Independence which gave liberty not alone to
the people of this country, but hope to the world for all future time.
It was that which gave promise that in due time the weights would
be lifted from the shoulders of all men, and that *all* should have an
equal chance."

(3) American nationality was not a narrow thing intended only for
the benefit of Americans. The Union and the idea it represented
made men free in America and sooner or later by the power of its

example would make them free everywhere. Lincoln was supremely conscious of the world mission of his country. Always during the Civil War he tried to lift the Northern cause to a higher level than victory for one section or even the nation. Always he attempted to show that the preservation of the Union was important for the universal family of mankind. The war was "a people's content" to maintain "in the world, that form and substance of government, whose leading object" was "to elevate the condition of men." The "great republic . . . the principles it lives by, and keeps alive" represented "man's vast future." It was "the last, best hope of earth."

IV

The great problem that faced the men of Lincoln's time was slavery. In his thinking about slavery Lincoln applied to the problem all four of the principles that formed the substance of his general political faith. He was opposed to slavery on moral, democratic, and economic grounds. He thought that it was wrong for one man to own another. He feared that the presence of slavery in American society would subvert the idea of equal opportunity. If the notion that Negroes did not possess equal economic rights became fixed, he said, then the next easy transition would be to deny the same rights to white laborers. He believed that slavery gave a tone of hypocrisy to the claim that the United States symbolized the democratic cause and thus endangered the success of America's world mission.

Yet in his approach to the problem of slavery, Lincoln was completely pragmatic and practical. He outlined his position as early as 1837 in resolutions which he and a colleague presented in the Illinois legislature declaring that slavery was founded on "injustice and bad policy" but that Congress had no power to interfere with it in the states where it existed. To Lincoln one fact in the situation—a fact that the abolitionists and other sincere antislavery people ignored—was of vital importance: slavery existed in the United States and millions of people believed in it. The physical presence of slavery and the feelings of its Southern supporters, he argued, had to be taken into account by the opponents of the institution. "Because we think it wrong, we propose a course of policy that shall deal with it as a wrong," he said. But, he immediately added, "We have a due regard to the actual presence of it amongst us and the difficulties of getting rid of it in any satisfactory way and all the constitutional obligations thrown about it."

Again differing with most antislavery men and showing a keen awareness of social behavior, Lincoln refused to criticize the Southern people for supporting slavery. "They are just what we would be in their situation," he said at Peoria in 1854. "If slavery did not now exist amongst them, they would not introduce it. If it did now exist amongst us, we should not instantly give it up." In this Peoria speech Lincoln dealt with the racial problems that would inevitably follow the destruction of slavery. The question of racial adjustment was inextricably connected with emancipation. If the Negroes were freed, what would be their place in society? The abolitionists favored, at least abstractly, a status of complete equality for the colored people. But most antislavery men, particularly if they were politicians, which was usually the case, hardly ever discussed the position of the Negroes *after* freedom. They had not thought the problem through, probably did not want to think it to a conclusion. Perhaps this was one of the tragedies of the antislavery movement.

Lincoln admitted at Peoria, as he did on other occasions, that he did not know any absolutely satisfactory way of dealing with slavery and the related racial problem. If all earthly power were given him, he said, he would not know what to do. His first impulse would be to free the slaves and remove them outside the United States, but he conceded that this "colonization" plan was impractical and impossible. What of the proposal to give the freed slaves an equal place in society? This would not do, Lincoln thought, because the mass of white people South *and* North would not agree to such a status for colored people. And whether the feelings of the whites were just was beside the point, he said, because "A universal feeling, whether well or ill founded, cannot be safely disregarded." Lincoln's own feelings about race are not easily comprehended by modern men. Personally, he had no color prejudices, as his relations with Negroes while President amply attest. But like perhaps ninety-nine percent of Americans in the nineteenth century, he believed that the colored race, either by nature or by cultural inheritance, was inferior to the white race. Under any system of racial relations and even if the Negroes were free, the superior whites would seek to oppress the lesser race. Immediate emancipation, Lincoln feared, would not therefore benefit either race and would create for the Negroes problems almost as troublesome as those of slavery. As Professor Donald has pointed out, Lincoln's views may not be palatable to the modern reformer but they were an accurate analysis of current American opinion.

Lincoln opposed slavery, but he also opposed the abolitionists— the ideologues who wanted to destroy it immediately and who were certain that they had an absolutely satisfactory way of solving race relations. He disliked their readiness to impose their inner opinions on others, their eagerness to enforce a great social change based on a moral theory. He distrusted their abstract approach to a complex situation and their refusal to admit that all kinds of practical problems would result from a sudden change in that situation. Above all, he was appalled by their willingness to give up the Union if they could not make it over in their image. To him the preservation of American nationality was infinitely more important than the accomplishment of immediate emancipation. "Much as I hate slavery," he said, "I would consent to the extension of it rather than to see the Union dissolved, just as I would consent to any great evil, to avoid a greater one."

At the same time that he attacked the abolitionists' solution, Lincoln put forward his own plan to deal with the problem of slavery. It was to prevent slavery from expanding into the national territories, to pen it up in the states where it already existed. His proposal, he liked to say, would place slavery where the public mind could rest in the assurance that it was in "the course of ultimate extinction." If slavery could not grow, he argued, it would eventually wither and die a natural death. During the interim years, as the institution declined in social health, plans could be worked out for its orderly demise. The slaveholders themselves, perceiving the inevitable, would consent to emancipation and would receive financial compensation from the national government for the loss of their property. This kind of patient abolition, Lincoln thought, would bring in its wake no unfortunate results for either whites or blacks. Lincoln's plan would have taken years to effect, possibly a generation or more, but, and this is often forgotten by some of its critics, it was intended as a fundamental settlement of a problem that had to be settled finally. Lincoln's whole position on the slavery issue was in the finest American pragmatic tradition. He opposed immediate abolition because it would make a right change at the wrong time, would wreck the machine of the Union. He proposed to keep the machine going and to make the change later when the time was right.

Lincoln's plan for a gradual solution of the slavery problem never had a chance. There were too many men in the North and the South who could not wait that long, who were determined to settle the issue immediately, even if they had to resort to force. And so the Civil War came, and Lincoln became the President of a divided Union. He became also the leader of a divided North, of a people who differed among themselves as to the objectives of the war they were fighting. Specifically the question in issue was whether emancipation should be made one of the war aims. The discord in Northern opinion was reflected in Lincoln's own Republican party in the struggle between the Radical and the Conservative factions. The Radicals wanted to use the opportunity of the war to strike down slavery; they demanded that the Union be restored without slavery. Lincoln and the Conservatives hoped to avoid turning the war into a crusade for social change; he and most Conservatives preferred to restore the Union with slavery still intact.

To Lincoln the preservation of the Union, of American nationality, was the great overriding object of the war. The Union dwarfed all other issues, including slavery. Lincoln intended to save the Union by whatever methods he had to use. As he told Horace Greeley, to accomplish his purpose he would, if necessary, free all of the slaves or free none of them or free some and keep others in bondage. At the same time he understood clearly the dynamics in the war situation. He knew that slavery was the provoking cause of the conflict. Slavery was "the disturbing element" in "the national house," he said, and it would continue to generate strife until it was removed. He knew, too, that the antislavery impulse would receive a tremendous impetus from the war. Lincoln approached slavery during the war in the same pragmatic spirit with which he had dealt with it before the war. He was ready to end it, as he would any other social evil, if he was convinced that the time was right and that greater evils would not result from its destruction.

At the beginning of hostilities Lincoln proposed that the sole objective of the war should be restoration of the Union. His immediate purpose was to bring all parties and factions in the North together in support of a war for the nation. This required a statement of war aims so simple and so national that all groups could unite behind it. But beyond the exigencies of public opinion, Lincoln did not want emancipation to become one of the war aims. He did not want slavery to be destroyed suddenly in the anger of civil conflict. If slavery was uprooted as a part of the war process, the change would be too violent; such a change would make it difficult, if not impossible, to solve the related problem of race relations. At the same time he realized that the situation created by the war demanded a more urgent approach to emancipation; a plan had to be worked out *now* to place slavery in the course of extinction. In an effort to provide such a plan, Lincoln, on several occasions, asked the border states congressmen to join with him in initiating a scheme for compensated gradual emancipation. With singular blindness they ignored his ideas.

Inevitably the facts of the war made Lincoln's hopes and plans for a gradual, orderly reform of the slavery problem impossible. Only in a short war, as he probably realized, could he have carried his policy. The longer the struggle continued, the more hostile Northern opinion became to slavery. It was unnatural that the Northern people would fight and sacrifice, for any period, to preserve an institution that in the opinion of most was the cause of the war. By the summer of 1862 every political sign indicated that the Northern masses wanted slavery destroyed as a result of the war. Now Lincoln faced a dilemma. If he opposed the popular will, if he persisted in postponing a settlement of the slavery issue to some future date, he would divide Northern opinion and perhaps wreck the entire war effort. He would, and this was the vital point, defeat his larger objective of preserving American nationality. If he wanted to keep the machine running, he had to make a change; if he did not, the machine might break down.

For Lincoln there could be only one response and one action. It was at this time that he decided to issue the Emancipation Proclamation and to make emancipation a second aim of the war. He changed his position because the impelling dynamics of war had created a new situation that demanded a new policy. To the theoretical moralist, to the intellectual reformer, to the prophet of blueprints, his shift may seem unprincipled and opportunistic. Actually, Lincoln's stand on slavery was always completely moral. Before the war he had opposed abolition because it would destroy the Union. During the war he used abolition to save the Union. He opposed a right change at the wrong time and supported the same change at the right time. His course is the supreme example in our history of the union of principle and pragmatism in politics.

The Louisiana Unification Movement of 1873

In the early months of 1873 conditions in "reconstructed" Louisiana verged on anarchy. To all outward appearances, carpetbag-Republican government and its political reflex, intransigent white-Democratic opposition, had divided the state into two sullen, bitter camps of racial and political hatred. In one, the Republican, were the great mass of the Negroes and their white leaders, and sometimes exploiters, the carpetbaggers and scalawags. In the other, the Democratic or conservative, were most of the whites, especially those in the country parishes. The Democrats had made a supreme effort in the election of 1872 to gain control of the state. They claimed that they had elected their candidate, John McEnery, to the governorship. The Republicans claimed the same thing for their man, William P. Kellogg. The federal government, acting in a spirit more partisan than objective, resolved the dispute by installing Kellogg with federal bayonets.[1] To the Democrats the Kellogg government was a rank usurpation. Many refused to pay taxes to it. McEnery, announcing that he was governor, issued proclamations and instructed Democratic legislators not to attend the sessions of the Kellogg legislature.[2] Savage violence gripped the state. One bitter individual tried to assassinate Kellogg, Republican officials received threatening letters, tension

Reprinted from *Journal of Southern History*, XI (August, 1945), 349–69, copyright 1945 by the Southern Historical Association, by permission of the managing editor.

between the races culminated in bloody clashes and riots, and mob action seemed the order of the day.[3]

Such conditions naturally had an adverse effect upon the state's economic development. Business and trade languished, and capital investment was retarded. At least so thought many businessmen of New Orleans, who had seen their city torn by brawls and killings and who believed the great port metropolis needed political stability to achieve economic prosperity. Crying for a return to the ways of peace, one newspaper wailed, "What a reputation is that for a city to have abroad; and how can we expect to prosper politically, or commercially, under such circumstances?"[4]

In this convulsed and uncertain hour of Louisiana's Reconstruction history, a group of whites and Negroes in New Orleans came forward with a plan to compose the differences agitating the state and to end at one blow the process of Reconstruction. They proposed to unify the two races into one gigantic political organization that, sweeping everything before it, would gain control of the state government and restore harmony and stability. They proposed to guarantee to the Negro complete political, civil, and, if possible, economic equality. The white sponsors of the plan represented the flower of the wealth and culture of New Orleans. They called their project the "Unification Movement." It seems to have escaped the notice of historians of Reconstruction and the state.[5]

The origins of the unification movement were in the election of 1872. In that year a group of New Orleans conservatives organized to achieve a reform of the city government. They soon decided that it was fruitless to work for improvement of the municipal administration as long as the state government was corrupt. Expanding their objectives, they created the Reform party, dedicated to honest, economical state government, and invited the support of like-minded people throughout the state. The guiding spirits of the party were Isaac N. Marks and William M. Randolph, of whom more later; it was almost entirely a New Orleans movement, drawing but small support in the country parishes. Eventually the Reform group fused with the Democrats or conservatives in the hope of thus defeating the Republicans and corruption. Noteworthy in the Reform campaign was the emphasis placed by the leaders upon better race relations. They invited Negroes to places on committees and to their rallies. They stressed the necessity of friendship between the races and advocated acceptance of the Negro's political and civil rights as guaranteed by the Fifteenth Amendment. The Reform platform recognized in extremely general terms the legal equality of the races.[6] The overtures of the Reformers attracted some Negroes to the party. The colored people had a real admiration for Marks, whom they considered a sincere champion of their race. The sincerity of some of the other Reformers they doubted, and the vague terms of the platform repelled them. Therefore the Reformers failed to secure any mass Negro support.[7] After the Reformers fused with the Democrats, they dropped their emphasis on race co-operation to concentrate on defeating the Republicans. The Reform leaders, however, had become convinced that the salvation of Louisiana lay in a political union of the races, and in the dark days of 1873 they turned again to their ideas of the previous year. They brought forth now a specific and detailed plan to combine the races and dignified it with the new name of "Unification."

In the spring of 1873 the first hints were heard in strife-weary New Orleans that a political movement to unify the races was in the offing. The leading journalistic champion of the proposed organization was the New Orleans *Times*, conservative organ of the business interests, and the leading champion of race co-operation on the *Times* was the reporter who conducted the sprightly column of political and social gossip called "Round About Town." On March 29 "Roundabout" announced that a unification party would be formed. Immediately approving letters flooded his column.

Claiming that he spoke for the young men of the city, "Juvenus" described New Orleans' withering commerce, the fall of real estate values, and the decay of the sugar industry. These sad conditions, he said, made it imperatively necessary for the whites to rise "superior to past traditions, party lines, and dead or useless issues. We believe the hour has come for immediate action on a broad and liberal plane of honesty and good faith to the interests of all citizens, white and black, in Louisiana."[8] A writer signing himself "F" said that the Negroes, disgusted with their carpetbag leaders, were anxious to enter into "an agreement with the white people by which both parties may be enabled to dwell in concord and pull together in political harness. . . . Unless the two races adopt some platform on which they can stand on friendly terms, Louisiana has nothing to look forward to but debt, dissension, anarchy."[9] Encouraged by such approving sentiments, Roundabout proceeded to create in his column a fictitious character named Mr. Chucks, a symbol of Louisianians coming to their senses on the race issue. In his first public statement, Mr. Chucks declared that if the refusal of the whites to grant political rights to the Negroes was the cause of the prevailing commercial prostration, "why, I think we're making asses of ourselves, that's all."[10]

Many *Times* readers agreed with Chucks. "Audax" wrote that the 70,000 Negroes in the state were entitled to a representation in the government commensurate with their numbers and denounced the white supremacy Democrats as an incubus weighing down Louisiana as the Old Man of the Sea did Sinbad.[11] "Radical Democrat" condemned the leaders of the Democratic party as "political highwaymen."[12] Many writers begged Roundabout to keep the professional party bosses out of the proposed new party, to bar the "noisy demagogues" of the Democratic party who had aroused the whites against the blacks as surely as the carpetbaggers had aroused the Negroes against the whites.[13] The chorus of approval for racial cooperation even penetrated into the columns of the *Picayune*, the organ of extreme Democrats.[14] A prominent conservative white man was quoted as saying: "We are completely in the hands of a set of men whose interest it is to keep alive this ill-feeling. They live on it. . . . We must get rid of party hacks and political jobbers, and satisfy the reasonable demands of the negroes."[15] The jubilant Roundabout exclaimed that a new era had arrived in which "the mass of men are fast receding from old landmarks of intolerance and prejudice; when they are casting about them for better guidance than that beneath whose auspices they have been well nigh stranded."[16]

The *Times* attempted to strengthen the movement for the talked about unification party by running interviews with business men who, according to Roundabout, were supporting it as the only agency that could restore peace to Louisiana.[17] A prominent merchant declared that he favored giving the Negroes the bulk of the state offices: "I am not afraid that they will in any considerable degree, abuse their privileges, and, for ourselves, we want nothing but peaceful government."[18] A business man, described as one of "our oldest and best," said: "Approve of it! It is our only hope of salvation. . . . We want a party that will embrace a broad and comprehensive view of things, that will say to the negro: Here, we want your political influence to restore an honest government. . . . You want civil equality; you shall have it, if you forsake the Northern adventurer who has plundered poor Louisiana until she is penniless."[19] A plaintive real estate dealer cried: "On with unification for God's sake, if it will give us an honest government; our present lot is insupportable."[20]

As the rumors of the formation of the new party ran through the city, other newspapers voiced their approval of unification. The *Herald*, an extreme Democratic journal, calling upon the whites to "commit to an eternal oblivion the stubborn and ancient prejudices which are now at war with the fundamental ideas of our democratic system," endorsed the proposed movement.[21] The influential French-language paper *L'Abeille* announced its support of the principle of unification, but withheld complete approval until it could see the specific plan which the co-operation party was expected to present.[22] Most important of all for the success of the unification movement was the indorsement of the *Picayune*, the leading organ of the conservative Democrats. This paper came around slowly to a support of unification, and at first its approval was grudging.[23] But it finally proclaimed complete ratification: "Let there be a union, then, on terms of the broadest liberality. Let there be an end of prejudice and proscription, and for the future let there be no differences of opinion dividing our people except upon questions of governmental polity."[24] The only sour notes in the New Orleans press came from Republican papers. The state-subsidized *Republican*, obviously confused as to the motives of the sponsors of unification, warned Negroes and Republicans that unification was a sinister, disguised Democratic plot to sabotage the Kellogg government; said it was absurd and should be ignored; said it was dangerous and should be defeated; and invited the unifiers, if sincere, to join the Republican party.[25] Another Republican organ said that the Negro leaders supporting co-operation were the educated former "free colored men" who had no mass following among the race and who could not deliver the Negro vote.[26]

This question of how "representative" the Negro supporters of unification were and what they might demand of the new party bothered whites who were disposed to accept co-operation.[27] To resolve these uncertainties, the *Times* interviewed Dr. Louis C. Roudanez, Paris-educated, wealthy, cultured Negro leader. Shrewdly, Roudanez denied that his race wanted social equality. All they asked was civil equality and honest government. "Let your people come out fairly and squarely and guarantee us [our rights], and a party can be formed that will sweep the State like wildfire," he stated. "A carpet-bagger, white or black, will become a thing of the past, and the vocation of agitators in either party will be forever gone."[28] Colonel James Lewis, Negro member of the city council, told the *Times*: "If the gentlemen who propose this movement are in earnest; if it is given without any mental reservations, and there is really to be a total abandonment of the prejudices which have so long kept us in the humiliating position we now occupy, we're with you heart and hand."[29] A delegation of the most prominent Negroes in the city called at the *Times* office to pledge the support of their people to unification.[30] State Senator James H. Ingraham assured the whites: "We have no disposition to Africanize this State. . . . [W]e are still willing to trust you; to confide our destiny to your keeping; to place the administration of affairs under your control."[31] Without exception all these Negroes said that they had allied politically with carpetbaggers only because the native whites had spurned association with them.

While the press discussed the issues of unification, the actual sponsors of it, white and colored, were holding a series of secret meetings. Their identity was for the moment unknown, but the whites were pronounced to be "Southern gentlemen" and the Negroes the "wealthiest and most intelligent colored men."[32] Finally it became known that a Committee of One Hundred, fifty from each race, was at work.[33] Then it was announced that the Committee would meet on June 16 to hear a report from a sub-committee appointed to draw up a platform upon which the races could unite. The meeting and the platform were crucial, said the *Times*, and would determine the future of Louisiana.[34]

The meeting of June 16 revealed to an intensely interested public the backers of the unification scheme. Isaac N. Marks was in the chair, and General P. G. T. Beauregard, Louisiana's great Civil War hero, headed the committee on resolutions. The white sponsors were the business, legal, and journalistic leaders of the city.[35] The Negro sponsors were the wealthy, cultured aristocracy of the race; many of them were the so-called "Creole Negroes" who had been free before the war.[36] The roster of the important resolutions committee read like a Who's Who of white and colored New Orleans. Of the white members, Beauregard, not satisfied to bask in his war glory, was president of the New Orleans and Carrollton Railroad. James I. Day was president of the Sun Mutual Insurance Company, a former president of the Bank of Louisiana and of the New York, Providence and Boston Railroad, a commissioner of the Fair Grounds Association, and a member of the board of directors of the Louisiana Equitable Life Insurance Company.[37] Marks was president of the Firemen's Charitable Association, which represented all the fire companies in the city, the Louisiana Fair Association, the New Orleans, Florida, and Havana Steamship Company, and the Mutual Aid and Benevolent Life Insurance Association; chairman of the board of commissioners of the fire department; a director of the Sun Mutual Insurance Company; and the owner of a grocery company.[38] Auguste Bohn was president of the Mechanics' and Traders' Bank, a director of the Louisiana Mutual Insurance Company and of the New Orleans Cotton Exchange, and a stockholder in the Vallette Dry Dock Company.[39] Judge William M. Randolph, a native of Virginia and a scion of the great Virginia family of that name, was a leading member of the Louisiana bar and one of the state's popular orators.[40]

Lieutenant Governor Caesar C. Antoine headed the list of Negro members. His inclusion was a grave tactical error on the part of the unifiers. He commanded a following among his race, but his name was anathema to the whites. He was a member of the "custom house" faction of the Republican party, despised by the whites as the most corrupt segment of a corrupt organization.[41] Aristide Mary, Creole Negro and wealthy philanthropist, was almost universally re-

spected by both races.[42] State Senator George Y. Kelso had some
standing as a Republican legislative leader but was known mainly
and dubiously to the whites as a follower of the recent governor,
Henry Clay Warmoth.[43] By far the most distinguished of the colored
members was Dr. Louis C. Roudanez. Educated in Paris, wealthy
and refined, he was a sincere leader of his race. To advance their welfare, he had founded the New Orleans *Tribune*, the first Negro daily
newspaper in the United States. He was convinced that the carpetbaggers were using the Negroes as tools to build up their own power
and had no real interest in the colored race.[44] Last on the Negro list
was Charles H. Thompson, well-known preacher and member of the
New Orleans school board.[45]

The resolutions committee submitted a majority and minority report. After a brief debate, the meeting unanimously adopted the majority report and appointed a committee to arrange a mass meeting
of the citizenry of New Orleans to give the stamp of popular approval to its decision.[46] The approved report was a significant document in the history of Reconstruction and race relations. It represented the efforts of conservative business men to meet and solve
one of the grave problems of the postwar South: Who would determine the place of the Negro in southern society—Southerners or
outsiders? Certainly no group of Southerners in the Reconstruction
era was willing to go farther in harmonizing race relations than the
authors of this document, which appeared in the New Orleans newspapers under the title "An Appeal for the Unification of the People of
Louisiana."[47] The complete statement read as follows:

> Whereas, Louisiana is now threatened with death in every vital
> organ of her normal, material and political being;
> And whereas, her dire extremity is but the fruit of unnatural divi-
> sion among her natural guardians—the children of her soil and of her
> adoption,
> And whereas, we have an abiding faith that there is love enough for
> Louisiana among her sons to unite [them] in a manful and unselfish
> struggle for her redemption:
> Be it therefore resolved—
> FIRST—That henceforward we dedicate ourselves to the unification
> of our people.

SECOND—That by "our people," we mean all men, of whatever race, color or religion, who are citizens of Louisiana, and who are willing to work for her prosperity.

THIRD—That we shall advocate, by speech, and pen, and deed, the equal and impartial exercise by every citizen of Louisiana of every civil and political right guaranteed [by the constitution and laws of Louisiana],[48] by the constitution and laws of the United States, and by the laws of honor, brotherhood and fair dealing.

FOURTH—That we shall maintain and advocate the right of every citizen of Louisiana, and of every citizen of the United States, to frequent at will all places of public resort, and to travel at will on all vehicles of public conveyance, upon terms of perfect equality with any and every other citizen; and we pledge ourselves, so far as our influence, counsel and example may go, to make this right a live and practical right, and that there may be no misunderstanding of our views on this point:

1. We shall recommend to the proprietors of all places of licensed public resort in the State of Louisiana, the opening of said places to the patronage of both races inhabiting our State.

2. And we shall further recommend that all railroads, steamboats, steamships, and other public conveyances pursue the same policy.

3. We shall further recommend that our banks, insurance offices, and other public corporations recognize and concede to our colored fellow-citizens, where they are stockholders in such institutions, the right of being represented in the direction thereof.

4. We shall further recommend that hereafter no distinction shall exist among citizens of Louisiana in any of our public schools or State institutions of education, or in any other public institutions supported by the State, city or parishes.

5. We shall also recommend that the proprietors of all foundries, factories, and other industrial establishments, in employing mechanics or workmen, make no distinction between the two races.

6. We shall encourage, by every means in our power, our colored citizens in the rural districts to become the proprietors of the soil, thus enhancing the value of lands and adding to the productiveness of the State, while it will create a political conservatism which is the offspring of proprietorship: and we furthermore recommend to all landed proprietors in our State the policy of considering the question of breaking up the same into small farms, in order that the [our] colored citizens and white emigrants may become practical farmers and cultivators of the soil.

FIFTH—That we pledge our honor and good faith to exercise our moral influence, both through personal advice and personal example, to bring about the rapid removal of all prejudices heretofore existing against the colored citizens of Louisiana, in order that they may hereafter enjoy all the rights belonging to citizens of the United States.

Be it further resolved, That we earnestly appeal to the press of this State to join and cooperate with us in erecting this monument to unity, concord and justice, and like ourselves forever to bury beneath it all party prejudices [all past prejudices on the subject of race or color].[49]

Resolved, also, That we deprecate and thoroughly condemn all acts of violence, from whatever source, and appeal to our people of both races to abide by the law in all their differences as the surest way to preserve to all the blessings of life, liberty and property.

Resolved, That we pledge ourselves to the cultivation of a broad sentiment of nationality, which shall embrace the whole country, and uphold the flag [glory] of the Union.

Resolved, That as an earnest of our holy purpose, we hereby offer upon the altar of the common good, all party ties, and all prejudices of education which may tend to hinder the political unity of our people.

Resolved, That in view of numerical equality between the white and colored elements of our population, we shall advocate an equal distribution of the offices of trust and emolument in our State, demanding, as the only conditions of our suffrage, honesty, diligence and ability; and we advocate this not because of the offices themselves, but simply as another earnest and proof upon our part, that the union we desire is an equal union and not an illusive conjunction brought about for the sole benefit of one or the other of the parties to the [that] union.

The motives animating the whites who helped to draw up this report invite analysis. It can be speculated that some of them did not wholly approve of the sentiments but saw in the proposed movement Louisiana's only hope of securing economic stability and honest government. Others, doubtless, believed that the state was faced with the prospect of permanent Negro suffrage, supported by the national government, and resolved to put the best face on the matter and try to control the Negro vote. Two of the white signers explained their support of unification. Beauregard had long believed that the whites could lead the Negroes to vote the right way.[50] Now he issued a public statement detailing his views. He argued that the Negro already had political and civil equality, guaranteed by the national and state constitutions, and that the whites might as well accept the fact. Continued Negro co-operation with the carpetbaggers would ruin the state. Therefore the whites must persuade the Negroes to leave the Republicans. The recipe was simple—let the whites recognize the Negroes' rights. Once this was done, the Negro would desert the alien carpetbagger and join his natural friend, the southern white man.[51] If Beauregard's reasons were predominantly pragmatic, Marks' were completely philosophical. He was opposed to any form of racial discrimination. "It is my determination," he proclaimed, "to continue to battle against these abstract, absurd and stupid prejudices, and to bring to bear the whole force of my character . . . to break them down. They must disappear; *they will disappear.*"[52]

At the meeting of June 16 the sponsors of unification laid their plan before the people for discussion. The reactions came fast, and in New Orleans they were generally favorable. The *Times*, as befitted the unifiers' first journalistic champion, was approving and optimistic of success.[53] The *Picayune* voiced unqualified support of the unification platform: "It is a Louisiana proposition, for Louisiana alone—to save the People of Louisiana from being garrotted by the thieves and tyrants who now hold us by the throat. We heartily support the great end sought to be obtained."[54] The *Republican*, which had at first denounced unification, was now a vigorous supporter, although it could not resist taunting the whites for having adopted Republican principles.[55] Influential individuals came forward to endorse the new movement. The Catholic archbishop of New Orleans, Napoleon Joseph Perche, asked Catholics to give it their support.[56] Ex-Governors Paul O. Hebert and Alexandre Mouton announced their approval in letters to the press.[57] The French-language journal, *L'Abeille*, ratified the general principles of unification, but raised a question which was troubling many whites. Were not the whites making all the concessions? Where was the Negro promise to vote out carpetbag government?[58] The unifiers replied that the Negro leaders were pledged to deliver the colored vote to them.[59]

Unification seemed to have won New Orleans, but it was soon evident that it was not taking among the whites in the country parishes and that it took less and less the farther north it traveled from

the city. It was noted that most of the Democratic country newspapers denounced the movement.[60] "Unification on the basis of perfect equality of whites and blacks!" exclaimed one angry editor. "We
abhor it in every fibre of our being. We know no necessity that can
bring us to such a pass."[61] Said the leading white supremacy organ of
North Louisiana: "The battle between the races for supremacy . . .
must be fought out here . . . boldly and squarely; the issue cannot be
satisfactorily adjusted by a repulsive commingling of antagonistic
races, and the promulgation of platforms enunciating as the political
tenets of the people of Louisiana the vilest Socialist doctrines."[62]
Another editor stated: "They have not seen, as we in the country
have, that the colored man will never vote with the white man, but
always against him."[63] There was, however, some white support in
the country, from individuals and newspapers, for unification.[64] One
Democratic editor asked: "Is there anything in it? Will we be any
better off? Shall we resign our last remaining privilege? Gentlemen,
that privilege is hollow to the core, and the experiment . . . is worth
a trial."[65] The Republican country papers divided in their opinions
on unification. Some gave it enthusiastic support, others advised the
Negroes to have nothing to do with it or invited the unifiers to join
the Republican party.[66]

While the state debated unification, the Committee of One Hundred went ahead with its plans to hold a great mass meeting in New
Orleans to ratify publicly the co-operation platform. This meeting, it
was believed, would decide the fate of the unification movement.[67]

At Exposition Hall, on July 15, the unifiers held their make or
break public meeting. The hall was jammed. Over the platform
hung a banner with the inscription: "Equal Rights—One Flag—One
Country—One People." Marks took the chair and made the opening
address. "We came here to-night, I hope and trust in God," he said,
"to lay upon the altar of our country all the prejudices of the past,
to recognize all citizens of the United States as equals before the
law. . . . [W]e have got to determine among ourselves that we will
reunite the population of Louisiana, and that we will work together
as one people for the redemption of the State." The next speaker was
a Negro, State Senator T. T. Allain, born a slave, widely respected by
whites. He criticized those whites whose prejudices had prevented

racial co-operation in the past, praised the unification platform but called for a practical application of its principles, and ended, "I maintain that all my race demands is pure and simple justice, and I call upon you, Louisianians, to give it."[68] Then James Davidson Hill, one of the owners of the *Picayune*, appeared and made a brief plea for racial harmony. The choice of the following speaker was a prime political blunder. He was State Senator J. Henri Burch, a Negro. He was long-winded, he was a carpetbag Negro from Connecticut, he was a member of the corrupt customs house faction of the Republican party, and he was thoroughly disliked by the whites.[69] He made a bad speech. He said, in effect, with a patronizing manner: We Negroes congratulate you whites upon overcoming your silly prejudices; we will help and guide you upward on the path that leads to complete tolerance; and if you are sincere, we will co-operate with you politically. His speech went a long way toward ruining the meeting, and the next speaker completed the work. This was James Lewis, administrator of improvements in the city council and one of the colored leaders of New Orleans.[70] He read a pledge, signed by eight Negroes,[71] designed to answer the criticism that the whites were making all the concessions to achieve unification and the Negroes none. Nothing could have reflected more strikingly the deep distrust which the colored people felt for the whites than this curious and politically inept document. It stated that when the Negroes received full recognition of their civil and political rights, then, but not until then, would they unite with the whites to overthrow the carpetbaggers and give Louisiana honest and economical government. This conditional promise rang down the curtain on the meeting like a wet blanket.[72]

Not even the *Times* could pretend that this had been a successful meeting. Dourly it commented that the unification movement was "fairly afloat," but that rough seas lay ahead.[73] Other papers, more realistic, labeled the meeting and movement as a flat failure. The *Republican*, noting that most of the crowd had been Negroes and that Beauregard and Randolph had not been present, decided that the white unifiers were not ready to carry out their part of the contract. It concluded that neither the white nor the colored leaders could really bind their people to support unification.[74] The *Picayune* charged that Negroes had killed unification by their refusal to co-operate with the whites until their rights were recognized: "They are unwilling to meet the white man on common ground, with common laws and common privileges, and struggle with him to achieve the redemption of all from ruin, and thus overcome the prejudices which divide and ruin; but they demand that the white man shall come with bated breath and stoop that they may step beyond."[75] In similar vein, the *Herald* accused Lewis, with his pledge, of being the murderer of unification: "He was the ruthless bird who killed Cock Robin, with the arrow furnished him by the customhouse managers. That pledge inflicted the fatal stab at the very heart of the Unification, and it fell at the foot of Pompey's statue."[76] The Shreveport *Times* congratulated New Orleans for having "repudiated this vile thing. In this she has been true to the State; in her capacity she has not fallen."[77] By the end of August the press had written off unification as a thing of the past.[78] The best obituary of unification was pronounced fittingly enough by Roundabout:

> It's a subject he isn't sweet on just now—chiefly, however, because he thinks it has been villainously murdered. The traditional impracticability of this community stepped in and finished it. . . . The trouble was that Gen. Beauregard & Co., being thoughtful gentlemen, appealed to a sense of kindness and justice and magnanimity that was slightly inaccessible. They saw that it was right, but forgot that the most available argument would have been that of expedience. . . . It has been misjudged; its spirit distorted; its deductions falsely and illogically stated.[79]

The failure of the unification movement demands analysis. The primary reason, of course, was that its platform was not acceptable to the whites. They would not support the concessions made to the Negro because they were afraid that these concessions would lead to racial equality.[80] The surprising thing is that there was so much white acceptance of a position of equality for the Negro; this suggests that in some respects the traditional picture of Reconstruction needs to be revised so far as white attitudes are concerned. One other reason for failure suggests itself. Unification was a reform movement run by amateurs. Its leaders made the mistakes that amateurs often make. The unifiers boasted that they had barred professional politicians from their organization.[81] Yet the hand of a professional would have saved the movement from some of its blunders. Any good ward heeler, for example, would never have let Burch speak at the meeting of July 15. The worst effect of excluding the politicians was to cause those of both parties to fight unification.[82] "And that's what's the matter," said one sage editor. "The Democratic politicians and the Republican politicians will oppose any movement that will break up their political organizations, and thrust them into retirement."[83]

A recent study of Reconstruction politics in Mississippi questions the validity of the usual classification of the leaders in two extreme groups—on the one hand the Republicans, composed of the carpetbaggers, a few renegade scalawags, and the Negroes, striving to maintain their corrupt hold on government, and on the other the Democrats, the native whites, fighting to restore white supremacy—and, noting that many former Whigs became Republicans, suggests that the role of the scalawag in Reconstruction has not been adequately portrayed.[84] The Louisiana unification movement projects on the Reconstruction scene still another group whose importance has not been recognized—the business men, not closely affiliated with politics, who saw the strife of parties and races destroying the stability they desired and who tried to harmonize political and racial extremes to restore peace and profits.[85]

An Analysis of Some Reconstruction Attitudes

In late years revisionist historians have done much to correct the existing and often distorted picture of the Reconstruction period in American history. Earlier writers on Reconstruction, whether they were Republican politicians or southern polemicists, journalists, or historians, exhibited a number of historical deficiencies, but in general it may be said that they told a story that was too simple and naïve. It was simple in that the terrible complexities of Reconstruction were presented in the easy terms of stereotypes—the good white Southern Democrats fighting against the bad colored Republicans and their insidious northern allies, or vice versa. It was naïve in that virtually no analysis was made to explain why people acted as they did. Thus carpetbaggers were dishonest because they were bad men or Republicans, but no attempt was made to describe the forces which contributed to their dishonesty. The revisionists have forced several modifications in the Reconstruction story. They have demonstrated, among other things, that the corruption of the Reconstruction state governments has been exaggerated and that in any case corruption was a national, not a purely southern, phenomenon, with an expanding capitalism as the chief corrupting agent; that

Reprinted from *Journal of Southern History*, XII (November, 1946), 469–86, copyright 1946 by the Southern Historical Association, by permission of the managing editor.

Democrats were quite as willing as Republicans to be bought by business; that the supposed astronomically high appropriations of the Reconstruction governments seem so only in comparison with the niggardly budgets of the planter-controlled governments of the ante-bellum period; that although the Reconstruction governments were corrupt and dishonest, they must be credited with definite progress in the fields of popular education and internal improvements; and that the national reconstruction program was radical only in a superficial sense in that it gave political power to the Negro but failed to provide economic power through the promised confiscation and ownership of land, and thus that because the position of the Negro had no lasting basis his rule was easily overthrown.[1]

These new viewpoints have provided a desirable balance and proportion to the traditional historical treatment of Reconstruction. Still debated and in part unexplored in research are the motives of the northern and southern people during this period. Who supported Reconstruction and why; and who opposed it, and why? In analyzing the motivation of Reconstruction, historians have devoted most of their attention to northern political and economic groups and have produced certain conclusions which have been generally accepted. What may be termed the Beale thesis, because it has been most competently developed by Professor Howard K. Beale, offers a sectional-class explanation of Reconstruction. According to this thesis, Reconstruction was a successful attempt by northeastern business, acting through the Republican party, to control the national government for its own economic ends: notably, the protective tariff, the national banks, a "sound" currency. To accomplish its program, the business class had to overthrow from the seats of power the old ruling agrarian class of the South and West. This it did by inaugurating Reconstruction, which made the South Republican, and by selling its policies to the voters wrapped up in such attractive vote-getting packages as northern patriotism or the bloody shirt.[2] Another student of the period, while accepting the Beale thesis, points out that northern business men supported Reconstruction not only because of national issues but also because they thought it would enable them to exploit the South through protected capital investments, and that Republican bosses supported Reconstruction because they believed that if the South could be made Republican they could stay in power.[3]

The Negro author W. E. Burghardt Du Bois, conceding the part played by industry in formulating the Reconstruction program, contends that there was in the North a substantial mass opinion of liberal idealism, which he calls "abolition-democracy," that stood for a democratic reconstruction plan, including equal rights for Negroes. This group, he insists, represented in politics by men like Thaddeus Stevens, was equally influential with business in determining the nature of Reconstruction.[4] The existence of such a body of opinion cannot be disputed. That it was as extensive as Du Bois thinks or that it was animated by as much idealism for the Negro may well be doubted; unfortunately there is no way to document accurately its numbers or influence. One thing is certain. The leaders of abolition-democracy did not succeed in incorporating their ideas into the Republican reconstruction scheme. They demanded universal suffrage, universal amnesty, and confiscation of the land of rich Southerners and its distribution among the freedmen. The Republican politicos, being economic reactionaries, discarded confiscation because they had no interest in bringing about a social revolution, and they rejected universal amnesty because it would have made a Republican South improbable. It would seem that the party bosses, instead of being influenced to any considerable degree by abolition-democracy, used it for whatever it was worth to marshal support for a program designed to benefit a plutocratic minority.

An interpretation of northern motivation that differs in part from both Beale and Du Bois has come from Marxist historians and writers.[5] The Marxian thesis has been elaborately presented by James S. Allen,[6] who regards Reconstruction as a plan formulated and carried through by big business to enable it to dominate the nation. Up to a point, this is only the Beale thesis dressed up in Marxian jargon. Allen, however, proceeds to advance the claim that the business program was "democratic," because industry, in achieving power, smashed the old, feudal planter class of the South and thus helped prepare the way for the coming of the industrial state which, after business itself was smashed, would evolve into a perfect democracy of the Marxist variety.[7] In recent years writers of Marxist persuasion have dropped Allen's emphasis on the class struggle, and have presented Reconstruction as a straight-out plan of equalitarian democracy. The new departure has been most strikingly expressed, in fictional form, by Howard Fast, who flatly states that the Reconstruction acts of 1867 were intended "to create a new democracy in the South."[8] The Marxian thesis in any of these forms has little validity. No amount of historical legerdemain can transform the economic reactionaries of the Republican party into great liberals or make the protective tariff and the gold standard into items of the democratic faith. Furthermore, as will be shown, the Marxists are wrong when they try to develop the corollary that Reconstruction was also a democratic process in the South.[9]

The sectional-class thesis of Beale would seem to be the most nearly correct analysis of northern motivation, although Beale did not fully explain how northeastern business persuaded agrarian Republicans from the Middle West to support industrial measures and a reconstruction policy designed to insure the rule of business in the South. It has since been demonstrated that this was done in part by giving the Middle West exceptionally generous appropriations for internal improvements and in effect buying its support;[10] and to this should be added such other inducements as free land, pensions, and railroads, as well as such emotional and psychological appeals as habitual use of the bloody shirt. Du Bois was also undoubtedly correct in contending that idealistic forces played a part in shaping reconstruction policy, and his point is a good, although minor, corrective to the purely economic analysis. But the major fact remains that the men who made Reconstruction were moved by issues of economic and political power far more than by democratic idealism.

While the question of northern motivation has been fairly well established, there has been little attempt to prepare a systematic analysis of southern attitudes toward Reconstruction. Most of the professional historians writing on southern reconstruction have been members of or followers of the so-called Dunning school. They are largely responsible for the familiar stereotypes of Reconstruction. According to their interpretation, Reconstruction was a battle between two extremes: the Democrats, as the group which included the vast majority of the whites, standing for decent government and racial supremacy, versus the Republicans, the Negroes, alien carpet-baggers, and renegade scalawags, standing for dishonest government and alien ideals. These historians wrote literally in terms of white and black. This is not to say that they did not recognize the fact that there were differences between Southerners on such issues as Negro suffrage. But they explained the differences in terms of individual motivation. Thus Southerners who advocated the vote for Negroes were either bad men, or wartime Unionists who hated "rebels," or kindly planters who knew Negroes well and wanted to control their votes in the right direction. Although the Dunning writers sensed an apparent disagreement between the planter-business class and the small farmers on the Negro question, with the planters being willing to accept a position of greater equality for the Negro, they did not explore the difference or try to ascertain whether there were economic and social causes for its existence.[11]

No such reluctance characterizes Du Bois. He boldly proclaims that Reconstruction was a labor movement, an attempt by the white and black proletariat to control the South, "a vision of democracy across racial lines."[12] A basic error invalidates most of his thesis. There was no white proletariat of any significant numbers; the great mass of the whites were yeoman farmers who thought in terms of racial supremacy instead of class solidarity. Furthermore, he exaggerates the readiness of the former non-slaveholding whites to unite with the Negroes. He himself recognizes that there are factual weaknesses in his theory. He knows that the common whites furnished the power by which the Republican state governments were overthrown; but he explains this disturbing fact by claiming that the planters cut off the developing interracial co-operation of the proletariat by appealing to the prejudices of the poorer whites and organizing them on the color line.[13] Closely paralleling Du Bois' interpretation, and even going beyond it, is that of the Marxists. They, too, present Reconstruction as a biracial movement of the laboring class which was finally destroyed by a counter-revolution of the planters.[14] According to Howard Fast, the Negroes and poor whites joined hands in the Republican party and created "a fine, a just, and a truly democratic civilization," but the reactionary planter class refused to permit this experiment in social democracy and wiped it out with force.[15] That the validity of such assertions is open to serious question can be shown by examining the attitude of the planters and business men in Louisiana toward Reconstruction and the Negro and placing the results in the larger setting of what is known about the general attitudes of the southern whites in other parts of the region.

First of all, despite the opinions of the Marxists, the overwhelming mass of the people—the yeoman farmers, middle class whites, and poor whites—were fiercely opposed to Negro suffrage and to any condition of equality for the Negro. The evidence on this point, while not voluminous because of the general inarticulateness of the common whites, is strong; it is best expressed by the fact that the small-farmer, white-belt areas of the southern states voted heavily against Republicans and Republican measures in election after election.[16] As Horace Mann Bond puts it, the farmers hated equally slavery, planters, and Negroes.[17] The attitude of the common whites of Reconstruction is consonant with the known attitude of the poorest whites, economically, today; that is, racial antipathy toward Negroes is always sharpest when accentuated by economic competition. The teachings of social psychology can be adduced to support the generalization concerning the reaction of the whites. In a caste system based on a fixed status for groups, any attempt by a subordinated element—in this case the Negroes—to achieve a higher status unlooses feelings of tension and fear in the next higher group, which will exert itself, often violently, to keep the subordinated group down.[18]

The most powerful group in the South was the planter-business class and its professional allies; its position on Reconstruction was of decisive importance. In the beginning days of Reconstruction, the planters and business men strongly opposed the central proposal of the Radical Republican program—suffrage for the Negro. But they opposed it for economic rather than racial reasons. This fact is crucially important in understanding their reactions. To use modern terms, they feared that the grant of the ballot to the Negro would add to the strength of the liberal or progressive vote. This is not to say that they did not regard the Negro as an inferior being of an entirely

separate race. But it is to say that they reacted to a proposal to en-
franchise a laboring class as would any propertied minority in any
society—they opposed it because they believed it would lead to an
attack upon property.[19] A few quotations selected from many statements appearing in conservative New Orleans newspapers which
were spokesmen of the planter-business interests will demonstrate
the point. Terming universal suffrage a menace to property, the New
Orleans *Times* said: "The right to vote should be given to those only
who can use it with discretion and sound judgment, and as our elec-
toral privileges are already too wide, it would be the maddest folly to
extend them at once to a class who have always been under control,
and who—without the ability to form a correct judgment for themselves—would be left to the tender mercies of party tricksters." Let
the Negro wait until he acquired property before he became a voter.[20]
In a fuller and more philosophical exposition of its views, the *Times*
stated:

> Wherever voters greatly outnumber property holders, property will
> assuredly be unsafe. When voters have property and intelligence, there
> is some hope that they may "find their interest in the interest of the
> community" and be anxious to secure a consistent, honest, econom-
> ical and straight-forward administration. But the selfish interest of the
> non-property holding voter lies in an altogether different direction. He
> wishes to secure rich pickings, and, too frequently, soils his fingers by
> base bribes. Were universal negro suffrage to be added to the white
> universal suffrage now existing in the South, the security of both life
> and property would be greatly weakened. . . . With our present too
> widely extended suffrage it is difficult even now to steer between
> the rocks of the political Scylla and the whirlpool of its Charybdis,
> and with universal negro suffrage added, the task would be wholly
> hopeless.[21]

Becoming frankly specific, the *Times* later declared that "If representative institutions are to be preserved in this country, the control
of taxes must be left to those who pay them, and the protection of
property to those who own it."[22] The New Orleans *Crescent*, endorsing the proposal of South Carolina's planter leader, Wade Hampton,
to extend the vote to Negroes who had acquired property and an education,[23] asserted: "Southern conservatives ask nothing more on the
subject of suffrage than that its distribution shall be determined by

the test of character and intelligence. They have asked for nothing more from the time that, by one of the irreversible results of war, the Southern negroes became a part of the free population of the country. It is not their fault if such a test has been rejected in favor of another that proscribes a large proportion of the highest intelligence on the one hand, and opens all political functions to the maximum of ignorance on the other."[24] Expressing the conservatives' fear of the economic implications of Negro suffrage, the *Crescent* said: "It seems to be practically absurd and dangerous to commit the decisions of those difficult questions to numbers of extemporized citizens incapable of forming any accurate or rational opinions; and likely to imagine that the right to vote means the right to live without work, and to rob the industrious classes for the benefit of the idle and thriftless."[25] The *Picayune* denounced Negro suffrage because it did not believe that common men of any color should vote; manhood suffrage was "the unlimited suffrage of the ignorant, landless and lawless."[26] "We look upon it [voting] as a duty rather than a right," said the *Picayune*, "and regret that there is so much of it among the whites."[27] To the *Picayune*, Reconstruction was a process that proscribed "intelligence, probity and property" and elevated propertyless nobodies to power.[28]

To the testimony of conservative newspapers can be added representative statements of conservative planter-business leaders. In 1867, when Congress was considering the radical reconstruction acts, various southern newspapers asked prominent individuals to give their reactions to the proposed measures. More frank and philosophical than most was J. W. Robb of Mississippi. He warned conservatives that all republics in history had fallen when they had extended the ballot to a laboring class, "an ignorant horde of stupid and besotted men." "I believe," he continued, "that from the introduction of negro suffrage, the worst form and spirit of agrarianism will arise to disturb the peace and order of the State, and that it will require our utmost exertions to keep it down, and retain for ourselves political existence and individual security."[29] Francis T. Nicholls, who became governor of Louisiana in 1877 when white supremacy supposedly was restored, told a Congressional committee that conservatives were opposed to Reconstruction because it had endangered property interests by placing ignorance in power. Before Reconstruction, he said, there had been a relatively small group of ignorant white voters whom the rich could control, but Reconstruction had made ignorance "the dominating power." He favored a law that in the interest of property would disfranchise the ignorant of both races.[30]

Congress ignored the opposition to Negro suffrage of the planter-business class, based primarily on economic grounds, and of the common whites, based primarily on racial grounds. In 1867 it passed the reconstruction laws of the Radical Republicans; and Negro suffrage and, in many states, Negro rule became a reality. There followed a period of years, varying in different states, in which the Republican party, led by white carpetbaggers and scalawags and composed predominantly of the Negro masses, controlled the South. The political record of its rule was a compound of blatant corruption and forward social legislation. It was an expensive program. Money was needed to gratify the desires of the white and colored politicians for graft and of the colored masses for social services furnished by the state. The Republicans had to resort to higher and higher taxation, and necessarily they laid the heaviest taxes upon real property. While taxation affected all property holders, large and small, the brunt of it fell upon the large holders. This, as Du Bois points out, is a crucial fact in Reconstruction history—a war-impoverished propertied class was being compelled by the votes of poor men to bear an almost confiscatory tax burden.[31]

Faced with extinction by taxation, the planter-business class reacted again and characteristically in economic rather than racial terms. Negro votes had imposed the tax burden. Negro votes could lift it. If in order to persuade the Negroes to do so it was necessary to grant them political and civil equality or even to let them run the state, well and good. Get the tax rate down, cried one New Orleans conservative, "even if every office in the State, from Governor to the most insignificant constable, were filled by a negro."[32] Urged another: "We must get rid of party hacks and political jobbers, and satisfy the reasonable demands of the negroes. This accomplished, Louisiana will again blossom as the rose. It is our only salvation."[33] A prominent merchant declared: "I am in favor, in case we ever have another election, of giving to the colored people the bulk of the lucrative positions. . . . I am not afraid that they will, in any considerable degree abuse their privileges, and, for ourselves, we want nothing but peaceful government."[34] "You want civil equality; you shall have it," a leading business man pledged the Negroes, "if you forsake the Northern adventurer who has plundered poor Louisiana until she is penniless."[35] On with political co-operation with Negroes, exclaimed a property holder, "for God's sake if it will give us an honest government; our present lot is insupportable."[36] A blunt Natchitoches planter asserted that it was imperative that the whites detach the Negroes from the Republicans: "When the war was over we wouldn't have anything to do with the niggers, and let the Radicals gobble them up. . . . I am in favor of anything to get them. Drop the name of Democracy, I say, and go in for the niggers."[37]

What practical political action did the planter-business class take during Reconstruction to protect itself from excessive taxation and to foster its economic interests? In local elections in New Orleans, for example, the business men contemplated putting up Negro candidates for Congressional and city offices to compete with white Republicans. On Carondelet Street, the city's great business center, it was planned to nominate a colored foreman of one of the leading cotton presses for Congress. Such a man, asserted the business reporter of the New Orleans *Times*, "Will protect and do more for the South than any white Radical which can be selected to run against him. Carondelet street will go for the gentlemen with the cotton press."[38] The business men, this journalist explained, "are taking an unusual interest in being represented in Congress by a representative born in the South. The nearer approach to a real African, black in color, the more confidence will be placed in him."[39] Since the records do not show that the Carondelet magnates got their foreman nominated, it is probable that the Democratic leaders in New Orleans refused to take a Negro candidate, or even more probable that the cotton press gentleman, if he had political ambitions and an eye for the future, became a Republican. Regardless of the outcome, however, the episode demonstrated that these hard-headed business men placed their economic interests above racial differences and that they preferred to entrust those interests to an understanding and amenable Negro rather than to an untried white.

A second device adopted by the conservatives was to enter the Republican party and seek to control it. A recent study by David H. Donald illustrates how this was done in Mississippi.[40] After Radical Reconstruction went into effect most of the former Whigs, in antebellum times the party of the big slaveholders, became Republicans. "Such action is not hard to understand," writes Donald. "The Whigs were wealthy men—the large planters and the railroad and industrial promoters—who naturally turned to the party which in the state as in the nation was dominated by business interests."[41] At first these planters, or scalawags, to use a familiar term, dominated the party, but they lost their leadership to the carpetbaggers who, in the struggles for power within the party, were willing to promise more to the Negroes. Donald points to the planters' fruitless opposition to the Republican program of big budgets and high taxes and their revulsion against the social equality claimed by the Negroes as sources of their difficulties. Finally, repudiated by people they could not control, they drifted "slowly and reluctantly over to the Democratic camp."[42]

Still a third device employed by the planters and business men was to invite the Negroes to leave the Republicans and join with them in a new political organization separate from the Democratic party. The conservatives promised in such case to respect the Negro's civil equality and his right to vote and to hold office. Such movements were tried in several states,[43] the most elaborate being the so-called "Louisiana Unification Movement."[44] Inaugurated in 1873, this movement was headed by General Pierre G. T. Beauregard and was supported by the flower of the wealth and culture of New Orleans and South Louisiana.[45] Its platform advocated complete political equality for the Negro, an equal division of state offices between the races, and a plan whereby Negroes would become landowners. The unifiers denounced discrimination because of color in hiring laborers or in selecting directors of corporations, and called for the abandonment of segregation in public conveyances, public places, railroads, steamboats, and the public schools.[46] The Louisiana movement, like the others, failed for lack of support from the white masses. The unification program was popular in New Orleans and in the plantation belt of South Louisiana, but in the small-farmer areas of other parts of the state it was received with loathing and execration.

It is evident that a basis existed for an alliance of the planter-business class and the Negroes. "If they [the planters] had wished," writes Du Bois, "they could have held the Negro vote in the palm of their hands."[47] Why did such an alliance fail to materialize? In the first place, the leaders of the unification movements could not persuade any significant number of whites to support the concessions which the planters were willing to accord the colored people. The common whites, animated by racial motives, refused to follow planter leadership, and without any mass white support the unification movements could not succeed. In Louisiana the movement failed to develop much mass support even from the Negroes because professional Negro politicians, secure in their place in the Republican party, advised their followers to shun co-operation and because those Negro leaders who favored co-operation could not suppress their suspicion of the sincerity of the planter-business class. "We know that, by an alliance with you, we can have more privileges than we now enjoy," one Negro spokesman told the conservatives. "We will not then have to cling to the carpet-baggers for protection, but can ourselves take whatever share of office and representation falls to us fairly. Still, we have *some* rights now, and we don't intend to give them up. Rather than do that, we will cling to the carpet-bagger forever, and let him share our power."[48]

In the second place, the planters and business men, while willing to make far-reaching concessions to the Negroes, did not make them because they believed in the principles of racial equality. They made them because of pressing economic reasons and because they wanted to control the Negro vote. They never ceased to regard the Negroes as inferior creatures who by an unfortunate turn of fate had become politically powerful in the state. Hence there was a limit to their concessions, its line marked by anything that seemed to suggest social equality. The carpetbaggers, unhampered by such reservations, could always outbid the conservatives. Thus in states like Mississippi, where the planter tried to dominate the Republican party, the carpetbaggers took the leadership of the Negroes away from the scalawags. Finally, the differing economic aspirations of the wealthy whites and the Negroes prevented any lasting alliance of the two. The Negroes demanded a program of social services financed by the state, which meant high taxes. The planters wanted to control the colored vote in order to reduce these services and lower taxes which they considered almost confiscatory. The Negroes wanted higher wages and shorter hours; the planters wanted a serf-like system of sharecropping. The planters simply lacked the capital to finance the Negro's social or labor program;[49] but in view of the obvious conflict between the desires of the two groups it is doubtful whether such a program would have received support from the planters even if they had possessed the necessary means for financing it.

And so the planters and business men, unable to prevent the establishment of Negro suffrage and unable to control it after it was established, joined with the common whites to overthrow the Republican state governments. By 1877 the Democrats controlled every southern state, and what the textbooks call white supremacy was restored. Actually, Negroes continued to vote, although in reduced numbers, and white supremacy was not restored until the 1890's. As Professor C. Vann Woodward has ably demonstrated, the men who came to power after Reconstruction were not in the old agrarian, planter tradition. They were often of the planter class, but in reality they were industrialists or would-be industrialists. They preached the industrialization of the South through the importation of Yankee capital, a policy of low taxes to attract business, and a political alliance with the Northeast instead of with the South's traditional ally, the West.[50] These men reacted to Negro suffrage as had men of their class during Reconstruction. As the vote of labor, it was something to be feared and kept in hand, but as the vote of an inferior people, it was also something that might be manipulated for the benefit of the wealthy. As events developed, the bosses of the New South sometimes found that they could use the colored vote to beat down attempts of the farmers to take over control of the Democratic party. In the election of 1880 in Georgia, for example, the rich defeated the farmers through a combination of a minority of the white votes and a majority of the colored ones.[51] The southern champions of industrialism, therefore, took no action to disfranchise the Negro; they used him to maintain the supremacy of a few white men over other white men. Disfranchisement finally came as a result of the efforts of small-farmer leaders like Ben Tillman.[52]

Placed in the general setting, therefore, the interests and activities of the Louisiana planter-capitalist group serve to confirm the fact that the Reconstruction period was one of the most complex in American history. It witnessed the ending of a great civil struggle and the travail of postwar adjustment, the consummation of a momentous economic revolution, and a wrenching change in race relations. No less complex than the times were the motives that impelled people—northern and southern, white and black, rich and poor—to act as they did. No simple or generic explanation cast in the form of sectional stereotypes will supply the key to what happened. Economic, social, and political stimuli affected groups in the South in different ways, and Southerners differed among themselves on the issues of Reconstruction in about the same degree as did groups in the North. The planter-capitalist class of the South thought and acted in terms of economic self-interest in a fashion similar to the industrial magnates of the North. The important difference was that the business men carried the northern people with them while the planters were unable to convince the white masses in the South that economics transcended racial supremacy.

PART II
Military Policy

Interlude: 1918–1939

After the close of the World War the United States entered on a period of peace that extended officially until 1941. In that year the nation was drawn into a conflict that had begun in Europe in 1939, the struggle that as it widened in area came to be called the Second World War. The date of entrance is, however, deceptive as to the length of the peace. For two years preceding its formal intervention the United States was involved in various ways in the war, offering sympathy and material aids to Great Britain and France and at the same time strengthening its own military machine. So open and active was the United States that the governments of Germany and Italy, and their distant ally, Japan, viewed America as an actual participant. Their interpretation was naturally biased, but it has become generally accepted by recent scholars as being essentially correct. The interlude of peace, therefore, actually ended in 1939.

The American decision to intervene in the World War in 1917 seemed to herald a departure in foreign policy. Important objectives had presumably led the United States to enter the conflict—a desire to advance the cause of international morality, the goal proclaimed by President Wilson, or a determination to preserve national security by putting down an aggressive Germany, the aim probably in-

This essay has not been previously published.

fluencing a majority of the people. Whichever objective was upper-most, in combination their force persuaded the nation to abandon its traditional policy of avoiding international entanglements and to become a member of a European diplomatic-military coalition engaged in a European war. That coalition emerged from the war victorious, and the United States apparently had reason to remain a member of it, if only to safeguard and further the objectives for which it had fought. But the course that seemed dictated by logic and self-interest was not followed. In one of the most abrupt reversals of national policy in history, the United States quickly disengaged itself from its allies and retired into its historic position of diplomatic isolation.

The first indication of withdrawal came when the Senate refused to ratify the peace settlement of Versailles, which included Wilson's cherished project of a League of Nations to preserve peace in the future. There was little objection in the Senate or elsewhere to the terms accorded the defeated nations, as was seen in the fact that soon after rejecting the treaty, the United States easily concluded separate peace agreements with Germany and its other enemies. It was the inclusion of the League in the Versailles document that caused the Senate to balk. Adherence to the treaty would obligate the nation to become a member of the League and, with membership, to assume a set of heavy international responsibilities. It was a minority of senators that blocked ratification, but they clearly represented a majority public opinion. Wilson's Democratic party lost to the Republicans in the election of 1920, and the Republicans, remaining in power throughout the decade, kept the nation out of the League.

Isolationism is the label most frequently employed to characterize American foreign policy during the 1920s. However, some historians object to the term, contending that it suggests an exaggerated image of America's world position, an apartness from other nations that did not exist. The United States did not retire into isolationism, these scholars argue. It maintained close diplomatic contacts with a number of other countries and engaged with other governments in several important endeavors. The United States was, in fact, more globally minded than at any previous time in its history.

The dissenting scholars cite various examples of American action to support their thesis. Although the United States refused to join the League of Nations, on numerous occasions it sent unofficial representatives to sessions of the organization. The government sponsored a conference of the principal naval powers in Washington to reduce naval strengths, and it cosponsored a meeting at Paris to draw up a statement renouncing the use of war by the signatories. The United States promoted two agreements to stabilize conditions in the Far East, where it had important trade relations and a territorial commitment in the Philippine Islands. The Four Power Pact (1921) required the principal Pacific powers, the United States, Britain, France, and Japan, to respect each other's Far Eastern possessions; the Nine Power Pact (1922) committed the above signatories and other concerned nations to observe the sovereignty and territorial integrity of China. Lastly, the government acted vigorously to protect America's expanding economic interests. When its late allies complained that they could not meet their war debts because Germany was not settling the reparations agreed upon at Versailles, the United States cooperated in adjusting the payments. And when American businessmen sought government support to further trade and investments abroad, the Republican administrations of the 1920s negotiated favorable agreements with receptive countries.

The revisionists' catalog of American interventions in world affairs is a useful corrective to the traditional picture of a United States immured in a shell of isolation. A definitive conclusion, however, is open to question. These incidents demonstrated an American willingness to act with other nations, but they did not constitute departures from traditional American policy: none of them involved the government in any permanent or binding international arrangement. The much mentioned unofficial participation of American delegates in League of Nations sessions had no political significance; the sessions that the Americans attended dealt almost entirely with cultural, technical, and humanitarian matters. The heralded declaration of Paris renouncing the use of war was merely a statement of intention; no signatory to the pact was bound to observe it if self-interest dictated a resort to war. The Four Power and Nine Power pacts were also statements of intention. The United

States, knowing that it lacked adequate force to preserve its interests in the Far East and that public opinion would not allow a use of force, sought to preserve those interests by asking other powers to agree to maintain the existing situation in the region. Any one of the signing powers could break away from the agreements whenever it chose to do so, and Japan shortly proceeded to violate them.

If American policy during the 1920s was not as interventionist as some historians have thought, it was still not as isolationist as others have concluded. Leaders and the public both recognized that the United States had to assume some kind of role in international affairs, had some responsibilities it must bear. Some of the American actions revealed that the idealism in the national psyche to which Woodrow Wilson had appealed lived on. Thus, American sponsorship of the Paris peace pact reflected a belief that war could be outlawed if enough nations publicly declared that it was evil. Again, although the United States had motives of self-interest in pushing the Four Power and Nine Power pacts, in so doing it cast itself as the champion of the integrity of a weak nation threatened by imperialist powers—China. The most sensational expression of idealism concerned Latin America, an area in which the United States had long claimed hegemony under the Monroe Doctrine. The Republican administrations of the 1920s unofficially disavowed a right to intervene in the Latin countries with force, and a Democratic administration coming into power in 1933 formally renounced that right. Hereafter the United States might interfere in affairs to the south, but it would restrict its actions to exercising economic and political influence.

In entering World War I, the United States had broken with its traditional policy of avoiding foreign entanglements, but this break had been caused by the appearance of an enemy, Germany, that seemed to threaten American security. Once that enemy was defeated, Americans saw no need to continue in the wartime alliance, and they clearly did not intend to take up the moral leadership of the world that Wilson wanted them to exercise in the League of Nations. They might assume moral positions and advocate moral causes but not as a committed member of an organization and, above all, not if they had to engage in the use of military force. Avoiding the use of force was, in fact, the distinguishing mark of American foreign policy during the 1920s and stretching into the 1930s. Not until other enemies threatened would Americans change this outlook.

The people's conviction found ready acceptance in Congress and with most national leaders. Congress's reaction was of key importance, for it would determine the size and structure of the military establishment assigned to carry out national policy. A policy of avoiding use of force carried to the legislators an obvious lesson: the nation did not need to support a large military establishment. Because a major land war seemed unlikely, a substantial land force was not required—a regular army adequate to defend the continental boundaries and the overseas possessions was sufficient. The sea force presented a more troublesome problem. The only possibility of war seemed to be with Japan, the one nation that could threaten American interest in the far Pacific, and this struggle would have to be fought by the navy. Congress, with some reluctance, agreed that the navy might have to be maintained near its present level of strength.

Congress found an opportunity to demonstrate its opposition to a large land force soon after the end of the World War. Asked by the War Department to authorize a regular army of more than 500,000 officers and men, and a three-month universal training system to produce citizen soldiers in event of war, it summarily rejected the recommendation. While the legislators studied what program of their own to enact, the demobilization of the drafted host raised during the war went on apace. The process was accomplished in less than a year's time, and in 1919 the land strength of the United States consisted of 225,000 men in the regular army, all of them volunteers.

Congress unveiled its concept of a proper land force in the National Defense Act of 1920. Enacted after months of study, which included taking testimony from various army officers, the law was a compromise of conflicting viewpoints. Its authors rejected the continuing argument of the War Department and the General Staff that the nation should rely for its defense on a regular army of half a million men or more, and also the urgings of a minority of regular officers that America needed a citizen army of men subjected to a compulsory training program. The War Department was allowed a regular army of a maximum size of 280,000, the largest force yet authorized in peacetime. The advocates of a citizen army received two concessions. The National Guard was to be expanded to a maximum size of 435,000 and given greater control over its own affairs. Another civilian component was established in the Organized Reserve, to be made up of officers and enlisted men who had served in the late war. The Reserve corps was to be of approximately the same strength as the National Guard, and the officers and the enlisted men were expected to engage in serious part-time training.

In giving the civilian components of the new system a numerical preponderance, the framers of the National Defense Act clearly indicated that they believed these components would have to do most of the fighting in a future major war. They indicated their opinion again in stipulating that one of the principal tasks of the regular army was to train both the National Guard and the Organized Reserve. To ensure that an adequate supply of trainers was available, the act increased the number of officers in the regular army to almost 18,000 men, three times the number in service before the World War. Half of the new officers were to be chosen from nonregulars who had served in the war. Another infusion of nonregulars was anticipated when the civilian components developed their own officers.

The army, called upon to train these masses of civilians in addition to its own personnel, depended on its educational system. Basic schooling for junior officers was provided at the United States Military Academy at West Point and in the Reserve Officers' Training Corps in colleges and universities throughout the country. The latter program, which antedated the World War, graduated each year about 6,000 men who accepted commissions in the Officers' Reserve Corps. Education above the basic level was available at thirty-one special service schools and at three general service schools. Of the latter, the one at Fort Leavenworth, now known as the Command and General Staff School, prepared officers for divisional command and service on the General Staff. The Army War College trained the most senior and able officers to assume top command and staff positions. The new Army Industrial College furnished instruction in logistics.

The act of 1920 provided the United States with a land force that was adequate in numbers to carry out national policy as then defined—a force that in conjunction with the navy could repel an attack on the continental mass and possibly defend any but the most distant of the insular possessions. Even this limited capacity was soon lessened by Congress. The legislators, certain that no enemy was likely to attack the United States, saw in the land establishment an unnecessary expense to the government, one that could be cut down in size without danger to the country. They began by chipping away at the regular army, a traditional target for advocates of economy. An act of 1921 reduced the army to 150,000 enlisted men, and a subsequent act brought it down to about 119,000, a level at which it remained until 1936. At the same time Congress reduced appropriations to the civilian formations envisioned in the act of 1920, with the result that these elements were never able to attain their authorized strength. The National Guard could enlist no more than 180,000 men. Suffering even more for lack of funds was the Organized Reserve, which depended on financial incentives to induce men to join it. The enlisted men's corps did not come into existence. An officers' corps of 100,000 men was formed, but the numbers were not organized in units and were not encouraged to engage in systematic military study. Some of them tried to keep in touch with latest developments by studying individually or with others in small groups, but many did just enough to retain their rank.

The skimpy appropriations allowed by Congress impaired the efficiency of the army at almost every level. Organization of the troops into corps and armies proved impossible to achieve, and the largest tactical unit was the division. Weapons consisted of abundant stocks left over from the World War and were used until they wore out. Progressive officers realized that these weapons were becoming obsolete and urged the adoption of new ones—a 105-mm. artillery gun to replace the French 75 as the standard artillery piece and a semi-automatic rifle that had been developed in the Ordnance Department, the Garand, to supplant the 1903 Springfield as the standard hand gun—but their efforts failed because of lack of funds to buy the requested items and opposition to change by more conservative officers.

The twin influences of pinched budgets and officer conservatism were responsible for the army's cautious approach to using new combat techniques. A tank corps had come into being during the World War, but a similar organization was not authorized in the National Defense Act. The approximately 1,000 tanks that survived the war were assigned to the infantry, and attempts to create an armored force with an independent mission failed to find favor with the War Department. The only new technique that did gain approval was the air service. An air branch as a part of the army was authorized in the act of 1920 and was given added status in 1926 as the Army Air Corps. However, airmen were still under the command of the infantry officer to whom they were attached. Demanding more autonomy, they won it in 1935 with the creation of General Headquarters, Air Force, subject to the General Staff. The Air Force was infatuated with a doctrine that it existed for one mission: to engage in long-range strategic bombing. It therefore concentrated its building on a heavy bomber, the B-17 Flying Fortress, to the neglect of fighter planes and cooperation with ground forces.

At the end of the World War the United States navy stood second in size and armaments only to that of Great Britain. It contained nineteen capital ships as compared with Britain's forty-two, a host of auxiliary vessels, including its first aircraft carrier, and a personnel of almost 500,000. Although boasting fewer of the largest ships than the British navy, the U.S. fleet was generally superior in the quality of its vessels, which were of a later design. The Americans were also ahead of the British in adopting recent technological advances. Conversion from coal to oil, combined with an efficient method of refueling at sea with tankers, gave the American fleet an expanded range of action. Improved radio communications enabled the high command to maintain contact with distant vessels and to exercise a greater control of remote operations than had ever before been possible.

A building program to add to the number of capital ships had been authorized by Congress in 1916. Construction had barely started when the nation became involved in the World War, and the program was suspended to enable shipyards to turn out antisubmarine vessels. However, at the conclusion of the war the General Board of the Navy proposed that the building program be resumed and even enlarged, and President Wilson, while at the peace conference, approved the request. The projected program would provide the navy with ten new battleships and six heavy cruisers, bringing the total number of capital ships up to thirty-five, a fleet that would be quantitatively superior to the British fleet.

Wilson's motives in endorsing the enlargement are not clear. He must have known that Congress would be reluctant to vote the vast appropriations required to support the program. And, although ignorant of military matters, he surely realized that the United States did not need the huge fleet desired by naval planners. America had no enemy to defend against except possibly Japan, who was reaching for domination in Asia; Germany had been defeated and the navy of friendly Britain controlled the Atlantic crossings. Wilson's probable reason for backing the construction program was to pressure Britain into supporting his League of Nations. In return for British support he slowed down new building, apparently indicating to the British that the issue of naval strength could be settled at a later conference. Britain, anxious to avoid an expensive competition, gladly accepted the compromise. Thus the situation stood in 1921, when the Republicans came into power.

The Harding administration viewed the project of a race in naval construction with distaste. Not only would it require great expenditures of money, which were anathema to a party dedicated to economy in government, it would place the Republicans in a position of seeming not to care about furthering world peace, a role that they were anxious to avoid after having led the rejection of the League of Nations. Weighing these considerations, Republican leaders decided to put a brake on the Democratic naval program. In 1921 the administration invited the governments of the other principal naval powers, Great Britain, Japan, France, and Italy, to attend a conference in Washington to discuss limiting "armaments" and settling Pacific and Far Eastern "problems."[1] The American sponsors of the Washington meeting gave it an official title, the International Conference on Limitation of Armaments. While it was in progress, they often referred to it as the Peace Conference. Both designations were pretentious. Although the invitation had proposed armament reduction, all the governments accepting understood that only naval reduction, and Pacific problems, would be discussed. In history textbooks the gathering is more accurately entitled the Washington Naval Conference. The grander titles were Republican attempts to prove that they were devoted to furthering world peace.

The conference, which stretched into 1922, was hailed at its conclusion as a triumph of American diplomacy. Then and during the immediate ensuing years the tribute seemed deserved. Most of the decisions arrived at had been sought by the American delegates and apparently favored American interests. The governments agreed to limit their total naval tonnage and to observe a ten-year moratorium in building capital ships. The two leading naval powers, the United States and Britain, were allowed 500,000 tons each, and Japan, the third power, was allowed 300,000 tons, the famous 5-5-3 ratio. France and Italy were permitted 175,000 tons each. In order to keep within the allowable tonnage limit the United States agreed to scrap a number of capital ships already built or being built. So also did Britain and Japan, but they needed to scrap fewer vessels to achieve their limits.

The American negotiators and political leaders generally took great satisfaction in the Washington agreement. Computing its benefits, they saw that a costly competition with Britain and possibly with Japan had been averted. At the same time the navy's rank in comparison with other fleets had been maintained at a safe level; the tonnage limits set in the treaty allowed the United States to keep a force second to none. Particularly gratifying to American leaders was Japan's acceptance of a lesser tonnage. Japan's agreement to reduce her fleet seemed to promise peaceful intentions. So too did her adherence to the Four and Nine Power pacts that followed immediately on the Washington conference. American interests in the Far East seemed to be safe.

Subsequent study of the Washington agreement revealed that the original American interpretation of it was much too favorable, and that the American interpretation of Japanese intentions was too benevolent. The inferior status imposed on Japan still left her the dominant naval power in the far Pacific; her fleet was concentrated in waters where the United States and Britain maintained only squadrons. Moreover, in return for accepting a lesser ranking, Japan wrung a far-reaching concession from the two other powers. Each nation agreed not to arm or fortify specified bases in the Pacific. The bases held by Japan were relatively close to the home islands and not important to her defense. But U.S. and British bases were vital to support operations of their fleets in the western reaches of the Pacific. Nevertheless, the western powers agreed to the restriction. Britain was barred from fortifying the Aleutian Islands, Samoa, Guam, and the Philippines, roughly all its sites west of Hawaii. Naval experts estimated that the limitation doubled the value of Japanese tonnage available for operations in the Pacific. It certainly left in doubt the capacity of the United States to defend the Philippines or Guam against a Japanese attack.

Also proving to be ill-founded was the American expectation that the Washington agreement would end competitive naval building. Why the United States had cherished this hope is hard to understand. The conference limited construction of only capital ships. No strictures were placed on auxiliary vessels—cruisers, destroyers, submarines, and other craft. Japan immediately began to build large numbers of cruisers, and other nations followed her lead, although to a lesser extent. Although the United States and Britain did not for several years lay down any cruisers, it was clear that the naval arms race was resuming. Japan showed increasing restiveness at the restraints imposed upon her, and in 1934 announced that she would no longer be bound by them. The American reaction was predictable. A Democratic administration had come into office in 1933, and the president, Franklin D. Roosevelt, was a "big navy man." With his blessing, Congress voted increased naval appropriations in 1934 and in succeeding years, and the fleet began to build back to strength in ships of all classes. It had a long way to go, but it was moving.

The army General Staff emerged from the World War with enhanced prestige. After undergoing reorganization in 1918, it had performed efficiently—indeed, in the opinion of persons in position to observe its work, brilliantly; Secretary of War Newton Baker went so far as to say that without the General Staff the war could not have been won. The new reputation of the agency permeated even Congress, and was obviously in the minds of the framers of the National Defense Act of 1920. Army advocates of an expanded General Staff found for the first time an understanding attitude among the legislators.

The act of 1920 did not give the army quite what it asked for. The request had been for a staff of 226 officers in Washington. Congress allowed 93 officers but placed no limit on the number serving with troops. The officers assigned in the War Department were enjoined to "prepare plans for national defense," for the use of the "military forces" for that purpose, and for the mobilization of men and material resources "in an emergency."[2] While laying down these broad duties, Congress stipulated that the staff was not to engage in routine administrative tasks. In short, the General Staff might plan and supervise, but it was not to command.

The somewhat Rootian language of the law left in doubt the authority of the chief of staff. His position was not appreciably clarified in a War Department regulation issued in 1921. This document stated that the chief of staff was the immediate adviser of the secretary of war and was charged by the secretary "with the planning, development and execution of the military program." He was to issue in the name of the secretary "such orders" as would ensure that the plans of the War Department were "harmoniously executed" by all agencies of the military establishment. This was more Rootian obfuscation. The regulation could be interpreted in different ways by different readers. A strong chief of staff might read it to mean that under the secretary he could command.

A strong chief assumed office in 1921, John J. Pershing, bearing the immense prestige conferred by his war record. Pershing strengthened the General Staff in several directions. First, he reorganized it on the model of his A.E.F. staff, creating five divisions concerned with personnel, intelligence, training and operations, supply, and war plans. His most important innovation was a surprise, for it was a reversal of his position on command that he had held during the war. He decided that in the event of war the chief of staff and the General Staff should do more than occupy themselves with building up an army at home. In addition, they should assume the direction of combat operations. These operations would be prepared by the War Plans Division, and the chief of staff, taking with him whatever staff groups he wanted, would move to the theater of war as commanding general. This was a fundamental change in the command system—the chief of staff would not only supervise in peace but would direct in war. Pershing's system was retained by succeeding chiefs of staff, with important results in the future.[3]

In Pershing's instructions to the War Plans Division, he assumed that any war in which the United States became engaged would be a single-theater conflict. His opinion was influenced by the American experience in the World War and was shared by army officers concerned with planning, and by the chiefs who came after him. The single-theater concept also controlled the thinking of naval theorists and was the basis of the joint planning of the two services throughout the twenties and into the early thirties.

The task of coordinating interservice planning fell to the Joint Army and Navy Board, usually referred to as the Joint Board. This agency had been created in 1903 by executive order of the service secretaries and consisted of the chief of staff and three officers of the General Staff and the chief of naval operations and three officers of the General Board. It had functioned with indifferent results, concentrating on devising plans for coastal defense, and during the World War it had held practically no meetings. The service secretaries, feeling a need of professional advice, reconstituted the Joint Board in 1919. Its personnel varied somewhat from year to year as the services saw a reason to add officers with special knowledge; each, for example, appointed a chief air officer as aviation became more important. To facilitate the making of strategy, a joint planning committee was added.

The Joint Board recognized two situations in which the services would have to act together. One was a war in which they operated for the most part separately but to attain a common objective. The other was a war in which they combined forces in a particular theater to attain a common objective; in the latter event the service with the paramount interest or strength in the area would appoint the commander of the combined force.

Guided by these principles, the board devised plans for possible war with the major powers. Each enemy was designated by a color; red for Britain, orange for Japan, and so on, and the designs were collectively referred to as the "color plans." Much of this scheming was, admittedly, busy work. The plans were directed almost entirely at nations who had no interests that conflicted with those of the United States and who were therefore improbable enemies. There was only one exception, Japan.

The board planners assumed that Japan would begin a war with a surprise attack on the most distant island possessions of the United States, the Philippines and Guam, to attach them to her expanding empire. Plan Orange was devised to prevent this. The plan underwent several variations from year to year, but its basic features remained unchanged. The army units in the Philippines were to conduct a desperate defense until help could arrive from the United States. That assistance would come in the form of the navy, which would advance westward from Hawaii bearing troop reinforcements. The expedition would relieve the American garrisons, the navy would engage and defeat the Japanese fleet, and the war would be won.

The plan seemed easy to promulgate—on paper. But when the planners came to consider such problems as mobilizing men and ships and transporting them across the Pacific, some of them, and especially the army officers, began to doubt that the movement could succeed. The skeptics pointed out the immense advantage that proximity to the Philippines gave Japan: she could have a sea and land command off the islands within days, whereas the United States would require several weeks to transport a defense force. Army officers feared that the small American garrison of some 10,000 troops would be overwhelmed before the relief expedition arrived, and seeing no strategic purpose in holding the islands, they advised abandoning them. Naval officers believed that the islands were a necessary Pacific base and insisted that they could be defended. However, as Plan Orange continued to undergo modification, the naval planners became vaguer and vaguer as to the length of time the fleet would require to fight its way to the Philippines, arousing suspicions that they hoped they would not have to carry out the plan. Probably no one seriously expected that the plan would be acted on. About this whole exercise there was an aura of unreality, its participants devising their projects with little relation to the military or political situation. There was no way in which the United States could defend the Philippines with its existing military forces. Nor was it national policy to try to hold the islands. Public opinion had decided that they were not worth holding, and in 1934 Congress enacted a law granting them their independence after a ten-year period.

While the Joint Board planners were reflecting on the problem of waging a one-theater war, events were occurring in Asia and in Europe that would cause the greatest war in history. The United States would become involved in this conflict, and it would have to fight on many fronts.

During the 1920s Americans had found it possible to view the rest of the world with feelings of detached superiority. They liked some nations better than others, but not with enough warmth to form alliances with any of them. They disliked the political systems of some nations, but not with such intensity as to lead them to act to weaken those systems. Above all, Americans felt secure. Isolated by the oceans, they feared no nation. Japan was the only power that appeared to harbor hostile intentions, and she threatened only the distant Philippines, which were not considered vital to the national defense. The world might not be "safe for democracy," as President Wilson had promised it would be, but it was clearly safe for the United States.

These comforting assurances began to crumble as the 1930s opened, and within a few years they would lie completely shattered. It was a dramatic change of attitude—the world that had seemed so safe suddenly became dark and dangerous. The influences that caused the change were not newly born; they had been forming for years but had gone unnoticed by most Americans. In Europe dictatorial leaders and parties had come into power in major countries: Benito Mussolini and his Fascists in Italy, Adolf Hitler and his Nazis in Germany, and the Communists in Russia. In the greatest power in Asia, Japan, a clique of militarists and their business allies had secured dominance over the emperor and asserted control over the government. All four movements seemed to threaten the values that were cherished in the United States and other democratic countries.

In the United States reactions to the rise of the new despotisms ranged from anger and alarm to indifference. The Russian dictatorship excited the least attention. The collectivist economic system espoused by the Communists was despised by Americans, but the Soviet government, preoccupied with solidifying its domestic authority, seemed little disposed to try to export its system. The Italian and German dictatorships, on the other hand, aroused real apprehensions. The Fascists and the Nazis advocated certain common principles: a belief in the innate superiority of their peoples over other peoples, a devotion to military virtues, a support of rearmament, and a justification of war as an instrument to achieve national ends. In American eyes these ideals were evil, and Italy and Germany had thus become dangerous nations. They might not attack the United States, although American military men had long suspected that Germany had designs on Latin America, but they could well turn on Britain and France and upset the balance of power in Europe.

Equally disturbing were the noises coming out of Japan. Already viewed as a possible enemy, Japan appeared even more dangerous after the accession of the militarists. The new rulers preached a doctrine of expansion in Asia that threatened to engulf all American interests in its wake. Viewing the aggressive attitude of Japan and of the European dictatorships, thoughtful Americans wondered if the nation was as insulated from the rest of the world as had been assumed or, with the advent of long-range navies and air power, as immune from attack.

The aggressive rhetoric of the authoritarian powers was soon translated into action. Japan was the first to move. Convinced that she had to expand to prosper, she saw large but weak China as one area vulnerable to her arms. In 1931 Japan seized the northern border province of Manchuria and converted it into a satellite state, disregarding protests in the United States and in the League of Nations. In 1936 she invaded China proper and brought the southern coast and extensive parts of the interior under her control. Again the

Japanese ignored American and League of Nations protests, and as if to show her scorn of the protesters, she withdrew from the League and announced that she would no longer be bound by the postwar agreements to limit naval armaments.

While Japan was marching in Asia, in Europe Mussolini and Hitler were rattling their swords. Mussolini, boasting that Italy was going to revive the imperial glories of ancient Rome, invaded the African nation of Ethiopia in 1935 and made it an Italian colony. Hitler's ambitions lay in making Germany the dominant power in Europe. In 1936 he occupied the Rhineland, which had been demilitarized in the Treaty of Versailles, and when he met no resistance from France and England, he boldly moved on to other conquests. In 1938 he seized Austria, and in the following year, Czechoslovakia. Hitler and Mussolini ignored protests raised in the League of Nations and withdrew their nations from the organization. Italy and Germany formed a new alliance, the Rome-Berlin Axis, and soon they were joined by Japan in an Anti-Comintern Pact that was ostensibly directed at international communism. Observers in other countries feared that the alliance might be directed at other targets as well.

Among Americans German and Italian aggressions overshadowed those of Japan. The reaction was natural in the circumstances of the time. Americans felt closer to Europe than to Asia and were, despite their colonial advances in the Pacific, still an Atlantic people. They believed that American security depended on a stable Atlantic community, and they regarded Britain, with her navy, and France as guarantors of that stability. Conversely, they regarded Germany and Italy as threats to it. Japan, in contrast, was engaged in distant China, and the victims of her aggression were other Orientals rather than Occidentals.

Although Americans were united in their dislike for what Germany and Italy were doing, they disagreed as to the nation's policy if the aggressions continued. A majority favored staying out of the whole European "mess," as the situation was often referred to; they were called "isolationists" as the debate took form. The popularity of their views was reflected in the passage by Congress of three neutrality acts in 1935, 1936, and 1937. These laws emphasized the current belief that American entrance into the World War had been caused by armament sales to the Allies, and they were designed to prevent its repetition. They required, among other things, that in event of war between foreign states the president had to prohibit the sale of arms and the extension of loans or credits to the belligerents.

Opposing the isolationists were the advocates of what was called "collective security," usually referred to as the "interventionists." Central to their thinking was a fear that the German and Italian dictators, unless impeded, would force Britain and France into an inferior status, possibly by making war on them, and would then dominate Europe, thus menacing the United States itself. Their greatest anxiety concerned the German dictator. Hitler boasted of his intention to extend Germany's might, and his threats to neighboring countries and persecution of the Jews made him seem a figure of evil as well as of danger. What the United States could do to stop Hitler and Mussolini the interventionists did not make quite clear. They talked about the necessity of the "peace-loving" nations banding together, "collective security," to arrest further aggressions. But they were not explicit in stating what would be involved. They presumably favored an arrangement in which American support in the form of weapons could be extended to nations opposing the dictators, and especially to the bulwarks of democracy in Europe, Britain, and France; some of them, although not saying so publicly, thought that the United States would eventually have to oppose Germany with its own arms. The interventionists were a minority when the debate on policy began, but they included some of the most influential leaders in the country, and many of the most vocal press and radio organs. Their most valuable recruit was President Roosevelt, who although having to proceed cautiously because of the strength of isolationist opinion, clearly supported collective security.

The policy debate focused new attention on the state of the nation's defenses. It was apparent that the United States existed in a perilous world, and interventionists and isolationists alike recognized that the existing military system was inadequate to fight a major war. Roosevelt was keenly aware of the deficiencies, and seeking to take advantage of the rising sentiment in favor of rearmament, he asked Congress in January 1938 to enlarge military appropriations. The burden of his message was the aggressions of Germany,

Italy, and Japan. In solemn conclusion Roosevelt said: "Our national defense is inadequate for national security and requires increase." The president later referred to the message as beginning a "vast program of rearmament." This was vast exaggeration. He asked Congress to vote money primarily for naval expansion. For the army he requested a smaller sum to be expended on shortages in equipment.

Roosevelt seemed to be thinking only of providing a force to defend the United States: the navy was traditionally the first line of defense and therefore should be strengthened. But by November 1938 he had changed his opinion. At a meeting of his civilian and military advisers he announced that the nation's air defenses were inadequate—the army Air Corps had about 1,600 planes on hand—and that he was going to ask Congress to appropriate enough money to enable the aircraft industry to produce within a short time 10,000 planes. Army officers at the conference, who had been pressing for a strengthening of the ground forces, noted with interest that the president was concerned only with procuring planes; he said nothing about enlisting and training pilots and crews or securing the other elements that make up a balanced air force. They suspected that the planes were intended not for the Air Corps but for eventual sale to England and France. Their suspicion was well founded. Roosevelt had learned that those countries considered their greatest danger to lie in the expanding German air force, and he had decided that in strengthening their air arms he would be contributing to the defense of the United States.

The army felt left behind in the rush to rearm. Neither the president nor the Congress seemed to think that it was imperative to strengthen the ground forces. In 1935 Congress authorized an increase of the regular army to 165,000 men, and a slow rebuilding process began. The General Staff had ambitions to create a much larger aggregation, an Initial Protective Force of 400,000, to be obtained by combining the regular army and the National Guard, and then to be followed by a Protective Mobilization Force of 730,000. These were dreams, for the moment. In 1939 Congress removed the limit to the army of a ceiling of 165,000 but appropriated only enough money to provide for 210,000.

On the eve of the outbreak of World War II in Europe, the regular army was approaching a strength of 190,000. The National Guard comprised about 200,000. Of the regular army total, about 50,000 were stationed in the outlying possessions. The 140,000 in the United States were dispersed among 130 posts. The largest combat unit was the division, and only a third of the divisions were at full strength. The army had adopted the Garand semiautomatic rifle and the 105-mm. artillery gun, but these moves were so recent that the new weapons had not been received in numbers; most of the regulars, and also the guardsmen, were still armed with the Springfield rifle and the 75-mm. artillery piece of World War I. The army was, in fact, a World War I force, significantly improved in recent years and highly capable of development, but not one prepared to engage in the war of air and armor that was about to be unleashed in Europe.

World War II: The American Involvement

Anyone who studies World War II becomes awed by its magnitude. The enormity of the effort put forth by both sides and the scope and scale of the military operations almost defy comprehension. This bigness imposes a problem on the historian who seeks to re-create the war for readers: he has either to enter into lengthy detail or to restrict his story to a broad outline. The latter approach has been chosen here as the more feasible.

The bigness of the war was recognized in the naming of it: it was truly a world conflict, much more encompassing than the earlier struggle of the same name. Operations were undertaken in almost every area of the globe, in Europe, Asia, and Africa, in fact, in every land mass except the Western Hemisphere, on the oceans and under them, and in the air. The nations aligned in the war ranged around the globe, although not all of them contributed men or arms. On one side were the Axis powers, Germany, Italy, Japan, and four small European nations. On the opposing side was an alliance that called itself the United Nations powers but is usually referred to, in a retention of World War I terminology, as the Allied powers.[1] Seventeen nations were active participants on the Allied side. The imposing number is, however, deceptive as to the strength of the alliance.

This essay was the last piece that Williams worked on, and remains incomplete. It probably would have gone into a second volume of *A History of American Wars.*

France, an important signatory, and a number of other European members, were conquered by Germany immediately after the outbreak of hostilities and were, except for irregular resistance, taken out of the war. China had to restrict her efforts to defending against the Japanese within her own borders. The brunt of the battle against the Axis was carried by Great Britain and her dominions, the Soviet Union, and the United States.

The war's dimensions were reflected in the size of the contending military forces. In no previous struggle had such hosts been called forth; the United States alone mobilized a total of 16,000,000 men,[2] or approximately four times the number of troops it had raised in World War I. A more realistic appraisal of the American accomplishment is afforded if one examines the peak strength of the armed forces, an imposing 12,300,000. Other Allied nations maintained comparable multitudes. The top strength of the forces of Russia, or the Soviet Union, was 12,500,000. Great Britain, although much smaller in population than the United States or Russia, supported more than 5,000,000. On the Axis side Germany achieved the greatest strength, a total of 10,000,000. But Japan sustained 6,000,000, and Italy, 3,700,000.

One of the distinctions accorded the war is that it was the most destructive in history. The perception is accurate as it pertains to ravaging of material things: buildings, residences, factories, whole areas of cities were leveled. The havoc was wrought in part by means used in earlier wars, opposing armies fighting for possession of territory, artillery firing into cities and towns. But most of it was produced by one of the new weapons of the air, the long-range bomber. Bombers have been called "flying artillery." They could reach targets deep in enemy territory that were impossible for conventional artillery, and could deliver much greater fire loads. Their raids caused such devastation that when it is reckoned in terms of money, the sums become meaningless.

The destructiveness of the war to human life raises many questions. Casualties were grievous, but they fell more heavily on some nations than on others. Civilian deaths, which were the greatest in any modern war, were most sore in countries that lay in the path of battling armies or that were subjected to repeated air raids. In Russia an estimated 2,500,000 civilians were killed; in Japan, 500,000; and in Germany, 300,000. Military or combat deaths were also unevenly distributed. On the Allied side Russia lost 7,500,000. On the Axis side Germany lost 3,500,000, and Japan 1,220,000. But other nations incurred only small losses: France, 210,000, Britain, 245,000, the United States, 318,000, Italy, 78,000. The total losses in the European armies were in astonishing contrast to those in World War I, and were remarkably light in relation to the strength of the several armies. One explanation for the paradox is that in the Allied forces only a portion of the aggregate strength were combat troops; a large part consisted of men in support roles. For example, in the American army for every three soldiers in the ground forces there were two technicians or administrators behind the lines.

The war has distinctions other than its destructiveness. Viewed in the context of world military history, it stands out as the most "technological" war. The new weapons or improved models of older weapons that appeared can be only indicated—tactical airplanes, strategic bombers, armored tanks, powered landing craft, amphibious vehicles, all united in what the historian Walter Millis called a great "automotive team." Also allowing but brief mention are the numerous ways in which technology was applied to conducting war, in the use of radio and radar and electronic communications generally, as one example, and as another, the methods employed by the United States navy to supply its vessels in the far reaches of the Pacific Ocean by constructing what amounted to "floating" bases. At the end of the war the United States produced what was believed to be the ultimate weapon, the atomic bomb, which seemed so terrible as to forbid war in the future.

The war is also distinctive in American military history. This was the first time that the United States had fought a global war—World War I had been a global conflict, but American forces had been involved in only one theater, Europe. In World War II American forces were active in widely separated areas, the European theater, which included Africa, and in the Pacific. The United States fought as a member of a coalition, as it had in World War I, but this time it was the dominant partner. America provided the greatest number of men to the Allied side, and the bulk of the supplies and weapons, and it determined the strategy of the Allies.

The United States joined the war for the same reasons that it had entered World War I, to preserve the balance of international power, against Germany in Europe and against Japan in Asia. It was an ironic result of the war that one of its partners in the Allied coalition, the Soviet Union, emerged from the conflict as the strongest nation in Europe, threatening a new imbalance of power on that continent and, although to a lesser extent, in Asia. The United States stood as the only counterweight to Russia, and it accepted its role. Refusing to retreat into isolation as it had done after 1918, the United States after 1945 became a champion of the democratic and the capitalistic world. The nation finally had a national policy.

The Course of the United States

The war that had threatened Europe since Hitler began his career of conquest finally erupted in 1939. After he seized Czechoslovakia, the British and French governments agreed that they must try to contain him from further aggressions, and thinking to intimidate him, the prime ministers announced that they would defend certain lesser nations against a German attack. They had not long to wait to make their word good. Hitler had fixed on Poland as his next victim, and although he did not believe that Britain and France could act effectively against him, he feared that the Soviet Union would resent an eastward extension of German power. He therefore concluded a pact with the Soviets, hitherto an ideological enemy, to partition Poland, Germany to take the larger part of the country, Russia to be allowed a smaller slice and leave to occupy the northern Baltic states. His plans complete, Hitler invaded Poland in September 1939 and in a lightning campaign of less than a month occupied his share. As the German army moved into Poland, Britain and France, in an apparent redemption of their promise, declared war on Germany. They did nothing, however, to aid the beleaguered Poles, merely stationing troops on the eastern border of France. The British and French leaders seemed to think that the presence of these forces and the threat of a naval blockade would eventually compel Hitler to come to peace terms.

They were underestimating the resolve and the ambitions of the German leader. While the opposing armies watched each other in what was becoming known as the "phony war," Hitler's restless mind was planning new moves. In April 1940 he unleashed his columns on Denmark and Norway, and after occupying these countries, he invaded the Netherlands and Belgium. (Three of these nations were neutral in World War I.) French and British troops entered Belgium to aid in its defense but could not stem the advancing Germans, who turned into France itself. As the invaders rolled toward Paris, Italy declared war on France and Britain and exerted additional pressure on the defenders from the south. The Germans captured Paris in mid-June and forced a new French government to agree to peace. While the French were being pressed into submission, the small British army had retired to a port on the coast and escaped to England. This was the only miscarriage in what otherwise was a great German victory. In a campaign of a few months Hitler had conquered five nations. A puppet French government sat at Vichy, but the Germans were in effective occupation of the country. The only power opposing Hitler now was Britain.

For a time after his triumph Hitler talked of completing his mastery of Europe by invading England. Whether he seriously contemplated this move or was merely trying to intimidate his last enemy has never been determined. Whatever the truth, after subjecting Britain to fierce air attacks he backed away; he was, perhaps, daunted by the failure of his air force to attain superiority over the British air force. Turning his eyes elsewhere, he joined with Italy in the spring of 1941 to overrun Greece and Yugoslavia. At the same time a German force occupied the Greek island of Crete and a German-Italian army based in Libya in northern Africa threatened Egypt, where Britain maintained forces to protect the Suez Canal. These thrusts seemed to portend a German advance into the eastern Mediterranean and the Middle East, but although Hitler was not averse to making gains in this area, he was reserving his main effort for a different theater. One enemy had always ranked above all others in his thinking, and he decided that he was now strong enough to strike at the Soviets. In June he ordered his generals to invade Russia, and German forces swept over the border. By the end of the year they had occupied large areas of western Russia and were approaching the gates of Moscow itself.

The spreading triumphs of the Axis powers excited to new heights the debate over foreign policy among Americans. The interventionists became strident in demanding that the United States must take some kind of action to halt the march of the Axis to hegemony in Europe, either by extending military aid to Britain and France, and after France fell, to Britain alone, or, as a last resort, by entering the war as an open participant. The isolationists, although appalled by the reach of German success, still insisted that the United States had no direct interest in the outcome of the war and should remain clear of it. They opposed sending aid to the Allies, believing that such assistance would tend to increase, inevitably involving the nation in the conflict. President Roosevelt and his advisers sided with the interventionists. Already sympathetic to the Allies on ideological grounds, they further feared that an Axis victory would place a hostile power in position to attack the Western Hemisphere and possibly even the United States.

The division on policy did not extend to thinking about national defense. Both parties to the controversy recognized that the United States existed in an uncertain world and must be prepared to defend itself; even isolationists conceded that the nation might be attacked by the ambitious Axis. Consequently, Roosevelt found wide popular support when he inaugurated measures to strengthen the military establishment.

The president acted first to build up the ground forces to somewhere near the strength permitted by the National Defense Act (280,000 men). Immediately after the war began, he authorized increasing the regular army to 227,000 and the National Guard to 235,000. These accretions seemed to provide an adequate defensive force late in 1939; at that time the war in Europe was in stalemate. But in 1940 came the great German victories that knocked France out of the war and left Britain standing alone against the Axis. The sudden shift in balance forced American leaders to revise estimates of their nation's defensive needs. Roosevelt, supported by Secretary of War Henry L. Stimson and Chief of Staff George C. Marshall, informed Congress that further additions to the ground forces were required. The legislators responded with alacrity, authorizing the creation of an army of 1,500,000 by 1941. This total was to be achieved by bringing the regular army up to a strength of 500,000, calling the National Guard into federal service for twelve months, and, in an action reflecting the popular belief that an emergency existed, imposing the first peacetime conscription in the nation's history.

A law to draft manpower had first been proposed by prominent civilians who were interested in national defense and who stressed that only conscription would produce an army adequate to defend the nation. Roosevelt and his advisers were reluctant to adopt the idea, fearing that a draft bill would fail in Congress and imperil other defense measures, but were finally won over. Once introduced, the measure passed with little difficulty. The Selective Service and Training Act of 1940 required all males between twenty-one and thirty-six years of age to register for possible service, forbade bounties and substitutes, and allowed exemption only to individuals supporting families, conscientious objectors, and persons engaged in tasks of "national importance." Reflecting the wish of the General Staff to put as many men as possible through a training program, the act limited service to a period of twelve months and stipulated that no more than 900,000 men were to be in service at one time. Conscription had been presented to Congress as a temporary peacetime measure, but when the international situation continued to be tense in the summer of 1941, the Roosevelt administration requested that the draft be extended to eighteen additional months. Isolationists cried that the government was creating a mass army to fight in the war in Europe and came within one vote of defeating the extension in the House of Representatives.[3]

The several measures adopted in 1940 ensured a steady flow of men into the ground forces, and by the middle months of the following year the army had achieved its planned strength of 1,500,000 troops. Large numbers of these men needed training—the National Guard units requiring additional instruction and the new regular units and the mass of selectees having to undergo basic drill. Recruit training was placed under the supervision of a new agency, General Headquarters, and as the various units were whipped into shape, they came under the command of four army headquarters. The army in 1941 was a stronger and more efficient force than it had been a short year before, well capable of repelling an attack on the United States. But it could not have engaged a major foe abroad. Many of the units required additional training—only twenty of the thirty-seven divisions were rated as combat ready—and most of them lacked adequate supplies of such items as ammunition, tank and antitank guns, and anticraft artillery.

At the same time that the government was striving to build up the land units, it was moving to strengthen other branches of the armed forces. Roosevelt had been eager to develop the nation's air power even before the war started, and after September 1939 he redoubled his efforts to persuade Congress to vote appropriations to expand the army's Air Corps. He got his way easily. By 1940 the air arm was training 30,000 pilots a year; the aircraft industry was gearing to produce 36,000 planes a year. In an important reorganizational move the Chief of the Air Corps was designated a deputy chief of staff, which gave him the right to sit with the chief of staff and the chief of naval operations in strategy discussions and which invested the air service with a measure of autonomy. Also undergoing expansion was the navy. Already engaged in a rebuilding program when the war began, the navy had little trouble in securing presidential and congressional support to create a two-ocean fleet that could cope simultaneously with Japan in the Pacific and the Axis powers, if they should defeat Britain, in the Atlantic. In 1941 the navy had in commission 17 battleships, 7 aircraft carriers, 37 cruisers, 171 destroyers, and 111 submarines. That many or more of each type of craft was being built, with emphasis placed on construction of carriers.

The rearmament program had been presented to the public as having a defensive purpose: the United States might be attacked by the Axis powers and must be prepared to defend itself. Defense was undoubtedly a factor in the thinking of Roosevelt and his advisers in 1939, but other elements entered into their considerations as the war continued to go in favor of the Axis. Through a subtle process the president and his civil and military planners moved from a policy of defending the nation to one of defending the whole hemisphere, and finally to a conclusion that in the cause of defense the United States would have to participate in the war offensively.

Roosevelt cultivated close relations with his military advisers. Even before the war broke out in Europe he had directed that the chief of staff, the chief of naval operations, and members of the Joint Board could on certain matters report directly to him rather than going through the service secretaries. He had previously approved a War Department regulation that clarified and enhanced the authority of the chief of staff; that functionary was in peace the commanding general of the field forces and in war he would continue to exercise field leadership until another commander was designated by the president. After 1939 Roosevelt exercised increasing supervision over the planners who were charged with devising strategy. With his approval the Joint Board abandoned its making of "color" plans, which envisioned war with one power, and turned to producing "rainbow" plans, which contemplated war against several powers and in more than one theater. Beginning with a proposal to defend merely the Western Hemisphere, the drafters worked out five plans, the last of which called for sending expeditionary forces to Africa or Europe. The last plan, "Rainbow Five," became the basis of American strategy when the nation entered the war. An additional document, called the Victory Program, recommended that after defeating Germany the United States should deal with Japan in the Pacific.

While the United States was trying to develop the capacity to wage war, it was extending various forms of military aid to France and Britain, and after France fell, on an increased scale to Britain. In 1939 Roosevelt persuaded Congress to repeal the prohibition in the 1937 Neutrality Act on the sale of munitions to belligerents, and heavy orders of arms came from France and Britain. In 1940, when the British navy was hard pressed to defend convoys of supply vessels in the Atlantic, Roosevelt announced that he was transferring fifty "over age" destroyers to the British in exchange for offshore Atlantic bases, and in the same year he directed that large stocks of planes and other arms be transferred to Britain. When this flow of materials proved insufficient to meet British needs, the president secured from Congress the Lend-Lease Act, which provided that the amount of supplies going to Britain or its allies would be determined by the wants of those nations rather than by their ability to pay for them—the United States was to become, in Roosevelt's words, the "arsenal of democracy." Nor did American aid stop at supplying foes of the Axis. In 1941 Roosevelt ordered that the navy take over from the British the task of patrolling the western Atlantic sea lanes and that American planes protect the air routes to Iceland and Greenland, where the British had bases. American ships also operated in the South Atlantic, convoying British troops to Cape Town in South Africa.

In taking these various measures the United States was not acting as a neutral. Roosevelt for a time tried to throw a guise of neutrality over what he was doing by declaring that the western Atlantic was included in the Western Hemisphere. However, he soon dropped this pretense and admitted that the United States was participating in the war—but in a limited way. In August 1941 he met with the British prime minister, Winston Churchill, in Newfoundland, and the two leaders agreed on a set of war aims and on the strategy that should be employed to achieve them. The agreement was in effect a military alliance, the first one that the nation had ever concluded before becoming involved in a war.

The American people approved, although with varying degrees of enthusiasm, the measures that the president had taken. It was obvious however, that they hoped to avoid open participation in the war, that they wished to limit America to being a supplier to the forces opposing the Axis. Roosevelt could not arouse them to want to do more. He tried to on several occasions, as when an American destroyer was set upon by German submarines near Iceland. "America has been attacked," he announced in words reminiscent of those President Polk had employed in 1846. "The shooting has started." The public response to this and other of his appeals was apathetic. Most Americans seemed resigned to the likelihood that Germany would engage in occasional retaliations, and it is very probable that if the Axis powers had continued to avoid a direct confrontation, the United States would never have entered the war actively. But even as Axis restraint was promising to keep the nation out of the European conflict, events were moving in another part of the globe that would change the situation dramatically. In December 1941 Japan committed an act that convulsed the whole nation with anger and that caused the shooting to start at last.

Pearl Harbor

While public attention was focused upon the war in Europe, the government had been edging toward a confrontation with Japan in Asia. American policy makers had long feared that Japan was determined to make her dominion of the Far East absolute, and in the late 1930s events added to their apprehensions. The Japanese had overrun large areas of China and had refused to withdraw their forces; they threatened, in fact, to conquer additional territory. Nor were their ambitions restrained to China. They were suspected, on evidence in intelligence reports, of planning to occupy most or all of Southeast Asia; French Indochina, Malaya, a British possession, and the Dutch East Indies. Possession of these areas would provide Japan with resources she needed to operate her industrial and military machine—particularly with oil and rubber—and would also place her on the flank of the Philippines, in position to attack them if she so desired. It was the latter possibility that particularly disturbed American leaders; the United States, while resigned to the islands' independence, was of no mind to let them become a part of Japan's expanding empire. Taking all these considerations into account, American planners decided that Japan had to be checked. They realized that opposition might provoke her to war, that they might involve the nation in an Asiatic conflict and a European one at the same time, but they were prepared to run the risk.

The means decided on to bring Japan into line was economic pressure—to deprive her of the raw materials she had to import to sustain her industrial system. In 1939 Washington angered Japan by announcing abrogation of a trade treaty that had been in effect for twenty-eight years. Other measures followed in rapid succession. In 1940 the United States forbade exporters to send to any country scrap iron and petroleum without first obtaining official license, and later in the same year placed an embargo on the sale of iron and steel scrap to any country except Great Britain. Rather than deterring

Japan, these actions provoked her to greater bellicosity. She concluded a new treaty with Germany and Italy in which the signatories pledged that they would attack any power not then a belligerent that made war on one of them. With Russia now involved in war with Germany, the pact was obviously aimed at the United States.

Japan continued on her expansionist course in 1941. She secured from the French government, subservient to Hitler, permission to send military forces into Indochina, placing that colony under effective occupation, a move that indicated unmistakably an intention to attack Malaya and the Dutch East Indies. The United States retaliated by putting an embargo on all trade with Japan, unless licensed, and freezing Japanese assets in the United States. At the same time the government dispatched army reinforcements and additional heavy bombers to the Philippines.

The freezing of Japanese assets was an especially provocative measure—in effect, an ultimatum to Japan. Without recourse to these assets Japan could no longer secure funds to purchase the oil, rubber, and other resources that she required. She would have either to abandon her plans of expansion or to launch a campaign to conquer Southeast Asia. The Japanese government was prepared to resort to conquest, but even while preparing its plans, it continued to negotiate with the United States. Japan offered to withdraw from Indochina but only after conclusion of a general peace and demanded that the United States not interfere in its quarrel with China; she also asked for a restoration of trade. The American government, for its part, pressed for a return to the status quo in the Far East. While Japanese emissaries were bargaining in Washington, the men in control of the government decided to act. Feeling compelled to resort to conquest, they resolved to destroy, or at least immobilize, the only instrument that could hinder their plans, the American Pacific fleet. On December 7, 1941, a Japanese strike force delivered a surprise and destructive attack on the great American naval base of Pearl Harbor, Hawaii.

The attack on Pearl Harbor came from the air. Six Japanese carriers approached undetected to within about two hundred miles of the base, their decks crammed with 360 bomber and fighter planes. Early Sunday morning, December 7, these craft took off for Pearl

Harbor, still undetected by the defenders. Suddenly appearing out of the sky, they rained bombs on the vessels moored in the harbor and on the planes parked on the air strips. The surprise was complete. Most of the ships were sunk quickly, and most of the planes were destroyed before they could get off the ground. Crippled and confused, the defenders could do little to fight off the attackers. The Japanese lost only 29 planes and fewer than 100 lives. American losses were appalling: 8 battleships and 10 other vessels sunk or put out of action, 188 planes, and over 2,000 deaths, most of them suffered in the sinking of the large ships. Fortunately for the Americans, the three large carriers normally in the harbor were at sea at the time, and the oil storages on shore escaped the attention of the attackers. Otherwise, the success of the attack was complete. The American fleet in the Pacific was for the time being out of commission. Most of the sunk ships were eventually refloated and repaired, but there was no American force immediately available to oppose the Japanese as they conquered one Pacific island after another. Pearl Harbor was a military disaster, the greatest in the nation's history.

In the aftermath of the debacle questions arose as to how the Japanese had been able to accomplish their surprise. The questioning became especially insistent after it was revealed that before Pearl Harbor the United States had broken the Japanese military code and had been regularly intercepting messages sent on it. Government leaders must have discovered that the Japanese were preparing a strike force, many persons decided. Why then had the military authorities at Pearl Harbor not been warned that an attack was impending? Was the failure the result of criminal negligence in the highest civil and military circles? Or, worse, had word of the danger been concealed because Roosevelt thirsted to involve the nation in war and realized that an apparent surprise attack would anger the populace into demanding war? The controversy raged for years, unchecked by the report of a special agency of inquiry that many considered a whitewash, and echoes of it are heard even today.

There is no mystery about what happened at Pearl Harbor. The tragic result was not caused by official stupidity or official plotting. High civil and military authorities were aware that Japan was preparing several naval concentrations. Where they went wrong was in interpreting the information. They concluded that the Japanese must be preparing to move in force on Southeast Asia and possibly on the Philippines. The commanders in Hawaii were alerted that the Japanese would be moving soon, but "we were not worried" about Pearl Harbor, as General Marshall explained later, because they thought the base was so strong that the Japanese would not dare to attack it. Their knowledge of Japanese intentions should have told them, however, where the blow must fall. Wherever the Japanese meant to go, they could not start while the American Pacific fleet was in operation. They had to destroy or cripple the fleet, and they therefore had to attack Pearl Harbor. In failing to recognize this elementary truth the American planners were committing a common military sin— they thought that the enemy would go elsewhere than where they were strongest.

Pearl Harbor brought the United States into war with Japan and also with her European allies. Congress, reflecting popular anger at the treachery of the attack, declared war on Japan with only one dissenting vote (Representative Jeanette Rankin of Montana, who had also voted against entering World War I). Japan retaliated by declaring war on the United States and Britain, and Germany and Italy joined her in her declaration on the United States. Congress thereupon declared war on the Axis powers.

The United States entered the conflict with a unanimity of purpose not seen in any previous war. No important group in the country opposed it. Americans of German and Italian descent hastened to avow their support of the government, and there was no persecution of these people as there had been of the Germans in World War I. The only ethnics who came under suspicion were Japanese or persons of Japanese descent living in Hawaii and California, many of whom were American citizens. Although there was no evidence to support the apprehension, it was widely believed that they were prepared to cooperate with Japanese invading forces. (For that matter, there was no evidence that the Japanese planned to invade Hawaii or California.) The possibility of removing the Japanese population from Hawaii was discussed but abandoned as being impractical; however, the islands were placed under martial law for the duration of the war. But in California removal was judged feasible. In an act of senseless hysteria, over 100,000 Japanese persons were rounded up and kept in internment camps until the end of the war.

The German Enemy

In entering the war the United States was pitting itself against two principal and powerful countries, Germany in Europe and Japan in the Pacific. But it was Germany that most concerned American planners at the beginning of the conflict, and it was against Germany that the first American effort was concentrated. The German enemy was almost completely the creation of one man, Adolf Hitler, who was both the head of the state and the director of its military forces. Hitler was that rare type of leader who literally changes history: a good case can be made that if he had not appeared, the war in Europe would not have occurred. He also influenced ways of waging war; and the events of the war, including the American participation, cannot be understood without examining this remarkable man.

Hitler first attracted attention during the 1920s, when he was only in his thirties. Before that time he had been an obscure figure, an artist of Austrian birth eking out an existence in Munich, a corporal in the imperial army in the World War. Returning to Munich at the close of the war, he turned his attention to politics, developing a set of ideas that remained with him for the rest of his life. His philosophy, if it can be called that, was an amalgam of convictions and prejudices held individually by many Germans: a belief in the superiority of the German people and in the inferiority and the evil nature of the Jewish people, a contempt for democracy and a hatred of communism, and a festering resentment of the humiliation inflicted upon Germany by the victors in the World War. German nationalism bulked especially large in his thinking. He preached that Germany should rearm in defiance of the limitations placed upon her in the treaty of Versailles and should become again a great military power. As one element in restoring Germany's greatness he advocated expansion to the east against her traditional enemy: Russia. The probability of war did not deter him.

Hitler's predilections led him to join the National Socialist Workers party, one of several restless organizations that scorned the republican form of government established after the war; its name became shortened to the Nazi party. He took over the direction of the party, eliminating rivals and imposing upon it his own ideas. Although the Nazis professed readiness to work within the system, running candidates for the national parliament and local offices, they attempted to subvert the working of the system. In elections they not only orchestrated the voting of their own followers but sent out armed, or "paramilitary," groups to intimidate opponents into not voting. Hitler himself specialized in fiery displays of oratory that transported audiences into frenzied adoration. Employing his powers to arouse, he planned to organize the German masses to place him in supreme power. His favorite dictum was "Go to the masses."

The masses responded to his appeal. Resentful of the postwar conditions imposed upon their country and suffering from inflation and a depressed economy, they were looking for a leader who could relieve their frustrations. In Hitler they saw this leader. The Nazis steadily increased their representation in the national parliament, becoming in 1932 the largest party. Two years later Hitler was awarded the offices of both president and chancellor and was granted authority to make laws by decree. He was almost absolute now, dictator if not in name. He preferred the title of Fuhrer: Leader.

Hitler was a leader with a dream. He intended to make Germany the master of Europe, controlling an empire stretching from the Atlantic Ocean into the western part of Russia in Europe, from Scandinavia to the Balkans. Other nations would have to submit to occupation by Germany or be subservient to her. "As long as I live I shall think only of the victory of my people," he once proclaimed. "I shall shrink from nothing and shall destroy everyone who is opposed to me." He would destroy possible opponents by making war against them; he had always recognized that war was necessary to achieve his dreams. In all his dreaming there was a demonic quality. He accepted the possibility of failure, but in failing he would also ruin his enemies. "We may be destroyed," he cried, "but if we are, we shall drag down a world with us—a world in flames."

The Military Systems of North and South

I

Trite it may be to say that the Civil War was the first of the modern wars, but this is a truth that needs to be repeated. If the Civil War was not quite total, it missed totality by only a narrow margin. Instead of ending a military cycle as historians once thought, the war began a new one that has not yet been completed. In two ways the Civil War differed from previous conflicts of the modern era in both America and Europe. First, as a war of ideas on the part of both participants, it was a struggle of unlimited objectives. The policy of the North was to restore the Union by force; the policy of the South was to establish its independence by force. Between these two purposes there could be no compromise, no halfway triumph for either side. One or the other had to achieve a complete and decisive victory.[1] Second, the Civil War was a war of matériel, bringing into full play for the first time the great transforming forces of the Industrial Revolution. Among the new techniques and weapons employed—either used for the first time or given their first prominent use—were conscription and mass armies, mass production of weapons, railroads, armored ships, submarines, the telegraph, breech-loading and repeating rifles, various precursors of the machine gun, and an incipient air force in the form of signal balloons. Because of these distinguishing qualities the Civil War was, compared with earlier con-

Reprinted from T. Harry Williams, *Americans at War: The Development of the American Military System*, © 1960 by Louisiana State University Press.

flicts, a ruthless, lethal, no-holds-barred war. In the high command arrangements, especially in the North, it witnessed an unprecedented measure of civilian participation in strategic planning and of civilian direction of the war.

II

At the beginning of the war there were only two officers in the service who had ever commanded troops in numbers large enough to be called an army. One was Winfield Scott, who was seventy-five years of age, and the other was John E. Wool, who was two years older, and both of them had had their active experience in the Mexican War, when the largest field armies numbered about 14,000. Besides Scott and Wool, not an officer on either side had directed as large a unit as a brigade; only a few had commanded a regiment. The largest single army that the younger officers, the men who would become the generals of the war, had ever seen, except for the handful who had visited Europe, was Scott's or Taylor's force in the Mexican War. The 30,000 troops collected by the Federal government at Washington in the spring of 1861 were the largest single American army yet assembled. The photographs of Civil War generals tend to mislead us. We look at those fierce, bearded faces and think of the subjects as being old and hardened warriors. But despite the hirsute adornments, most of them were young men, and none of them, regardless of age, had ever handled troops in numbers before the war. This explains many of the mistakes made by both Northern and Southern generals in the early stages of the conflict. They were simply not prepared to direct the huge armies that were suddenly called into being and thrust upon them. The West Pointers, with the advantage of their technical training, were able to learn their jobs, but sometimes the educational process was painful—for them and their troops.

Both sides at first attempted to raise their armies by the traditional American method of calling for volunteers, and in the first year of the war, when both sections were moved by emotional outbursts of patriotism and optimistic estimates that the war would be of short duration, volunteering served to fill up the armies. But after the initial flush of enthusiasm had flickered out, enlistments dwindled away, and it became evident that the volunteer system would not supply enough men to constitute the huge armies the war was going to require. Both combatants had to resort to conscription, the Confederate States in 1862 and the United States a year later—the first time in the American military experience that national conscription was employed. Because of faulty methods of keeping statistics the total number of men raised by either side can only be estimated. In the Confederacy 1,300,000 enlistments were counted, but this figure includes many short-term enlistments and duplicates. The same qualification must be made of the North's enlistment total of 2,900,000. The best estimates are that 1,500,000 men served in Federal armies for three years and 900,000 in Southern armies for the same period.

The field armies that appeared in the war dwarfed in size any force in previous American wars. Disregarding the many small army units that operated in various theaters, we will concern ourselves here with the maximum forces employed by North and South. In the Eastern theater the Federal Army of the Potomac varied from a minimum of 90,000 to a maximum of 130,000. The highest number attained by its opponent, the Army of Northern Virginia, was 85,000, but the average size of this force was smaller, ranging between 55,000 and 70,000. The largest Federal army in the West comprised 90,000 troops, while the biggest army which the Confederacy placed in the field in this theater numbered 70,000, a total far above the average, which ranged between 40,000 and 60,000.

The generals who commanded the large field armies were without exception professional soldiers, graduates of West Point. A large number of citizen soldiers in both armies proved themselves capable of directing divisions and corps, but the few amateurs who were given command of even small independent armies—as Benjamin F. Butler and N. P. Banks—were unequal to the task; N. B. Forrest on the Confederate side was a natural genius who probably could have led an army, but in actual experience he commanded only a cavalry force. It was the professionals, then, who in the area of battle operations fought the war and, for the North, won it. But it would be highly inaccurate to conclude from this that the trained experts demonstrated a consistent level of competence or manifested an immediate and perceptive awareness of the nature of modern war.

On the contrary, most of the Northern generals who came to prominence in the first half of the war were sorry field leaders— were, in fact, unfit for high-level command. They exhibited a number of excellent qualities: they knew how—or, more accurately, they readily learned how—to prepare, train, and administer armies. There was only one quality that they lacked, but it was a fatal inadequacy: they did not want to fight their armies. In the first of the modern wars, in a war that both sides were playing for keeps, they were ruled by the military concepts of the eighteenth century. They thought of war as an exercise in bloodless strategy, as a series of maneuvers to checkmate an enemy on a gigantic chessboard. Above all—and here George B. McClellan is the supreme example of the type—they envisioned a leisurely, gentlemanly kind of war; in short, a war of limited objectives: if you don't accomplish your objective this time, all right, try it again later, next month, next year. McClellan always saw the war as a kind of game practiced by himself and other experts off in a private sphere of action that had no connection with the political community. If the public demanded action, if the government might fall because there was no action, such considerations impressed McClellan not at all. Ignorant politicians and other people should not be interfering with the specialists, who would move when the conditions of the game were exactly right and not one minute before.

Generals like McClellan were simply not competent to command in a conflict like the Civil War—a rough, mean war and one in which, whether the military liked it or not, civilians were going to have their say. Instead of recognizing the reality of civilian interference and accommodating himself to it, McClellan wasted his energies by wailing that it should not exist—the same kind of futile protest that his supporters have advanced ever since. Not until 1864 did the North succeed in bringing into the important command posts, in the persons of U. S. Grant, William T. Sherman, Philip H. Sheridan, and George H. Thomas, men who possessed the hard, driving qualities required in modern war and who understood the political nature of the war. Although the South owned its share of fumbling generals, it can be said of most Confederate commanders that, from the beginning, they were at least willing to fight their armies. Doubtless the inferior human and material resources of the South, which compelled her generals to act when they could with what they had, explains their greater aggressiveness.

III

At the outbreak of war neither side had ready at hand a plan of general strategy. The newly formed Confederate government could hardly have been expected to possess a previously devised design, but such a measure of preparation was well within the capacities of the Federal military organization. That no plan existed is, of course, not surprising. Nobody had thought, until the crisis suddenly broke, that the difficulties between the sections would come to war, and—here is the crux of the matter—nobody or any agency in the military system, neither Scott nor the General Staff, was charged with the function of studying strategy or of preparing plans for a possible war. The strategy of the war, then, had to be worked out as the conflict developed in the light of what the planners on each side could learn about the strategic situation. So far as prior preparations were concerned, neither government approached the standards of President Polk and his cabinet, who had outlined a general plan of operations a year before the war with Mexico started.[2]

The policy of the North, or the United States, was to restore the Union by force; hence, Northern strategy had to be offensive. But the strategic objectives of the North were complicated by the fact that this was a civil instead of a foreign war. If it was to win, the North had to do more than occupy the enemy capital or defeat enemy armies. It had to do these things and, in addition, convince the Southern people that their cause was hopeless. In short, to conquer a peace the North had to subdue a population. Northern armies would have to invade the South, seize key points and areas, and occupy large regions of the enemy country—all of which would require a vast expenditure of human and military resources. Northern strategy, as it was finally formulated, set up three principal objectives to

be attained: (1) in the Eastern theater to capture Richmond and defeat the defending Confederate army; (2) to seize the line of the Mississippi River, thereby splitting the Confederacy into two parts; and
(3) after the second objective had been achieved, to occupy Chattanooga and the Tennessee River line, thereby gaining a base from
which an offensive could be launched to divide the South, east of the
Mississippi.

The policy of the Confederacy was to establish its independence
by force, and to accomplish this purpose the government decided on
a defensive strategy. In part, the South had no choice in the matter;
its decision was a forced reaction to Northern strategy. But the adoption of a defensive strategy was also in part a deliberate determination by its leaders, particularly by President Davis. For a power that
wanted only to be let alone and that harbored no aggressive designs
against anybody, a strategy of defense seemed so beautifully logical—and Confederates were always beguiled by logic. But the fact
that the South's only purpose was to resist conquest was not sufficient reason to rely on such an inert strategy. With equal logic, and
probably with more effect, the South might have achieved its policy
of independence by taking the offensive early in the war when its
resources were greatest, by demonstrating that it was too strong to
be conquered through victories on Northern soil.

Confederate strategy was pervasively and, in a sense, passively defensive. The high command decided to defend every part of the Confederacy, to meet every threatened attack, to hold every threatened
point—a policy which dispersed its resources, inferior to those of
the North, over a wide strategic circumference and yielded the strategic initiative to the enemy.[3] If the South chose to await attack, it
might have adopted an alternative defensive strategy; it could have
shortened its lines to inclose the most defensible areas or those containing important resources or possessing a symbolic value. It did
not do this, partly for valid reasons. For the new Southern government to abandon any of its territory would have seemed an admission of weakness and would certainly have lost it a measure of
popular support. But even without these practical political considerations, President Davis and other civil leaders seemed to think al-

most instinctively in terms of defending places for their own sake, of holding territory simply because it was their territory.

In general, at the highest command levels the North displayed a greater degree of efficiency and originality than did the South. The Confederates, so brilliant in tactical maneuvers and in battlefield strategy, never succeeded in creating a competent command system or in setting up a unified plan of strategy. The Northern strategy of offense was basically sound; the Southern strategy of defense was fundamentally defective. But it would be inaccurate and unfair to ascribe the differences between the strategic systems to the human beings who operated them, to say that one side had wise leaders and the other had not, to dismiss Davis and his advisers as inept and unintelligent men (as a matter of fact, they were very intelligent) who did not rise to their opportunities. Warfare should always be considered a social institution. As Clausewitz said, a nation's social system or culture will determine the kind of war it will fight. Davis and Lee and other Confederates were the products of their culture, and their culture decided and limited their military thinking. Whereas the North was a nation of the nineteenth century and looked to the future, the South was a confederation of sovereignties that refused to accept the nineteenth century and looked to the past. The Confederacy was founded on state rights—localism was imbedded in every segment of its system—and it fought a state-rights war and, on the strategic level, a traditional, eighteenth-century type of war. Just as it was difficult for Southern political leaders to envision centralism in government, so it was hard for Confederate military directors to see the war as a whole or to install centralism in its direction.

IV

At the head of the military systems of both countries and of their command organizations were the two presidents, Abraham Lincoln and Jefferson Davis. They form an interesting contrast and offer the materials for an instructive and fascinating study in civil-military relationships and in the higher direction of war. Judging them solely by their backgrounds, one would expect that the Confederate President would be a great war leader, that he would far eclipse his rival. Few civilian war directors have come to their office with Davis' technical advantages. He was a graduate of West Point, he had served in the regular army, he had had battle experience in the Mexican War, and he had been Secretary of War. Lincoln had been a civilian all his life, he had received no military education, and he had had no military experience except briefly as a militia soldier in the Black Hawk War, when, as he liked to recall, he had made some ferocious charges on the wild onions and engaged in bloody struggles with the mosquitoes. And yet the truth is that Lincoln was a great war president and Davis was a mediocre one. The command careers of the two men illustrate perfectly the truth of Clausewitz' dictum that an acquaintance with military affairs is not the principal qualification for a director of war but that "a remarkable, superior mind and strength of character" are more important.

We cannot pause here to measure Davis' defects as a political leader of his people, intriguing though such an analysis of this sincere and tormented man would be. But certainly the weaknesses that he displayed—his excessive pride, his sensitivity to criticism, his impatience of contradiction, his lack of passion for anything, even for the South—detracted from his effectiveness as President and contributed to the final defeat of the Southern cause. We are concerned with his qualities as a war director, and we are obliged to note that in this area he failed as surely as he did in the political sphere.

He failed because he did not seem to realize what his task was or what his proper functions were. He could not grasp the vital fact that the Confederacy was not a going, recognized government but a revolution and that, in order to win, it would have to act with remorseless revolutionary vigor. Always he proceeded on the theory that the Confederacy was a permanent government and could act like older established governments, and always he observed every nicety of legal punctilio and tied himself up in every possible piece of red tape. Because of his military background, he fancied himself a military expert; he would rather have been a general than the head of state. Somebody in our own times has quipped that Davis learned enough about war in a few minutes at Buena Vista in the Mexican

War to defeat the South; and during the war Richmond wags, referring to Davis' boasting about a formation he had led at Buena Vista,
said that the Confederacy was dying of an inverted V. His image of
himself being what it was, he concerned himself overly much with
military affairs. The criticism here is not that he interfered with his
generals—this point will be discussed later—but that he spent too
much time on unimportant routine items, on matters that he should
have left to subordinates. Once he even proposed to go through
1,500 documents bearing on promotions high and low. He could not
delegate authority to people he knew were not as competent as he.
Because he was a capable administrator, he loved to do the admin-
istrating himself. He had been an outstanding Secretary of War, but
as President he rarely rose above the secretarial level.

Nor can we take time to analyze the qualities that made Lincoln a
great war President. They are so well known, perhaps, that they do
not need repetition. We may note two factors, however, that reveal
something of his concept of the role of commander-in-chief and that
help to explain his success as a war director. First, Lincoln was, in
a technical sense, a poor administrator. Unlike Davis, who spent
much time in his office, Lincoln was rarely in his office. He was
often to be found in the offices of other people, generals and secretaries, ostensibly visiting around and telling stories, but really sizing
up subordinates and deciding whether he could delegate authority to
them. When he found a man whom he could trust to do a job, Lincoln was quite willing to let him handle the details of his office. In
short, he was interested in the big administrative picture, and he did
not, if he could avoid it, burden himself with petty routine—all
of which means that he understood perfectly his function and the
proper function of administration (or if he did not understand good
administration, he intuitively practiced it). Second, Lincoln realized
immediately that the war was a revolution, and he dealt with it on
that basis. Whenever he felt that revolutionary methods were necessary to attain the objectives of Union policy, he used them, even to
the length of violating law or the Constitution. He was not, he
explained, going to see the government and the nation go to smash
because of a squeamish regard for legal niceties. It is a curious
fact that Lincoln, who headed an established government, acted

with more revolutionary zeal than Davis, who led an experimental government.

As a director of war Lincoln displayed, almost from the beginning, a fine strategic sense. He was a better natural strategist than were most of his generals who were trained soldiers. Grasping the importance of economic warfare, he proclaimed a naval blockade of the South. Realizing that numbers were on his side, he called for 400,000 volunteers in 1861. Almost immediately he understood one of the great all-time strategic maxims, which his first generals seem never to have heard of, and applied it to his war: the proper objective of Union armies, he insisted, was the destruction of Confederate armies and not the occupation of Southern territory. Knowing the advantage that superior forces gave the North, he disregarded the traditional Jomini doctrine of concentrating at one point, and showing a startling originality in his strategic thinking, he urged his commanders to keep up a constant pressure on the whole strategic line of the Confederacy until a weak spot was found and a breakthrough could be made. Always, always, he prodded the generals to move, to execute an offensive strategy.

Both Lincoln and Davis have been criticized by historians and military writers for "interfering" with generals and military affairs. Most of these strictures seem misinformed. Judged by modern standards both presidents did some things that a civil director of war should not do. But it must be emphasized that they were operating without benefit of a formal command system, that they executed functions which, in the organization then existing, could have been performed by no other agency. Moreover, if the caliber of many of the generals, the so-called trained experts, is carefully measured, it is evident that the presidents were often justified in the supervision they exerted. Particularly for the Union cause, as will be demonstrated later, it was fortunate that Lincoln called his generals to account. But the vital point about such "interfering" is the purpose for which the war director intervenes—the strategic objective he is trying to accomplish. If the strategy is sound and if the director of war is a man of "a remarkable, superior mind," the results of his intervention will be generally good. Lincoln interfered to make a sound offensive strategy stronger, and Davis interfered to make a defective defensive strategy more defensive. One acted from a valid theory and the other from a faulty one.

V

In describing the machinery of the command arrangements of both sides, we will consider first the organization of the Confederate system, giving it relatively brief attention, not because in the history of the war it was less important than its Northern counterpart but because, unlike the latter, it contributed little to the development of modern concepts of command.

The formal organization of the Confederate military system was practically identical with that of the United States. The President acted as commander-in-chief of the armed forces, assisted by two civilian deputies, the secretaries of War and the Navy. Davis permitted his naval secretary a relatively free hand, but he supervised the War office with minute care. Something of his interest in this department is revealed by the number of men, five, who passed through its organization as Secretary; Davis was, in reality, his own Secretary of War. To assist the President and Secretary in administering the housekeeping branches of the army, the Confederate Congress authorized the establishment of a number of staff or bureau agencies—quartermaster general, adjutant general, and others—similar to the organs in the Northern General Staff.

Without being too inaccurate one could summarize Confederate command arrangements by saying that they consisted mainly of President Davis. He was general-in-chief as well as commander-in-chief, and he attempted to exercise both functions to the fullest. The most that he would permit his civil or military assistants to offer was advice—which, if they were smart, they offered only when asked. Early in 1862 Davis assigned R. E. Lee to Richmond to act "under the direction of the President" as commanding general of all Confederate forces. The phrases in the directive were impressive, but in practice Lee became a mere adviser who furnished his superior, when requested, with technical counsel. In the summer of 1862

Lee left the office to become field commander of the Army of Northern Virginia, and Davis did not name a successor until February, 1864. In the long interim Davis, acting without professional advice except that which he might choose to obtain from field commanders, formulated the basic strategy of the Confederacy. To the President's credit it should be noted that on at least one occasion he tried to delegate authority to a departmental commander. His plan, which was an interesting attempt to tighten up command arrangements, called for placing all armies in the Western theater under one general, Joseph E. Johnston, who, in modern parlance, would function as an army group commander. The experiment failed because Johnston refused to accept the responsibilities of his position.

In 1864, at a time when the government was under criticism after a series of disasters, Davis resurrected the office of General-in-Chief, naming to fill it Braxton Bragg, who as a field commander in the West had been responsible for many of the disasters. Public and political pressures had forced Davis to remove Bragg from field command, and his assignment of the general to service in Richmond may have been only a gesture of defiance to his critics and an affirmation of his confidence in Bragg. At any rate, Bragg, who possessed real ability in strategic planning, understood his position and his superior perfectly. He restricted his functions to providing requested advice and praising Davis' military wisdom. In February, 1865, the Confederate Congress, in a move designed to clip Davis' powers, formally created the office of General-in-Chief, and the sponsors of the measure made it plain that the post was intended for Lee and that Lee would be expected to direct the Confederacy's strategy and operations. Davis, having no choice, appointed Lee, but he announced that he was still the commander-in-chief and intended to continue. Lee, who had great respect for civil authority, accepted the commission on the basis offered by the President. The war ended before the new command experiment could be tested. It is doubtful whether Lee could have performed the dual functions of army commander and general-in-chief. Nor is it certain that Lee, who was a product of his culture and obsessed with the war in his native Virginia, could have adjusted his strategic thinking to the problems of national strategy on many fronts. The South did not achieve, and probably could not have achieved, a modern command system.[4]

VI

Northern command arrangements at the highest level consisted in 1861 of General Scott, who was general-in-chief, and the General Staff, comprising the bureau heads in the War Department. The General Staff, we must emphasize again, was not a collective agency, was not concerned with strategy, and according to modern military usage was a misnamed body. In the first months of the war Lincoln turned to General Scott and other officers for advice on strategic questions. At this stage he was perhaps too much inclined to defer to the professionals and tended to exaggerate the potential of the military mind.

His first shock of disillusionment came when he asked Scott to present a plan of general strategy. The old general, who had done no previous thinking about strategy for the war, responded with a scheme that demonstrated he was unable to envision the requirements of modern mass war and was not the man to direct general operations. His so-called Anaconda Plan proposed a naval blockade of the Southern coastline and the occupation of the Mississippi River line by a combined land and naval force. These objectives secured and the South inclosed in an iron circle, Scott would stop and do nothing more, waiting for the squeeze of the blockade to bring an alleged Union sentiment in the besieged section to the surface, after which the South would voluntarily seek peace. Although the plan had obvious merits—the blockade and the occupation of the Mississippi became major items in Northern strategy—Lincoln rightly rejected it, partly because it would take too long to accomplish its by-no-means-certain results. But, more important, Lincoln the civilian recognized the fundamental defect in Scott's thinking. The soldier was advocating the one-idea type of strategy: one kind of operation, one weapon, one branch of the service will win the war.[5]

Partly at his own request, partly because of pressure from above, Scott retired from service on November 1, 1861, and to the post of

General-in-Chief Lincoln named George B. McClellan, who was also the field commander of the Army of the Potomac. This is not the place to discuss McClellan's shortcomings as a battle captain, which were many and fatal, except as his qualities as a field general seem to be related to his course as general-in-chief. The one great defect that he displayed in both areas was an inability to see things as they were, to distinguish the actual factors in a situation from imagined ones. He lived much of the time in a world of fantasy of his own making. His incapacity to adjust his thinking to the realities was fully apparent in the one plan of general strategy he submitted to Lincoln. He proposed that an army of 273,000 (why he hit upon this rather odd number he did not explain) be assembled in the Eastern theater to operate under his command. With the support of the navy he would land this force on the Virginia Coast, march inland, and capture Richmond. Then he would sail down the coast and repeat the process with other important Southern cities, finally ending up at New Orleans. It was about as fantastic a proposal as Lincoln received from a military man, and he was to be the recipient of many.

On many counts the plan was defective. It concentrated operations in one theater to the neglect of others and it made places instead of armies the objectives. Worst of all, it was too grandiose to be supported by existing resources. At that time the government could not have collected so many troops in one theater and housed and fed them, nor did it have sufficient sea transport to carry them to McClellan's points of attack. And even if all these conditions could have been met, McClellan did not possess the staff organization to administer such a host. This incredible design, which must have astounded Lincoln and which he filed without comment, confirmed his developing doubts of the capacities of military men.

With the exception of this proposal McClellan offered no strategic suggestions worthy of Lincoln's consideration or our attention. During the winter of 1861–62 he was busy preparing his field army for operations in the spring. Whatever plans of strategy were advanced came from the President, who vainly urged McClellan and other field commanders to deliver simultaneous attacks along the entire strategic line of the Confederacy. This idea, which was eminently sound and which was the strategy eventually adopted by the North, was received with scorn by the generals, partly because it was the proposal of a civilian and partly because it violated the traditional Jomini concept of concentration at one point. On several occasions during the winter Lincoln prodded McClellan to undertake even a minor or diversionary movement to sustain popular morale, to demonstrate to the public that the armies meant business. That he refused was characteristic of McClellan and of the military tradition he represented. War was a game played by professionals and had no relation to political requirements; he would move when the game was right. It was also characteristic of McClellan that, when he did decide on a spring movement for his own army, he did not, for months, inform Lincoln of his plan. He did not seem to know how to form such a relationship with his civilian superior that he could counsel with him on strategy; in fact, he did not seem to realize that he ought to offer any guidance to his superior.

When McClellan took the field in March, 1862, Lincoln removed him as general-in-chief, presumably on the grounds that one man could not direct a field army and at the same time plan movements for other armies. The President did not immediately name a successor to McClellan. For approximately five months he left the position vacant, during which time he acted as his own general-in-chief. It may be surmised that Lincoln either had decided he could perform the function of directing strategy himself or that he was looking around for a suitable officer for the place. During this period he detached McDowell's corps from McClellan's army to insure the safety of Washington, planned the offensive movement in the Shenandoah Valley to trap Stonewall Jackson, and combined the separate armies in northern Virginia under the single command of John Pope. He not only framed strategy but on several occasions, as when he instructed one general on the proper use of signal fires, he got down to the tactical level. Some of his decisions were wise, others were open to criticism. Generally, his basic concepts were sound. When he erred, it was because he sometimes found difficulty in expressing his strategic notions in terms that the military mind could understand or because, as in the Valley campaign, he minimized logistical factors and exaggerated the strategic possibilities of a situation. And, it should be added, he asked too much of some very dull generals.

It must not be supposed, however, that Lincoln was running a one-man show, making decisions right and left without consultation. He conferred regularly with his executive deputy, Secretary of War Edwin M. Stanton, and other War Department officials. In the Civil War, for the first time, the civilian division of the department was placed on an adequate administrative basis. With three assistant secretaries authorized by Congress, the department was no longer an assemblage of clerks but a professional agency. Moreover, Secretary Stanton infused new importance into the bureau system. He set up an organ known as the Army Board, which consisted of the various bureau heads and was presided over by General E. A. Hitchcock. Although this was only the General Staff under another name, a forward step had been taken. The staff now had a chairman and could act as a collective body. Its members were not qualified to rule on matters of general strategy, but they were competent to advise on lesser strategic issues and to offer technical information. Lincoln frequently went to the War Department to talk with the Army Board before coming to a decision.

Whatever doubts Lincoln had come to have about professional soldiers, whatever convictions of growing strategic powers were stirring in his mind, he resolved to have one more try at intrusting the direction of strategic operations to a general. Perhaps he sensed that he, a civilian, was exercising too much control over the conduct of the war. In July, 1862, he called General Henry W. Halleck to Washington from the West and appointed him general-in-chief. Halleck seemed to be an ideal choice for the position. A graduate of West Point with long years of service in the regular army, he was known before the war as one of the few and one of the foremost American students of the higher art of war—of strategy and military history. Most of the great books on war had been written in French by such masters as Napoleon and Jomini, and only a handful of American officers had enough facility with the French language to read them. Halleck, a linguistic scholar, had translated several of these works and had written a book of his own on war, *Elements of Military Art and Science*, which followed Jomini closely. Even after he became general-in-chief, Halleck continued to interpret Jomini's writings, causing one of his critics to jibe that "General Halleck is translating French books at nine cents a page; and sir, if you should put those nine cents in a box and shake them up, you would form a clear idea of General Halleck's soul." (Jomini, with his doctrine of concentration at one point, had an enormous influence on Civil War strategists; McClellan's proposal to mass 273,000 men in one theater was a Jomini concept.[6]) In addition to theoretical knowledge, Halleck had another apparent qualification for supreme command: he seemed to be a successful general. Under his command in the Western department a number of victories, the first Union successes of the war, had been won. They had been won by other generals, notably by U. S. Grant, without Halleck having had much to do with them, but the departmental commander received the credit.

Lincoln installed Halleck in the office with the full intention that the general should function as actual general-in-chief, that is, with the President's approval, should plan and direct over-all strategy. Lincoln meant to keep his own hands off the details of military administration. When commanders in various departments wrote Lincoln asking for instructions, he referred them to Halleck who, he said, now had charge of the entire field. At first Halleck carried out the responsibilities of his job, but within less than two months he experienced a mental and military breakdown and refused to exercise his functions. Fundamentally Halleck was unfit for the post of General-in-Chief because he disliked to assume responsibility. He loved to offer advice and technical criticism to the President or to field generals, but he flinched from making flat decisions or issuing definite instructions. In August after the Union defeat in the battle of Second Manassas, he almost collapsed. His was an impossible position, he felt; to the field general went the credit for a victory, but upon the general-in-chief fell the blame for all failures. Therefore, he abnegated the duties of his office and deliberately assumed the role of a mere adviser. When Lincoln asked him for counsel, he furnished it, but he would do nothing more. When the President asked him to go to the Army of the Potomac, survey the situation, and order what should be done, Halleck replied that if he had to shoulder such a responsibility he would resign.

Halleck's refusal to execute the duties of his position forced Lincoln to resume the functions of general-in-chief, which he would perform until the early months of 1864. Although the President was disappointed in Halleck, he continued to keep him in the post of commanding general. He retained Halleck because he needed somebody near him who could provide technical military information and advice. In addition, he discovered that Halleck was extremely valuable as a medium of communication with the military. Often Lincoln and his generals failed to understand each other because, almost literally, they did not speak the same language. Lincoln, speaking the terminology of the lawyer and the politician, could not always frame his strategic concepts, particularly in writing, in words that the soldiers could grasp. The generals, using the jargon peculiar to their profession, could not always describe their plans in terms the President could understand. Halleck had associated so much with civilians and soldiers that he could speak the language of both and was able to explain Lincoln's ideas to the generals and translate the generals' notions to Lincoln. As Halleck became increasingly adept at formulating Lincoln's thoughts, the President intrusted to him more and more the framing of military directives. Lincoln did not, however, often turn to the general-in-chief for strategic counsel. In the planning of several important movements Halleck does not seem to have been consulted; apparently he first learned of General Joseph Hooker's crossing of the Rappahannock in the opening campaign of 1863 from a chance encounter with an officer on the streets in Washington.

In late 1862 and during 1863, when Lincoln was acting as his own general-in-chief, he had undoubtedly come to have something of a scorn for professional soldiers. Whereas in the first days of the war he had been too much inclined to defer to their opinions, he had passed to the opposite extreme of being too ready to impose his opinions on them. He had seen too many of his generals plead excuse after excuse for not fighting: they needed more men and then more supplies and then more transportation—and then they would start the whole cycle over again. He had urged too many of his generals to seek the final decision of battle, to make enemy armies instead of places their objective, only to see them shrink from the decision, to see them place the occupation of territory above the destruction of the enemy's forces. Always growing in stature as a strategist, Lincoln loomed high in ability above most of the generals whom he was forced to use. We may now examine some of his "interferences" with commanders and note what the effects on the Union cause would have been if he had not intervened when he did.

In the summer of 1863 General Lee started his Confederate army west from Fredericksburg to the Shenandoah Valley and then headed north toward the Potomac. This was the beginning of the offensive that would culminate in the battle of Gettysburg. North of the Rappahannock Federal General Hooker studied the movements of the man who had defeated him at Chancellorsville, and he soon divined that Lee was aiming an invasion at Maryland or Pennsylvania. The reactions of the trained soldier were almost incredible. First he proposed to Lincoln that he cross the river and attack Lee's rear area forces at Fredericksburg. When the President vetoed this scheme, Hooker came up with an even wilder one. Contending that the government should be able to collect a sufficient force of reserves to halt Lee, he asked for permission to take his army south to attack Richmond. In rejecting this plan, Lincoln pointed out the obvious. Hooker would shatter his strength against the Richmond defenses while Lee ranged through Pennsylvania without opposition. And even if Hooker captured the Southern capital, its possession would not compensate for the prestige the Confederacy would gain, especially in Europe, by a successful offensive into the North. Hooker's proper move, Lincoln instructed, was to move his army to a position where it could fight Lee, which was what Hooker, at the President's direction, finally did.

At the battle of Gettysburg, General George G. Meade, who succeeded Hooker as commander of the Army of the Potomac, threw back Lee's attacks and hurt the Confederate army badly. Meade had fought a skillful defensive battle, but he was satisfied with his victory as it was. He was content to see Lee leave his front, and his principal concern was to "herd" Lee back over the Potomac. Like other

Federal generals, he lacked the killer instinct, which all the great
battle captains have had, to finish off the enemy. After the engagement he issued a congratulatory order to his troops in which he
praised them for having driven the enemy from "our soil." After all,
this was a civil war! When Lincoln read the order, he exclaimed in
anguish, "My God! Is that all?" The President saw more clearly than
his commander the results of Gettysburg: the Confederate army had
been dealt a murderous blow and a decisive attack on it north of the
Potomac might complete its destruction. He also sensed that Meade
shrank from delivering such an attack, and through Halleck he urged
Meade to pursue Lee and finish him off. But Meade merely followed
his retreating foe and, even though Lee was held up by high water at
the Potomac, permitted him to escape. Weeks later the general came
to Washington for conferences, and during a conversation Lincoln
said to him suddenly, "Do you know, general, what your attitude towards Lee for a week after the battle reminded me of?" "No, Mr.
President, what is it?" asked Meade. "I'll be hanged if I could think
of anything else," said Lincoln, "than an old woman trying to shoo
her geese across a creek." As an analysis of Meade's psychology, this
was perfect.

During the siege of Vicksburg Lincoln was beset by fears that the
Confederates might detach troops from their army in eastern Tennessee to reinforce the Southern field army in Mississippi for an attack on Grant's rear. To protect Grant and to prevent the siege of the
vital river fortress from being lifted, Lincoln asked General W. S.
Rosecrans, the Federal commander in Tennessee, to mount an offensive to contain the Confederate army in Tennessee. Rosecrans replied with the kind of analysis of the situation that Lincoln often
received from his generals and that made him think soldiers were
maybe, as he put it, "a little crazy." The general said that it would be
unwise for him to undertake a forward movement, because if he
moved he would only push the Confederates closer to Mississippi.
His proper course, he explained, was to sit where he was, do nothing,
and occupy the enemy's attention. In all of Rosecrans' correspondence with the President there was one possibility that he never
discussed, that he did not even seem to consider. Like so many
of Lincoln's generals in a crisis, it did not occur to him that he

might advance and win a victory. Ultimately he did move, but, like Hooker, because the President made him.

VII

Although Lincoln wielded his great powers as war director with a certainty that came from ever growing confidence, he was willing, as he had always indicated, to yield those powers to a general who was competent and willing to exercise them. By 1864 he had found his man—and Congress and the nation ratified the choice—in U. S. Grant, who in the West had emerged as the greatest Union general of the war. In February Congress created the rank of lieutenant general, expressing a wish that Grant would receive the grade and the position of General-in-Chief, and Lincoln unhesitatingly named Grant to both. At last the United States was about to get a modern command system.

In the system arrived at in 1864, which was the joint product of Lincoln, Grant, and maybe of Halleck, Grant as general-in-chief was charged with the functions of framing over-all Union strategy and directing the movements of all Federal armies. As commanding general, Grant might have been expected to establish his command post in Washington, where he would be near the President and in quick contact with Federal field generals all over the country. But Grant disliked the political atmosphere of the capital, and he set up his headquarters with the Army of the Potomac in the field. He was always close to Washington, which he could reach in a short train trip, and he was in almost instant telegraphic communication with the President. Technically, Grant did not become commander of the Eastern field army—Meade continued to hold that position—but since he traveled with that army, it was subject to his close supervision.

Under the new arrangement Halleck received a new command office, the Chief of Staff. Again, as when we dealt with the nature of the General Staff, we must avoid confusion between nineteenth-century and contemporary usages of the same term. Halleck was not a chief of staff in the modern sense. In the present command system his position would correspond perhaps to the Secretary of the General Staff. Primarily he was a channel of communication between Lincoln and Grant and between Grant and the seventeen departmental commanders under the general-in-chief. Grant sent most of his dispatches for the President to Halleck, who, when necessary, briefed or explained them for Lincoln. Similarly, Halleck transmitted to Grant many of Lincoln's directives or inquiries concerning strategic matters. Because of Halleck's facility in the languages of both soldier and civilian, Lincoln and Grant never misunderstood each other, as Lincoln and McClellan so often had.

Halleck also served as a liaison between Grant and the department and field commanders. If Grant had had to read all the reports from these officers and frame detailed instructions for them, he would not have had much time for strategic planning. At Grant's direction, the subordinate commanders sent their dispatches for Grant to Halleck, who either transmitted them to the general-in-chief or summarized their contents for him. Grant sent most of his orders to subordinates through Halleck. Often he would tell the chief of staff in general terms what he wanted done and ask him to put the objective in a written directive, or he would delegate authority to Halleck to handle a particular situation. Although Halleck professed to think that his role in the command system was insignificant, it was really vitally important. Without such a co-ordinator of information the system would not have worked as brilliantly as it did.

But the key military man in the system was Grant. As general-in-chief, he proved to be the general for whom Lincoln had been searching. And because the President came to realize Grant's capacities, he gave him more latitude in determining strategy than he had permitted McClellan or Halleck. To a man who asked whether Grant did not have too much freedom of decision, Lincoln said, "Do you hire a man to do your work and then do it yourself?" Grant possessed the rare ability to see the war as a total picture and to devise what in later wars would be called "global" strategy. In fact, he was probably the only general on either side who could envision the war as a whole, the only one who was qualified to act as general-in-chief in a modern war. This is not the place to discuss his plan of grand operations for 1864, but it was a brilliant demonstration of strategic thinking and would do credit to the most finished student of a series of modern staff and command schools. Unhampered by traditional military doctrine, Grant was boldly original in innovating new strategic concepts. A young officer once asked him what he thought of Jomini. Grant said he had never read the French-Swiss master, the guiding authority for so many other Civil War generals. He then expressed his own theory of war: "The art of war is simple enough. Find out where your enemy is. Get at him as soon as you can. Strike at him hard as you can, and keep moving on."

It is not true, however, as Grant stated in his memoirs and as many historians have repeated since, that Lincoln gave him an absolutely free hand in deciding strategy and directing operations. According to Grant's account, the President was a military innocent who greeted him with relief when he came to Washington and said, in effect: General, I am not a military man, I don't understand war and don't want to know your plans—go ahead and do exactly as you please. Grant wrote under the influence of his own postwar myth, which cast him in the image of the great soldier who was the architect of victory. Actually, as the evidence in contemporary war documents amply demonstrates, Lincoln, while permitting his general-in-chief wide latitude of action, watched him closely and never hesitated to check him when the need arose. On at least two occasions, as when he forced Grant to come to Washington to supervise personally the launching of the campaign against Jubal Early in the Shenandoah Valley and when he restrained him from removing General George H. Thomas before the battle of Nashville, he saved the general from serious mistakes.

Moreover, as the documents again show, the victorious strategy of the North was the joint product of consultations between Lincoln and Grant. The general submitted to Lincoln the broad outlines of his plans, and the President, approving the objectives and trusting Grant, did not seek to learn the details. Indeed, Grant made his strategy conform to the strategy Lincoln had been advocating since 1862: make enemy armies the objective and move all Federal forces against the enemy line simultaneously so as to bring into play the Federal advantage of superior numbers. An offensive all along the line, violating the Jomini maxim of concentration, was the essence of Grant's strategy. When Grant explained to Lincoln this plan, so eminently sensible for the side with the greater numbers and the superior transportation, he remarked that those forces not fighting could still help the fighting by advancing. Grasping the point and recognizing the application of his own ideas, the President uttered a maxim of his own, one that for modern war was more valid than most of Jomini's dictums: "Those not skinning can hold a leg."

The 1864 command system was a major factor in the final victory of the North. By providing a sound basis for participation by the civil and military branches in the formulating of strategy, it gave the United States a modern command organization for a modern war. With a commander-in-chief to state policy and the general objectives of strategy, a general-in-chief to put the strategy in specific form, and a chief of staff to co-ordinate information, the United States possessed a model system of civil and military relationships and the finest command arrangements of any country in the world. Created in the strain of war, it expressed the national genius to improvise an arrangement to fit the requirements of the moment. The American system was superior to most command organizations then existing in Europe and was at least as good as the Prussian general staff machine. Indeed, it was probably the most efficient system that we have ever had.

The Macs and the Ikes: America's Two Military Traditions

The two generals were different, and they came out of the war with different reputations. One was folksy and friendly and had the common touch. He made the ordinary soldiers feel that he was interested in their smallest problem, and they loved him. The civilians on the home front admired him more than any general of the war. He won victories, he was a great general, but he seemed warm and real and close. He was Mars, but he could also have been Uncle Ned, sitting in the parlor talking about the children. For the most part, he got along well with the administration. He sometimes thought Washington wasn't supporting his army properly, and then he protested to the President through official channels. Before the war he had paid little attention to politics and had not followed or studied closely the issues dividing the two major parties. At first, after the war began, he continued to disregard politics. But when he emerged as a military and national hero, the politicians of both parties began to eye him as a presidential possibility and to woo him with offers of support. He probably could have had the nomination of whichever party he chose. Some of his admirers advanced the proposal—and he liked it—that he run as the nominee of both, as a national candidate to unify the nation. In the end, he accepted, perhaps instinctively, the nomination of the conservative party.

Reprinted from *American Mercury*, LXXV (October, 1952), 32–39, copyright 1952 by American Mercury Magazine, Inc.

The other general also won great victories. He was a brilliant field commander, and defeated the enemy in the campaign that ended the war. But this general never became the hero to the soldiers and civilians that the first one did. He was different from the first general in almost every way. Everything about him was dramatic—his appearance, his actions, and especially his speech. He wrote orders, proclamations, and letters crammed with splendid phrases and thunderous rhetoric. Most of the enlisted men didn't like him. To them he was a figure in bronze, a magnificent but distant spectacle who swaggered by the ranks at parades and other public ceremonials. He might win battles, he might look great, but he was never close to the common soldier. He didn't talk to them about their little everyday problems, he didn't know how to, he probably never thought it was important. To the civilians at home he was also majestic, faraway, and a little unreal. He could never have been Uncle Ned in the parlor. If he had come in the parlor, everybody would have been embarrassed and would have stood up, waiting for him to utter an Important Pronouncement.

This general did not get along well with the administration. He was convinced that he was smarter than the President and the latter's civilian advisers, and much better qualified than they to determine strategy and policy. He also had strong opinions on issues of domestic politics and had let it be known he wouldn't mind being in the White House. Because he felt deeply about things and because he liked to express his ideas in writing, he became embroiled in frequent and angry epistolary controversies with Washington. Sometimes these quarrels involved matters of strategy concerning movements of his army, sometimes they involved the larger issue of the policy of the war. Because he knew that he was more intelligent than the President and because he was so convinced that he was right, he was not always careful to keep his opinions private or to put his protests through channels. Some of both got into the newspapers. Finally, a furious and frustrated administration relieved him of command at the high point of his career and called him home. He was still an important figure in American life and would continue to be so, but he had little chance now to be President. His influence as a political force, even in the party he affiliated himself with, steadily declined. Or, to put it another way, as a military hero with political possibilities he faded away.

What I have written could stand, with a few minor modifications, as a description of the careers of Generals Eisenhower and Mac-Arthur in World War II. Actually, I have described in the order of their appearance Generals Zachary Taylor and Winfield Scott in the Mexican War. I have misrepresented the facts about Scott a little. Four years after the close of the war and the election of 1848 in which Taylor won the Presidency, Scott made a highly unsuccessful run for the highest office as the Whig candidate. Outside of that my account is accurate, and in essence Scott's political career parallels MacArthur's.

Eisenhower and MacArthur in our own time and Taylor and Scott in an earlier one represent two distinct military traditions in our national life, two patterns that have been fairly constant in our military history. Ike and Old Rough and Ready are in the tradition of those generals who have worked with their civil superiors with a minimum of friction and who did not try to impose their views of policy upon the civilian authorities. Dugout Doug and Old Fuss and Feathers represent the type who have conducted their relations with Presidents with a maximum of friction and who have at times pressed their ideas of policy upon Washington with such violence as to cause an open break between general and government.

Generals in the Taylor-Eisenhower tradition have been popular with soldiers and civilians. Those in the Scott-MacArthur tradition have not. The Ike-like generals have been men with warmth in their personalities, men who liked people—qualities which partly explain both their popularity and their success in dealing with Presidents. The Mac-like generals have been, or have seemed to be, cold, uninterested in ordinary folk; they were dashing, dramatic men who aroused passionate devotion in some but were never loved by the many, in uniform or out. The Ike generals have possessed a humility of mind and character which caused them to treat their civil superiors with a certain deference even when they disagreed with them. The Mac generals have been men with great intellectual arrogance, always certain that they were far superior in mental power to the

President above them (which sometimes they were), and always
ready to instruct him in matters of policy or to try to browbeat him
into adopting their ideas.

The fundamental difference between the two types has been this:
the Ike generals have exemplified militarily the ideals of our industrial, democratic civilization, which took shape in the nineteenth
century; the Mac generals have represented militarily the standards
of an older, more aristocratic society. At the same time that Western
civilization was becoming industrial, war was becoming total. No
longer did it involve only a clash of armies on the battlefield; all elements of a society might feel in some way the impact of conflict.
War became industrial, machinelike, and democratic. The act of carrying on war became increasingly a problem in administration and
production. Necessarily, the role of the civilian, whether President,
industrial mobilizer, or home-front worker, grew in importance.

Against this background, a new type of military leader emerged—
the pragmatic, scientific general of the military world, but close to
the civilian community, a sort of military businessman. The Mac-
type generals might readily grasp and employ the strategic concepts
of modern war and be outstanding battle captains, but they rarely
have understood the nature of modern democratic society or modern
industrial war-making. The spiritual roots of the Mac generals are in
the preindustrial age when war was primarily confined to armies
and confided to generals. They have thought of themselves as members of a warrior caste, apart from civilian society, and in their field
superior in judgment to the civilian authority. Where the Ike generals have been pragmatic, the Macs have been intuitive, military artists, who played it by their ear and not by civilian notes. Being artists, they have wanted a large area of freedom of action, in which to
create and improvise. Being aristocrats in spirit, they have resented
the restraints of democratic power. The generals of the Ike model,
being soldiers of a democratic civilization, have been better able to
integrate themselves into the pattern of the democratic tradition.
They have acted and talked as most Americans think American
leaders should act and talk. They have seemed natural, familiar, and

safe. Hence the people have trusted them, and have entrusted the high offices to them instead of to the exotic Mac-men.

The best prototypes of the two traditions, the two most fully documented case histories of the two types, are in the Civil War, in the persons of George B. McClellan and Ulysses S. Grant. McClellan stands for MacArthur, Grant for Eisenhower. I want to make it plain that in comparing MacArthur to the "little Mac" of the Civil War, I intend no disrespect to MacArthur's generalship or to his administration of occupied Japan. I think he was a great field general and administrator; I know McClellan was a poor general and suspect he would have been an indifferent director of an occupied area. Nor in describing McClellan's difficulties with the administration am I suggesting the least parallel between Lincoln and Truman. I am saying only that as military personalities the two Macs were cut from the same military cloth.

In one respect McClellan departed from the tradition of his kind. He was very popular with the GI's until near the end of his military career. The soldiers felt that he cared for their welfare and would not waste their lives in needless fighting. Their devotion to him has been exaggerated, however, and there is evidence that increasing numbers of them wrote him off as an inept commander. In every other way, McClellan conformed to the pattern. He was magnetic and dramatic. He loved pomp and display and was the central figure in every scene. He was master of a purple rhetoric and put too many things down on paper. He had a first-rate Messiah complex and believed that he had been called to save the country. "I must save it," he wrote his wife, "and cannot respect anything that is in the way." Admirers told him he should be dictator. "I have no such aspiration," he told his wife. "I would cheerfully take the dictatorship and agree to lay down my life when the country is saved." He had great contempt for Lincoln, whom he regarded as a simple oaf who unfortunately was his superior officer. In his monumental certainty of self, McClellan believed that he had the ability and authority to pronounce political policy for the administration. In a conflict of opinion between him and Washington, he assumed that he could treat with the government on an equal basis as a sort of contracting party.

The issue of war policy that divided the North was: should the destruction of slavery be made one of the aims of the war? Most Republicans favored emancipation, most Democrats opposed it. McClellan, who was general in chief of all armies for a short period at the beginning of the war and commander of the largest field army in the East until near the end of 1862, was an open, avowed Democrat and an opponent of emancipation. Although he made no public statement of his views, he engaged in intimate conferences at his headquarters with prominent Democrats who were talking him up for the Presidency. He corresponded with Democratic leaders and urged them to fight the antislavery forces. In the summer of 1862, McClellan made his big try to capture Richmond, and failed. Lincoln came down to McClellan's camp in Virginia to find out what had gone wrong. While he was there, McClellan handed him the famous document known as the Harrison's Landing letter. Ostensibly a statement from McClellan about strategy, it was actually a lecture on what policy Lincoln should follow. McClellan advised Lincoln to adopt a conservative, anti-emancipation program and then select a general in chief to carry it out. He did not ask the place for himself—but he was willing to serve. McClellan did not make the letter public, but its contents leaked out to the press.

Lincoln ignored McClellan's counsel, and in September, after McClellan's indecisive victory at Antietam, issued the Emancipation Proclamation. McClellan was enraged. He threatened to resign, saying he would lose his self-respect if he served a government that supported a policy with which he disagreed. One night he invited a group of officers to dinner. After the meal he told them that some of his admirers had urged him to oppose the Proclamation and that the whole army would follow him if he did. When the guests recovered from their shock, they begged him to do nothing to set the army against the government. He agreed he should not, but one wonders what he would have done had they encouraged him. A few days later he published a peculiar order to his soldiers, informing them of the nature of the Proclamation and what their attitude toward it should be. In a democracy, he said, the civil authority had the power to determine policy, and the proper remedy for political errors was to be found in the action of the people at the polls. In 1864 McClellan decided to give the people an opportunity to remedy Lincoln's errors. Relieved of command by Lincoln late in 1862, because he had failed as a general and not because of his political opposition to the administration, McClellan ran as the Democratic candidate for President and went down to a crushing defeat. He did not even secure much of the soldier vote on which he had counted heavily.

Grant was almost the exact opposite of McClellan. There was little magnetism and no drama in his appearance and personality. He was not a dazzling figure at parades. His dress was always informal and, to army martinets, seemed sloppy. One sensitive observer hit it exactly when he said Grant was an extraordinary person but didn't look it. He was a spare man with a pen and didn't think it was vital to the nation that he get his every thought on paper. He worked well with his military superiors and exceptionally well with his subordinate officers. As general in chief of all Union armies in 1864–65, he showed the same skill in human relations and human management that Eisenhower did in Europe. He possessed the great gift of knowing how to manage men quietly. Although he never inspired troops to frenzies of applause, he was genuinely popular with the GI's. They regarded him with quiet affection and great respect. "Ulyss is all right" and "Ulyss don't scare" were typical GI statements that expressed their regard for him.

Grant's relations with Lincoln were always smooth, always in correct form for a democratic command system. Since Grant started in the war as a field commander in the West, his first contacts with Lincoln were through the medium of official correspondence. He had never met Lincoln and knew little of what kind of person Lincoln was. Yet he always treated the President with marked deference because he had high respect for his office. After he became general in chief, with his headquarters in the East, and was thrown into close association with Lincoln, he came to have a great admiration for the President as a man and a war director. Part of Grant's success in dealing with his political superior can be ascribed to his human qualities: his skill with people and his humility of character. But the principal reason why he succeeded, why he was a great general in chief, why he was an effective administrator in a democratic command system, was his deep conviction that he should not pronounce on matters of political policy. Grant expressed this conviction in two letters written with what was for him unusual feeling. Early in the war his father asked him what he thought of emancipation. Grant replied: "I have no hobby of my own with regard to the Negro, either to effect his freedom or to continue his bondage. . . . I do not believe even in the discussion of the propriety of laws and official orders by the army. One enemy at a time is enough." In 1864, when he had become the hero of the war, people besought him to give his views on certain political issues, some of which involved the conduct of the war. To a friend he wrote: "So long as I hold my present position, I do not believe I have the right to criticize the policy or orders of those above me, or to give utterance to views of my own, except to the authorities at Washington. . . ." Grant's letters expressed a doctrine that the people believed was proper for a general in a democracy. McClellan's Harrison's Landing letter expressed one that they sensed with a vague instinct was improper and dangerous to democracy. They trusted Grant's military type; they feared McClellan's. Twice they elected Grant President; McClellan they rejected.

The Taylor-Grant-Ike type and the Scott-McClellan-MacArthur type have always been present in our military history and probably always will be. Both are products of the American tradition, and both may act a useful part in the military life of a democracy. In a country that puts a premium on the free discussion of all issues, it is obvious that generals of the Mac type will often arise to differ strongly and perhaps openly with the government over matters of policy. It is just as obvious that a democratic government cannot permit a general of the Mac type to continue in his position. His sustained opposition would unsettle the very basis of democratic authority. In such a situation the general can render a greater service to his cause and can stimulate democratic discussion of the issue involved by getting out of the army and taking his case to the people, as most generals in the Mac tradition have finally done. It is of great historical significance that each Mac general has employed normal political methods to advance his program. Scott and McClellan ran for President; Mac-

Arthur tried to influence the action of the Republican Party. Cromwell and Napoleon are not in our military tradition. It is also historically significant and a testimonial to the sound political instinct of the American people that in choosing generals to be Presidents they have always elevated those of the Ike type. They have favored with their votes only those generals who by their characters and in their actions have seemed to embody the spirit of the democratic tradition.

PART III
Biography

Freeman, Historian of the Civil War
An Appraisal

Long before his life had ended, Douglas Freeman had become a name and a legend.[1] To him was accorded the rare honor of being accepted, while still alive, as a great historian, as *the* authority in his field and of having his works acclaimed as classics that would endure permanently. Undoubtedly he was the most widely known writer of our times on the Civil War and perhaps the most widely bought. He may have been the most widely read. A surprisingly large number of lay readers seem to have plowed through at least a part of his volumes. In the last fifteen years most members of the reading public, if asked to name the best military historian of the Civil War, would have answered without hesitation, "Freeman." Most of the professors would have given the same reply. His tremendous volumes were received with deferential respect by the academic world. Only a few raised their voices to criticize, and these for the most part spoke in private and not in print. He sat in Richmond surrounded by a vast admiration without parallel in modern historiography.

Now, before his myth hardens into an unchangeable mold, seems an appropriate time to evaluate him and his work. I will discuss his books about Lee and Lee's lieutenants under three headings: the case for Freeman, the weaknesses of Freeman, and finally what

Reprinted from *Journal of Southern History*, XXI (February, 1955), 91–100, copyright 1955 by the Southern Historical Association, by permission of the managing editor.

might be termed the basis of Freeman or the basic quality of his work.

First in any listing of Freeman's virtues must be his literary style. Here was a historian who knew how to write. His pages are marked by grace, clarity, and eloquence. There are passages of vivid, moving action (Pickett's charge at Gettysburg in *R. E. Lee*) and others of haunting, moving beauty (the surrender at Appomattox in the same work). Freeman employed devices that only a literary master knows when and how to use. He had a talent for ending a chapter with a sentence that not only provided a transition to the next but also sustained the mood of the whole work. An example is the manner in which he concluded the chapter dealing with operations in 1864: "... surely, when the last December sun of 1864 set over the Petersburg defenses it brought the twilight of the Confederacy."[2] It may be conceded that his subject lent itself to, even demanded, the use of techniques that evoked a mood of sadness and impending doom. He was writing about that most appealing of tragic themes, the man who goes down to defeat battling against great odds. (Interestingly enough, his favorite adjective to describe the condition of the Southern cause at a given moment, repeated over and over in every volume, is "dark.") He rose to the requirements of his subject. Some of his chapters, such as "The Sword of Robert E. Lee" and "The Pattern of a Life," meet the standards of history as a form of literature.

A second strong point of Freeman's was his great sense of fairness and honesty. He tried to be objective and usually was. He did not, however, write without feeling. The Civil War was fought by passionate men. The historian of the war, to really tell the story, has to catch some of their passion. Freeman could feel as they felt. One gets the impression that Freeman said to himself: "I am going to be impartial. I will tell the truth, even about Lee." But he tried to tell the truth without wounding anybody. Here there is a curious parallel between Freeman and his hero. Lee was notoriously humble in dealing with other people whether they were his superiors or his subordinates. With the latter he was particularly tender. When he criticized a subordinate in a report, he usually did so with a vagueness that makes it difficult to determine what he was getting at.

That is, he tried to tell the truth without hurting. Freeman, in discussing Lee's relations with his colleagues, remarks that the general was "a gentleman in every impulse." Was this habit of consideration a weakness? asks Freeman. He answers that it was "a positive weakness."[3] It is evident, however, that he considers it a proper kind of weakness for a man like Lee to have had; more iron in Lee would have been unfitting. Likewise there is no dash and slash in Freeman. Several times he says that it is beyond the function of a Lee biographer to criticize the skill of Lee's opponents or to compare Lee with other generals. Why should he not have done so? Such comparisons would seem necessary in order to understand Lee and his war. But a gentleman historian speaks the hard truth no more than a gentleman general.

The quality of Freeman's which has been most censured is his attention to detail. Readers complain that they get lost in the rich abundance of his items; critics ask why he saw fit to record the state of the weather on a night when Lee did something. The answer to these complaints is that Freeman decided to tell the complete story of Lee. Unless the validity of his decision is open to question, the detail has to be accepted. Considering Lee's stature as an historical figure, Freeman seems to have decided correctly. There is much to be said for having the full record of Lee set down where the patient reader can work it out for himself. It has been conjectured that Freeman knew much more than he told. Probably so. At least he did not get lost in the detail which he presented. He could rise above it to grasp and describe the bigger picture: the growth of Lee as a general or the developing strategic features of a particular campaign.

Much of the criticism of Freeman's detail is really criticism of a kind of detail that is unfamiliar to many readers. Americans have been strangely reluctant to study seriously the history of war. Most reluctant have been the academicians. I have heard professors complain that they cannot understand Freeman and other military writers because they get confused by the multiplicity of names: Smith's division moved up on the right, Brown's regiment moved to the left, and so forth. The same professors will run riot in their own writings about elections, minor politicians, caucuses, factions, and subfactions. Their detail is as massive as Freeman's, but it seems less monolithic because it is familiar and couched in a familiar jargon. The reader who knows something about the war to begin with will not find that Freeman's volumes are overloaded with facts. In *Lee's Lieutenants* the detail is kept to a minimum. Some people have been turned away from Freeman because they tried to read a volume or two at a stretch. The cumulative effect of the detail in such cases is, of course, appalling. The best way to take military history is, like any other kind, in small, well-chewed bites.

Lastly, any table of Freeman's credits must include a tribute to his scholarship, which was of a high order. He used and mastered a tremendous number and variety of sources. The military documents of the Civil War are as difficult a set of sources as any historian ever had to use: incomplete, contradictory, and frequently inaccurate. From a number of conflicting accounts the historian has to try to reconstruct an approximately truthful story of *what* actually happened. Frequently he has to solve the problem of *when* something happened: At what time was an important order sent or received? The documents disagree or do not say at all. The historian has to deduce the time from other events mentioned by the generals in the case or by their subordinates. Freeman excelled in this type of reconstruction. Anyone who wishes to realize the appalling confusion in the documents has only to turn to the pages in *Lee's Lieutenants*, I, where Freeman examines such controversies as whether Beauregard's battle order before First Manassas was distributed to the regimental commanders and whether Ewell received Beauregard's order to cross Bull Run in the same battle. Freeman's analyses of these disputed points and of others are models of historical criticism and of historical detective work. Every historian of the war who has to describe a battle will find his task immeasurably easier if Freeman has worked it over first.

One quality of Freeman's that I think is a weakness is considered by his admirers to be one of his strong points. This is his "fog of war" theory. In a battle a general knows only a part of what is happening. He may not know where the enemy is or what he is planning; he may not know completely even the movements of his own forces. He operates in a fog of the unknown. This fog is a reality, said Freeman, and therefore the most scientific method is to write from the viewpoint of the general. That is, you tell the reader only what the general knew at a particular moment. In *R. E. Lee*, the reader, with a few exceptions, stays with Lee; he sees what Lee saw and no more. Curiously enough, in view of the criticism of his detail, Freeman says that one reason he adopted the fog theory was to avoid confusing detail; by restricting the story to Lee he hoped to simplify it.[4]

Freeman's bold decision to describe battles as they appeared to Lee has been compared to Lee's own audacity. Freeman's admirers claim that his technique produces a powerful dramatic impact and a story of superior literary artistry. Their argument can be illustrated by a hypothetical incident. Let us say that in a battle Lee saw an enemy force approaching on his right. Not knowing its size, he took vigorous measures to meet it. Now, say Freeman's defenders, if at any point in his narrative the historian lets the reader know that the enemy force was small, he ruins the effect of the whole episode. The reader must not know until Lee knows. To all of which, the answer is that drama and artistry are not necessarily the most important things in a description of a battle. The military biographer is depicting a scene in which his subject plays a dominating role. He has to tell enough of the scene to make the role intelligible. If he has to sacrifice drama in the process, so be it. After all, he is recounting an historical episode, not writing a story for the *Saturday Evening Post*. If a political historian writing about Eisenhower in the 1952 election were to adopt Freeman's method, he would leave out much of what the Republicans did and most of what the Democrats did. He would also leave out a necessary part of his story.

Freeman's "fog of war" device is likely to confuse even a fairly well-informed reader. As an illustration, take his application of it to Lee's pursuit of the Union army as it retreated from the York to the James in the Seven Days. Here is a vast, chaotic operation, puzzling to all but the specialists. Probably nine out of ten people cannot understand it unless they are told something about the general movements. Freeman almost ignores the Federals and does not even relate fully what all the units in Lee's command were doing. His whole account tends to break apart in his hands. By insisting on remaining at headquarters with Lee, he fails to give a clear and complete picture of Lee's campaign and hence of Lee himself. It is probable that many people who complain that they get lost in Freeman's detail are really lost in the fog of his presentation.

A second weakness of Freeman's is that he was a little too worshipful of Lee. Somebody has said that he always approached Lee on his knees. This is an exaggeration. He was more like the little girl in Richmond who came home from Sunday School and said, "Mama, I can never remember. Was General Lee in the Old Testament or the New Testament?" Although on occasion Freeman was capable of pointing out Lee's mistakes and deficiencies, he was more likely to concern himself with making excuses for his hero. Thus, in analyzing the reasons why Lee failed to destroy the Union army in the Seven Days, Freeman emphasized the lack of good maps, inadequate artillery, and a poor staff. It comes as something of a shock to hear Freeman say blandly that in the reorganization after the Seven Days Lee did nothing to remedy these shortcomings. Freeman speculates that Lee did not act because he realized Confederate success depended on utilizing the resources at hand without waiting to perfect them and that much had to be left to chance. Freeman's guess may be correct, of course, but it is just as possible that Lee did not understand the importance of certain branches of a modern army.

Freeman's tendency to worship Lee resulted in several chapters in the *R. E. Lee* that are open to serious question. In the section on Chancellorsville he stated that Lee had it within his power to destroy Hooker's army and was prevented from doing so only by the threat of the Federals at Fredericksburg to his right rear. His conclusion was based almost entirely on Confederate sources and seems to me to be at complete variance with the facts. Certainly the Union corps commanders never dreamed that their 70,000 massed men were in danger of destruction from 43,000 Confederates.

Perhaps the chapters that have been most criticized are those on Gettysburg. Here Freeman contended that Lee could have carried Cemetery Ridge on July 2 because the Federal army was not as yet concentrated and that Longstreet's pigheaded slowness was largely responsible for the Confederate failure. In *Lee's Lieutenants*, after more study and reflection, he retracted these statements. In discussing the causes of Confederate defeat at Gettysburg in *R. E. Lee*, he listed such factors as the absence of Stuart, Longstreet's delays, and the failure of Ewell to move. Here he exhibited a too common characteristic of Southern historians—that of assuming that the Confederates possessed the complete power to determine the outcome of a battle. This weakness too he corrected in *Lee's Lieutenants*. He named what he considered to be the mistakes of the Confederates and then added: There were 90,000 Yankees on Cemetery Ridge. Of course, it is to Freeman's credit that he could admit errors and modify earlier beliefs.

The weakest section in *R. E. Lee* is, in my opinion, chapter twenty-four in Volume III. Freeman has just finished describing the maneuvering after Cold Harbor in which Grant disappeared from Lee's front and eventually turned up at Petersburg. Freeman then writes a chapter that is almost pure special pleading to prove that Lee was at no time deceived as to Grant's intentions. Lee was partially deceived because he thought that Grant was trying to get into Richmond. The last thing that Grant wanted was to bring on a fight near the Richmond defenses. He was trying to entice Lee into a battle in the open. Lee did not understand Grant's purpose and neither, apparently, did Freeman. Freeman seems reluctant to admit that in Grant Lee had met his match. This chapter lowers the quality of the entire volume, which is in other respects one of the finest in the set. Freeman came close to arguing that whatever Lee did was right because he was Lee.

A third weakness of Freeman's is that he did not realize that the Civil War was the first of the modern wars. It marked a transition from the older, leisurely, limited-objective kind of war to the all-out for keeps, ruthless, total war of modern times. In this respect Freeman was as unmodern-minded as Lee. Both abhorred economic warfare as needless cruelty. In discussing Lee's reception of the news that McClellan had been removed as commander of the Army of the Potomac, Freeman quotes Lee as saying that he was sorry because he and McClellan understood each other so well. Freeman then adds: "He was sorry too that a man who had always conducted operations with science and humanity was supplanted by one whose respect for principle he had no means of determining until Burnside should begin field operations." [5] This is the old tournament notion of war. Did Freeman expect Burnside to send Lee a brochure announcing how he was going to fight?

Freeman's concept of war is displayed to the full in his description of the opening of the battle of Fredericksburg. The Federals were trying to lay a pontoon bridge over the Rappahannock so they could cross to attack the Confederates. Southern troops posted themselves in houses along the river front and proceeded to pick off the men working on the bridge. Finally the Federal high command, in order to root out the sharpshooters, ordered artillery to open on the houses. The guns fired into the dwellings "indiscriminately," writes Freeman. "The cruelty of it" aroused Lee. He exclaimed that the Federals loved to destroy the weak. [6] It is evident that Freeman too was aroused. The implications of his account are fascinating. Apparently it was perfectly scientific and humane for the Confederates to get in the houses and kill people, but it became cruelty when the Federals tried to get them out. What did he expect the Yankees to do—continue to let their men get killed or call off the battle? Maybe he thought that they should have taken the time to examine the houses and determine which ones held soldiers and which were empty!

A final weakness of Freeman's is that he does not relate Lee's military thought and actions to military developments before and after the war. He does not place Lee, a great general, in the nexus of American military history. His treatment of Lee lacks perspective. As an example, increased firepower was changing the nature of war. A strong force protected by field fortifications or trenches was almost impregnable against frontal assault by attacking infantry. The old style of advancing in regular lines was becoming suicidal. New and more flexible tactical formations were called for. There is hardly a hint of any of this in Freeman's accounts of Lee's attacks at Malvern Hill and Gettysburg. Surely the revolutionary military changes in which Lee was an actor are a part of the Lee story. In Freeman's volumes it is as though Lee and the Army of Northern Virginia are wrenched out of the context of military history to be presented brilliantly in a kind of historical void.

Perhaps the best way to summarize Freeman as a historian is to say that he was a Virginia gentleman writing about a Virginia gentleman. He could understand Lee because he was like Lee. The limitations of Lee are also the limitations of Freeman. As Lee's military genius was restricted because he was a Virginia gentleman, so are Freeman's historical talents. The problem of Freeman cannot be separated from the problem of Lee.

Lee persisted always in viewing the war as primarily an affair of Virginia. Operations in other theaters were almost a kind of side show. Freeman saw the war in the same way. In discussing the favorable situation Lee had created in Virginia as a result of Second Manassas, Freeman writes that this had been achieved when the Confederates on other fronts "had been able to do nothing to relieve the pressure on Virginia."[7] Needless to say, the commanders in Tennessee, Arkansas, Texas, South Carolina, Louisiana, and other places were not charged with the mission of lightening the pressure on Virginia. Again, in describing Lee when he crossed the Potomac as the invasion of Pennsylvania started, Freeman refers to him as "the man who carried his nation's hopes."[8] The hopes of the Confederacy at that moment rested as heavily on Braxton Bragg and John Pemberton as they did on the Virginian. The hills around Vicksburg and Chattanooga were as fateful as those in Pennsylvania.

Because Freeman is like Lee, he did not quite see the tremendous importance of Lee's motivation in joining the Confederacy. Nor was he quite able to explain why Lee did so. In discussing Lee's decision to go with the South, he speaks about Lee's faith, about something deep in his heart, about the spirit of Virginia: "He did not stop . . . to reason out the nature of his feeling, which was instinctive."[9] Lee was a strange, almost a baffling creature. He did not believe in slavery and he did not believe in secession, yet he elected to fight to defend both because his state seceded. He went into the war and waged war in almost an unthinking way. The pull of his home state—its houses, its soil, its rivers, its people—overpowered his mental or rational nature. He could not analyze this pull, nor could he resist it. Freeman understood Lee's feeling, but he did not realize that it constituted a tragic limitation in the man. The emotion that impelled Lee into the war also influenced the way he fought. He fought for Virginia. Freeman did not recognize Lee's limitation because to him too the war is in Virginia. It did not occur to him to examine the effects of Lee's preoccupation with Virginia on total Confederate strategy. Nor did he see the tragic result of Lee's limitation. In the end, all the brilliance and fortitude of the greatest Confederate general availed little to save his country. It fell to pieces behind his back, and most of his efforts in Virginia went for nothing.

The Gentleman from Louisiana
Demagogue or Democrat

Was it true, the reporter asked, probing deeper with his questions, that the state officials and the legislature of Louisiana were corrupt? [1] Governor Henry Clay Warmoth exploded. His answer reflected what one suspects was a common complaint of the carpetbagger caught up in the swashbuckling politics of Louisiana but at the same time demonstrated that he himself was rapidly adjusting to the realities of the Louisiana scene. "I don't pretend to be honest. . . . I only pretend to be as honest as anybody in politics, and more so than those fellows who are opposing me now. Here are these New Orleans bankers making a great outcry against the dishonesty of the Louisiana legislature. . . . I tell you . . . these much-abused members are at all events as good as the people they represent. Why, damn it, everybody is demoralized down here. Corruption is the fashion."

One may admit a certain exaggeration in the Governor's remarks, and also in the statement of a later critic that Louisianians are not interested in ideologies or principles but in the fundamentals—the whir of slot machines, the pounding of horses' hoofs at the Fair Grounds, and the clink of ice in a Sazerac cocktail. Nor is it neces-

Delivered at the annual meeting of the Southern Historical Association in Atlanta, Georgia, November 12, 1959.
From the Bobbs-Merrill Reprint Series in American History, with minor corrections therein. Originally in *Journal of Southern History*, XXVI (February, 1960), 3–21, © 1960 by the Southern Historical Association, and reprinted herein by permission of the managing editor.

sary to adopt the judgments of those commentators who say that Louisiana is not an American state but a banana republic, a Latin enclave of immorality set down in a matrix of Anglo-Saxon righteousness, a proposition whose basic assumption is highly dubious both in the light of history and present observation. And yet without question Louisianians have a concept of corruption not found in other states. They seem to accept it as a necessary concomitant of political life, and, on occasion, even to delight in it. It is an outlook peculiar to the state, perhaps an expression of Latin realism, and it has made Louisiana politics undeniably different. Corruption, which as defined by purists often means only the compromises that are required to keep the machinery of democracy running, has appeared in all states where it has been worthwhile and at all levels of government and has been practiced by all classes. In the Louisiana attitude toward corruption there is little of the sanctimoniousness often found in Anglo-Saxon communities; indeed, there is even a tendency to admire a "deal" if it is executed with skill and a flourish and, above all, with a jest. Louisianians, more than any other people in America, realize, with a kind of paradoxical honesty, the hard fact that politics is not always an exercise in civics book morality. In 1939 Gallup pollsters asked a sample group in the state, "Do you think elections in Louisiana in recent years have been honestly conducted?" Twenty-five percent answered "Yes," sixty percent answered "No," and fifteen percent sagely ventured no opinion. The frankness of the response would not have surprised Governor Warmoth.[2]

But we would be committing a common scholarly error if, in picturing the political anatomy of Louisiana, we emphasized unduly either the color or the proportions of the corruption. Academic people, as well as the general public, expect too much of politics; they are too prone to be horrified by departures from an ideal standard of morality that is largely imaginary. As Pendleton Herring has pointed out, a double code of ethics holds for politics. We judge politicians by a higher standard than we apply to men in spheres of private action. This is wrong and can even be dangerous, Herring tells us, because the politician, whose function is to compromise the conflicting desires of frail mankind, has to treat government as a problem of mechanics rather than as a question of morals. "The politician is concerned not with what should be but with what can be."[3] If strong men are forced out of politics by too puristic standards, lesser men will take their place. We may recall Emerson's warning in this connection: "Better, certainly, if we could secure the strength and fire which rude, passionate men bring into society, quite clear of their vices. But who dares draw out the linchpin from the wagon-wheel?"[4] But Americans have always had a curious bifocal view of corruption. Throughout our history we have tolerated corruption to an extraordinary degree, have even encouraged it for certain ends, and in some of the relations between government and business have put it to broad social and economic ends. Perhaps more research is required in this area of behavior, concentrating on the psychology of the corruptible rather than on the arts of the corruptor. It may be that one of our greatest scholarly needs is an honest history of corruption.

Rather than corruption being the hallmark of Louisiana politics, a zest for politics as a game and an appreciation of politics as a power lever have been the distinguishing qualities. Describing the political scene in the 1850's, one historian writes that to a greater degree than in most states "the active electorate revealed a peculiar enthusiasm for the dramatic clash of personalities, the stratagems of politics, and the winning of public offices."[5] Or, put in less academic terms, the state took its politics raw, like corn whiskey, and loved the diet. This fact was not lost on Governor Warmoth, who was an extremely resourceful and audacious operator, possessing in high degree that quality of ignoring existing rules and making up his own that in a politician we call genius. Coming into office with an insecure power basis and confronted by a constant, cunning, and sometimes unscrupulous opposition, he erected an imposing facade of laws that invested him with imperial authority. He could appoint and remove local registrars of voters, tax collectors, and assessors. He could appoint the board of police commissioners in New Orleans, which controlled the selection of all personnel; constables for all parishes except Orleans, Jefferson, and St. Bernard (which were subject to the Metropolitan Police, a state force accountable to the governor); and all members of the militia. He could fill all vacancies in local offices, including those in the potent parish police juries. He could order the arrest of persons anywhere in the state and direct local enforcement officers to execute the warrant, and authorize officers in one parish to aid those in another. On the noninstitutional level Warmoth invaded the floors of the legislature to lobby for his bills and to berate his own followers, and he required undated resignations from some of his appointees. All in all, it was an extraordinary performance in power, and the example most probably impressed a later leader of greater stature than Warmoth.

In 1893 in the north-central parish of Winn there was born a son, the seventh in what would be a family of nine, to Huey P. Long, Sr. The boy was named Huey P. Long, Jr. He grew up in an environment that physically was no different from other areas in rural Louisiana but that possessed a unique historical heritage. Winn was undeniably poor, a parish of small farms, cutover timber lands, and lumber mills. The people had a wry saying that they made a living by taking in each other's washing. The Longs were as well off as the average, perhaps slightly above, the father in 1900 owning 340 acres of land and other property assessed at $780. Historically Winn had a tradition of dissent not equalled by any other parish. In 1861 the delegate from Winn to the secession convention was one of seventeen members who voted against final passage of the secession ordinance and one of seven who refused to sign it. Although the parish furnished three companies to the Confederate service, most of the inhabitants seem to have sat the war out, many refusing to fight to save the rich man's slaves and some openly supporting the Union. John M. Long, Huey's grandfather, was not in the Confederate army, and Huey's father professed strong Union sympathies. The old man told a reporter, "Didn't Abraham Lincoln free the niggers and not give the planters a dime? Why shouldn't Huey take the money away from the rich and still leave 'em plenty? . . . Maybe you're surprised to hear talk like that. Well, it was just such talk that my boy was raised under and that I was raised under. My father and my mother favored the Union. Why not? They didn't have slaves. They didn't even have decent land." It is not surprising—but of great significance—that in his political career Huey P. Long never seriously employed the Con-

federate legend in his speeches. He stuck to economics in an era
when most Southern politicians entertained their audiences of rural
poor with the magnificent irrelevancy of how their grandpappies had
charged up the slopes at Gettysburg.

The parish added to its record of dissent in the farmers' revolt of
the 1890s, emerging as the leading center of Populist strength in the
state. In the election of 1892 the Populist gubernatorial candidate, a
resident of Winnfield, the principal town, swept the parish by a margin of almost five to one, and the Populists won every election in
Winn until 1900. The spirit of social protest represented by Populism carried over into a surprising support for Socialism. A strong
Socialist party appeared that elected half of the parish officials in
1908 and its slate of municipal officials in Winnfield in 1912. And in
the presidential election of the latter year Eugene Debs received almost thirty-six percent of Winn's popular vote. This was rural Socialism, of course, hardly distinguishable from Populism, but it is
significant that so many Winn residents were not afraid to wear a
label that was not popular in the rural South. No Long apparently
was a member of either the Populist or Socialist movement. In fact,
Huey Long, while still a schoolboy, once debated a touring Socialist
lecturer, upholding the merits of the Democratic party. But obviously Long's whole political philosophy was shaped and condi-
tioned by the tradition of his environment. If his program has to be
labeled, it was neo-Populism.

It is not so clear, however, where Long derived his later formula of
Share Our Wealth. Most commentators have ascribed its origins to
the Populism and Socialism that Long heard discussed in his youth,
and the plan does have overtones of both these creeds: Long himself
said that he got the idea from the Bible, but the appeal to Holy Writ
seems to have been window dressing. Indeed, Huey may have come
to the Bible late, although the evidence on this point is contradictory. According to one story, in the state campaign of 1920 a friend
quoted to him a verse that could be used to damage an opponent.
Huey, much impressed, peeled off a bill and said, "Go over to Hirch
and Lehmen's store and buy me the best damn Bible they've got."
Reliable evidence indicates that Long, a keen student of history and
thoroughly familiar with the Reconstruction period, drew the in-

spiration for Share Our Wealth from the experiment of the Freed-men's Bureau and its forty acres and a mule. And it may be that he took another leaf from the lesson of Reconstruction, for when he finally unseated the old political hierarchy in 1928, in erecting his own power structure he would employ, consciously or unconsciously, many of the techniques and devices of Governor Warmoth.

After the overthrow of Reconstruction, the sources of power in the South fell to, or were taken by, the upper income groups, represented roughly by the planters and the new industrial and commercial interests. In every state such an oligarchy dominated the political scene, exercising its power in the Democratic party through the medium of a machine or a combination of factions. Occasionally rebels rose here and there to challenge the existing hierarchies. These are the men we know by the much abused term of demagogue. As W. J. Cash explains them: although in their rise to power they exploited the aspirations of the masses, they did little for the masses when they got power—partly because they were more interested in place than in programs, partly because, although they built their own machines to perpetuate themselves, they were unable, or unwilling, to destroy the old machine, and hence their tenure was never secure.[6] No demagogue of this type appeared to defy the existing order in Louisiana. For almost fifty years after Reconstruction the oligarchy ruled serenely, made confident and smug by the knowledge that its network of influence and interest enveloped the entire state.

The Louisiana hierarchy contained the usual elements found in other Southern states and some peculiarly its own. In addition to the familiar planting groups, there were important business interests: lumber, railroads, and sugar. Above all, there was oil; in the 1920s the Standard Oil Company became a major economic and political force in the life of the state. In New Orleans there were shipping interests and gas and electrical utilities. And in the great urban center there was a genuine big city machine, the Old Regulars or the Choctaw Club, closely allied with the business and financial powers. The Old Regular organization was largely the creation of Martin Behrman, long-time mayor and author of the classic statement, "You can make corruption illegal in Louisiana but you can't make it unpopular." The machine performed some of the desirable functions expected of such associations and many of the undesirable ones. In the words of one friendly observer, "The Old Regulars were used to buying out and trading out and swapping out." By means of padded registration rolls, paid up poll tax receipts, and police pressure, the machine could swing the city to any side or candidate. In a gubernatorial election the machine would endorse a candidate with a strong country following in return for a pledge of control over state patronage in the city. The relationship was not, however, as tight or tidy as it sounds; it was almost wholly informal, and no rigid, state-wide machine existed.

Such was the ruling hierarchy, satisfied with things as they were, discreetly corrupt on occasion, devoted to the protection of privilege. It did not even trouble to make the masses feel important by appealing to them for votes, those that could vote; the small towns and the forks of the creeks rarely heard a candidate for governor. The leaders of the oligarchy were singularly blind to the signs of the time. Although the Progressive movement had touched Louisiana, its impact had been light, and what change had occurred had been mild, almost imperceptible. Riley J. Wilson, the hierarchy's candidate for governor in 1928, thought that Long's proposal to pave the roads was preposterous because it would cost too much money. Nor would the ruling classes accept the inevitability of change even when they saw Long swept into power on a program demanding change. Looking back today, many of them see that they made a fatal error in opposing every idea advanced by Long. But said one dolefully, "There is no reform from within, it comes only by defeat." Others still do not know what happened to them. Old patricians who stood apart from the machine or affected not to see its workings ask, Why should the voters have repudiated men who believed in honest, economical government? They do not know that the masses in any state are not impressed by honesty unless it promises to bring a better life. The Louisiana ruling class is a perfect illustration of an elite inviting destruction by its own myopia. As he well knew, Huey Long was fortunate in his enemies. "It has been my good fortune to have blind men like these in politics," he said. "They cannot see something after it has passed over them, and they have been knocked down by it a half-dozen times."

Before the advent of Long on the Louisiana scene, governors were elected by "leaders," who usually were the sheriffs of the parishes. The candidate who lined up the largest number of influential leaders could make a deal with the city machine and take the office. Abruptly and rudely Long destroyed this pattern. Often in his first campaigns he would invade a parish and denounce the boss. There was design in this. As he explained to one man, the boss had forty percent of the vote, forty percent were opposed to him, and twenty percent were in-between. "I'm going into every parish and cuss out the boss. That gives me forty percent of the votes to begin with, and I'll hoss trade 'em out of the in-betweens." Whatever the formula, it worked. In the rueful words of one opponent, "Overnight, one might say, the leaders found themselves without followers, and the mob was in control." Long then created his own local organization, the sheriff or leader being his man. "That man was sheriff and leader because Huey wanted him to be," explained one admirer. "He cut out the middleman in politics. He went directly to the people. Sometimes he would appoint two leaders to watch each other, and deal directly with the people. That's a system you can't beat."

If Long had stopped after creating an organization of his own, no matter how effective, he would merely have followed the path of previous politicians of his type. But he did more. As W. J. Cash shrewdly perceived, Long was the first Southern mass leader to set himself, not to bring the established machine to terms, but to overwhelm it and replace it with one of his own.[7] Long told a former teacher at Tulane University, "That damn political science class of yours with your talk of ideals held back my political career for years. I'm fighting a crooked machine in the Old Regulars and have to fight fire with fire. You have to protect your own damn fools." He did, indeed, face a powerful and implacable opposition. In fact, during Long's entire political career there was hardly a time when he was not under some kind of threat of removal or impeachment. "I have tried for about sixteen years to have it some other way," he once said, "and it has never been any other way, so now I have stopped trying to have it any other way." He was saying that the oligarchy was ruthless and that he would fight it on its own terms. Writers who discuss the so-called demagogues like to detail the methods by which these men supposedly corrupted politics, but they forget that the demagogues only utilized and sometimes improved techniques used for years by the elite and employed particularly against spokesmen of the masses. For instance, in the impeachment proceedings against Long in 1929 the opposition offered huge sums of money for votes to convict. Huey himself charged that Standard Oil brought enough money into Baton Rouge to "burn a wet mule." In addition, the crudest kind of economic pressure was applied. Long retaliated with promises of jobs and favors. Often quoted is Long's remark that he bought legislators like sacks of potatoes. This was made when one legislator who had announced he would vote for conviction switched to Long's side. Asked how he had secured him, Huey replied, "Just the same way they got him. It's just like going to market and getting a sack of potatoes. They got a fixed price. You bought him that way and I bought him the same way."

Of necessity, Long had first to create an organization to pass his program in the legislature. He went into office with a minority of pledged supporters. In the lower chamber he could count on only nineteen votes, whereas, as many of his measures had to be cast in the form of constitutional amendments, he needed a two-thirds majority or sixty-seven. Gradually the desired control was built up, but in the frank words of one Long leader, "They all didn't come for free." The basis of the Long machine was patronage. Deliberately, Long as governor extended his power over existing boards and other agencies, and through the creation of new agencies to perform new functions he continually enlarged the patronage at his disposal. Eventually he was able to deprive the opposition of almost all political sustenance, and then he finally brought the Old Regulars to their knees. In the last phase of his career he reached out for more and more power, too much power, pushing laws through the legislature that repeated Warmoth's program of control of local government and election machinery and went even beyond it.

Like countless other politicians before and after him, Long built a powerful machine. But being a supreme realist, he knew that there were certain areas of government that had to be immune from politics. That is, some jobs had to go to men who would not be interfered with by anybody. This was necessary both to insure the proper functioning of government and to preserve the life of the machine. He insisted that appointees to certain positions enjoy complete freedom of decision and action. Said one not altogether friendly observer, "He was smart that way. He knew where to fit men into positions—nonelastic men." When a judge told him that Long followers were trying to influence his decision on a case, Huey told him to disregard the pressure, "Remember that a crooked judge is no credit to Huey Long." To some heads of departments he would say, "The only thing I ask you is not to hire any of my enemies." The federal Resettlement Administration feared that Long would try to politicalize its program, and sent a man to Louisiana to watch him. This official found to his surprise that it was the opposition that demanded the patronage. One day Huey called him in, assured him that he wanted the program to succeed and would not interfere with it. Then, thinking of his enemies, Long added, "The first time I catch you appointing somebody because one of those sons of bitches tells you to, I'll drive you out of Louisiana."

Political machines have to have money, to sustain the strength of the organization and to perform certain welfare functions expected by their followers. This was particularly true in the 1920s and the early 1930s, before the impersonal welfare of the New Deal and later of the states substituted for the services of the machines and hence undermined their power. Long leaders are completely frank in explaining how the machine raised money for campaigns and for other purposes, notably publicity. Because most of the press was in opposition, Long hit on the idea of disseminating his ideas through printed circulars, some 26,000,000 being distributed. During Long's administration the state engaged in a tremendous road building program. The road contractors and contractors on other public works were called on for regular contributions in elections. So also were the distributors of highway machinery, who enjoyed lucrative relations with the state, and the companies that wrote the state's insurance. For obvious reasons, these interests met their assessments. The number of state employees was deliberately maintained at a high level, the jobs being spread around lavishly, and the occupants had to contribute a percentage of their salaries to the machine war chest. Some officials were required to render monthly payments, but in Long's time lower salaried workers were assessed only before elections. In addition, there were approximately a thousand leaders and subleaders who stood ready to supply money for critical needs. As one of these told the writer, "He would send for me and all these other men to come to his room in the Roosevelt, and he would say 'I need $60,000 to pay the poll taxes,' and we would all shell out and that is how Huey got his money. He didn't have to graft it." Not only do Long leaders frankly detail these financial dealings, they insist passionately that the machine's system of raising money was moral, certainly more moral than the system of the opposition. The opposition, they say, asked for money from the interests under the table and hence was subject to the power of a minority, whereas the Long organization took money openly and hence was free to act for the majority.

And act for the majority the machine did. Huey Long was the first Southern mass leader to leave aside race baiting and appeals to the gold-misted past and address himself to the social and economic ills of his people. The record of accomplishment can only be summarized here. In 1928 Louisiana had 296 miles of concrete roads, 35 miles of asphalt roads, 5,728 miles of gravel roads, and three major bridges within the state highway system. By 1935 the state had 2,446 miles of concrete roads, 1,308 miles of asphalt roads, 9,629 miles of gravel roads, and more than forty major bridges within the state highway system. In the field of education, free textbooks were provided (stimulating a twenty percent jump in public school enrollment), appropriations for higher education were increased, and over 100,000 adult illiterates, of both races, were enrolled in free night schools. Facilities in state hospitals and institutions were enlarged, and the services were modernized and, more important, humanized. The money to pay for this tremendous program came partly from increased taxes, bearing largely on corporate interests, but mostly from bonds, the state debt jumping from $11,000,000 in 1928 to nearly $150,000,000 by 1935.[8] Moreover, the costs were based on sound financial practices, the legislature appropriating no money without collaterally providing the revenues and bond issues being capitalized by taxes. Not the least accomplishment in Long's record was his revitalizing of state politics. He created a new consciousness of politics on the part of the masses. By advancing issues that mattered to the masses and by repealing the poll tax, he stirred voter interest to a height unmatched in any other Southern state, and he left Louisiana with an enduring bifactionalism that has many of the attributes of a two-party system.

The secret of Long's power, in the final analysis, was not in his machine or his political dealings but in his record—he delivered something. One man, trying to put through to the writer the impact of Long on the masses, could say only, "They felt the hand of Huey." But how is his record to be evaluated? In looking at various judgments of Long, we discover again that curious tendency of scholars to hold politicians to an ideal and impossible standard. Thus one writer lists Long's accomplishments and concedes them to be impressive, but then says, aha, they amount to nothing because he didn't touch the problem of sharecropping and tenantry.[9] Another, forgetting that Long acted in a largely rural state, cries, yes, but he did little for labor.[10] Such complaints are like saying, why didn't Franklin Roosevelt nationalize the banks? The answer to such queries is, of course, that seemingly ideal solutions may not be politically possible or feasible at a given moment. The politician does what he can, not what he should do. If he acted otherwise, he would cease to be a politician and the democratic system would cease to exist.

Was Huey Long a dictator? The term was thrown at him freely in the 1930s by a generation impressed with the example of the Fascist leaders in Europe, and it has passed into many of the books. The trouble with the dictator label is that it has a European connotation and does not fit the American scene. Long was an American boss, a very powerful and sometimes ruthless one, who in his last phase had too much power. He probably knew that this was so, because he repeatedly told the men who would be his successors that they could not wield his authority. But he was never more than a boss. As one of his associates shrewdly put it, "Huey wouldn't have acted as a dictator on any issue that might have alienated the majority of the voters."

Certainly he had none of the qualities we associate with the Fascist leader. Not even his worst enemies accused him of having religious or racial prejudices. Once Dr. Hiram Evans of the Klan denounced him as un-American and threatened to campaign against him in Louisiana. Long came into the press gallery at the state senate and said he wanted to issue a statement: "Quote me as saying that that Imperial bastard will never set foot in Louisiana, and that when I call him a son of a bitch I am not using profanity, but am referring to the circumstances of his birth." His knowledge of the philosophy of European dictators was only perfunctory, although his evaluation of them was reasonably accurate. Asked if he saw any similarity between himself and Hitler, he said, "Don't compare me to that so-and-so. Anybody that lets his public policies be mixed up with religious prejudice is a plain God-damned fool." The symbols of Fascism excited in him only an amused scorn. Discussing the NRA in the Senate, he said, "However, Mr. President, I hope that if we give it the sign of the Fascisti, known as the 'blue eagle,' or the 'double eagle,' or whatever they call it, we will at least let the eagle have a chance to live. . . . It is all right that the Germans have the Fascist sign in the form of a swastika; it is all right that the Mussolinites . . . in Italy have their sign in the form of a black shirt, and it may have been all right that the Fascisti in America have their emblem in the form of a double eagle, but at least we ought to have given that emblem the right to have lived and to have thrived. I really believe, Mr. President, that we almost condemned that eagle to death in advance when we published [it] looking squarely into the countenance of . . . Hugh S. Johnson. . . ."

Political observers of the 1930s were led to level the dictatorship charge by Long's actions when as United States Senator but still boss of the state he returned to Louisiana to jam laws through the legislature. Special session after special session was called, and Long would dominate committee hearings and storm onto the floor of either house to shout at his followers. On one occasion forty-four bills were passed within a few hours. In seven special sessions between

August 1934 and September 1935, a total of 226 bills was enacted. Some bills started out as one thing in one house and became something entirely different in the other. Thus a House measure to codify existing license laws turned at the last minute in the Senate into a bill to tax Standard Oil, much to the consternation of the Standard lobbyists, who had innocently gone home.

But the observers who were horrified at this seeming travesty of the legislative process missed some things. For one, the most important bills had previously been explained in detail by Long in a closed caucus of his supporters. For another, many measures were passed as constitutional amendments and had to be submitted to a popular vote. Fourteen amendments adopted in one special session were ratified by the voters by a margin of seven to one. Still, one wonders if Long's methods comported with the spirit of democratic government. He apparently wondered too. "They say they don't like my methods," he said once. "Well, I don't like them either. . . . I'd much rather get up before a legislature and say 'Now this is a good law; it's for the benefit of the people, and I'd like for you to vote for it in the interest of the public welfare.' Only I know that laws ain't made that way. You've got to fight fire with fire." But in the later stages of his career he did not have to employ fire. He still faced an unrelenting opposition, it is true, but he had it well in hand. Having been forced to overthrow the oligarchy by ruthless methods, he continued to use the same methods after his victory was assured. Either he feared the recuperative genius of the oligarchy or he had become too fascinated with the exercise of sheer power to give it up. Undoubtedly he had been hardened by the constant attempts of the opposition to destroy him, especially by the try at impeachment. There is some kind of personal and sectional tragedy in the Long story. He might have been, lamented one critic, such a leader as the South had never had. But it was not entirely his fault that he did not become Dixie's peerless Progressive. Perhaps the lesson of Long is that if in a democracy needed changes are denied too long by an interested minority, the changes, when they come, will come with a measure of repression and revenge. And perhaps the gravest indictment that can be made of Southern politics in recent times is that the urge for reform had to be accomplished by pressures that left in leaders like Long a degree of cynicism about the democratic process.

Was Huey Long, then, a demagogue? Here again we encounter semantic difficulties. The Greeks gave us the term, and we have accepted their definition. The demagogue was "a man of loose tongue, intemperate, trusting to tumult, leading the populace to mischief with empty words." He was "foul-mouthed, . . . a low mean fellow." Implicit in Greek thinking about the subject was the assumption that in politics the masterful leader manipulated the mindless mass with the mere turbulence of his rhetoric. We know that for the American scene, at least, this concept has little validity, yet we permit it to affect our judgments of American politicians. Scholars particularly have been influenced by the notion that violent language is the peculiar mark of the demagogue. They seem to think that popular leaders have risen to power simply because they could excite and entertain the voters. Certainly Huey Long was a master in the use of scathing invective and also of effective satire, as witness his elucidation of the possible meanings of NRA: National Racketeering Association, National Ruin Administration, Nuts Running America, or Never Roosevelt Again; or his application of damaging and durable nicknames to his aristocratic Louisiana foes: "Kinky" Howard, "Liverwurst" Nicholson, "Shinola" Phelps, "Turkeyhead" Walmsley, "Feather Duster" Ransdell, and "Whistle Britches" Rightor. But his skill with words was only one of several factors that explain his success, and a minor one at that. And only a cursory reading of the literature of Louisiana politics will reveal that extreme language was not a Long patent. Among the terms applied to Long—by the best people—were: "an ultra Socialist" whose views went "beyond Marx, Lenin, and Trotsky," "an impeached thief and scoundrel," "a political freak, cringing coward, and monumental liar," a man with "the face of a clown, the heart of a petty larceny burglar, and the disposition of a tyrant."

Long himself was deeply interested in the application of the term of demagogue and perceptively aware of its limitations. In one especially realistic analysis he said, "There are all kinds of demagogues. Some deceive the people in the interests of the lords and masters of creation, the Rockefellers and the Morgans. Some of them deceive the people in their own interest. I would describe a demagogue as a politician who don't keep his promises." On that basis he denied that he deserved the label. But on another occasion, changing the definition, he accepted it. Referring to his program, he said: "I shall have to admit, it is a demagogy, because in the old Greek parlance that meant the language that was acceptable to the majority. That is not meant as a derogatory term, and I do not take it as such, because when I advocated free school books in Louisiana that was termed demagoguery; when I advocated free bridges instead of toll bridges it was called demagoguery; and when I advocated paved highways instead of dirt roads that likewise was called demagoguery."

Let us dispense with the word demagogue in dealing with men like Long and employ instead a term suggested by Eric Hoffer, mass leader. As listed by Hoffer, the principal qualities required in a mass leader are—and Huey Long had all of them—audacity, an iron will, faith in his cause or in himself, unbounded brazenness, and a capacity for hatred, without which he may be deflected from his goal.[11] To these we may add others. The mass leader must have an abnormal and combative energy. Long was, as Henry Adams said of Theodore Roosevelt, "pure act." The mass leader must know which enemies he should destroy and which ones he should maintain as symbols of the continuing evil he fights against. "Corporations are the finest enemies in the world," Long once remarked. "You got to know how to handle them." After he had broken the power of Mayor Walmsley in New Orleans, an associate asked why he simply did not get rid of Walmsley. "He said, 'No, that would be bad psychology. You always leave a figurehead for your boys to fight against. If you don't, they start fighting against themselves. Walmsley is a perfect target for us to fight. He's impotent and can't do us any harm.'"

The quality above all others that the mass leader must have is audacity—a boundless self-confidence which lets him give full rein to his ideas, a brazen courage which enables him to disregard conventionality and consistency, and a daring imagination which equips him to ignore existing rules and create his own. Examples of Long's audacity are too numerous to be considered here, but a few must be cited. During one of the several financial crises of the early 1930s a run developed on the New Orleans banks, threatening a general collapse. The problem was to close the banks over a weekend until money could be secured from the RFC. Aides feverishly sought for a holiday that could serve as an excuse. Huey easily supplied one. A proclamation by the governor announced that the banks would be closed because, Whereas, on this date Woodrow Wilson severed diplomatic relations with Germany. . . .

The triumphant climax of Long's many savage jousts with Standard Oil came when the legislature, at his bidding, enacted a tax of five cents a barrel on refined oil. From the viewpoint of the Standard Oil this was bad enough, but worse was to come. Another legislature, also at Long's bidding, authorized the governor to suspend any portion of the tax. The suspension would come, of course, only if the Standard conformed to certain conditions, and the full tax could be reapplied at any time. It was a completely effective device to keep the great corporation in line. At the height of the controversy over the tax measure the company sent an emissary, a close friend of Long's, to ask him to desist. Long listened to this man but then remarked that he was not particularly interested in the tax anymore. "Pete, I'll tell you what I'm going to do. Tell the Standard Oil to get the hell out of Louisiana and I'll exappropriate that plant and the legislature will appropriate enough money to buy it and we'll operate it. And from the funds the first year we will educate the top boy and girl in every high school in the state at LSU free, and as the profits begin to grow we will educate the second and third ones and so on. . . . It will take a constitutional amendment but the people will vote for it when I tell them that we will use that money to educate the boys and girls of Louisiana free from the profits." The emissary departed hastily.

It is possible that we have been too apologetic about and too patronizing toward all the Southern demagogues. Some of them were hopelessly confused and some were merely clowns. Some did nothing to control the interests they attacked and some sold out to those interests. But the best of them tried to do something for their people. Throw out the crudities they had to employ to arouse a submerged electorate and the race baiting, and these men are the Norrises, the La Follettes, and the Borahs of another section. Even such an object of hatred to the righteous as Theodore Bilbo meets the test for admission to the liberal heaven, a straight New Deal voting record in the Senate. Indeed, many of the Southern demagogues, in their genuine concern for the welfare of the masses, in their essential respect for the democratic system, conform in their own peculiar fashion to Eric Hoffer's picture of the good mass leader—the leader who does not hesitate to "harness men's hungers and fears" to weld a following in the service of a cause but who, because of his faith in humanity, does not attempt to use the frustrations of men to build a brave new theoretical world.[12] Or, to shift to another formula, many of the demagogues conform, again in their own manner, to Jacques Maritain's image of the prophet leader, whose main mission is "to *awaken* the people, to awaken them to something better than everyone's daily business, to the sense of a supra-individual task to be performed."[13] Certain it is that without the driving force supplied by the demagogues a static society would not have been renovated as quickly—or as painlessly—as it was.

One night in Long's hotel room in New Orleans, while he seemingly dozed on the bed, a group of visiting correspondents fell to analyzing his political personality. Finally arousing himself, he said, "Oh, hell, say that I'm *sui generis* and let it go at that." In a class by himself he certainly was. He stands without a rival as the greatest of Southern mass leaders. He asked the South to turn its gaze from "nigger" devils and Yankee devils and take a long, hard look at itself. He asked his people to forget the past, the glorious past and the sad past, and address themselves to the present. There is something wrong here, he said, and we can fix it up ourselves. Bluntly, forcibly, even crudely, he injected an element of realism into Southern politics. Not without reason did Gerald Johnson, who disliked him, say that Huey Long was the first Southerner since Calhoun to have an original idea, the first to extend the boundaries of political thought.[14] Above all, he gave the Southern masses hope. He did some foolish things and some wrong things. He said some things that he should not have said and some that he did not believe. But this we may be certain he meant: "Nevertheless my voice will be the same as it has been. Patronage will not change it. Fear will not change it. Persecution will not change it. It cannot be changed while people suffer. The only way it can be changed is to make the lives of these people decent and respectable."

Huey, Lyndon, and Southern Radicalism

The president of a scholarly association is, by consent or resignation, allowed a wide latitude in choosing the subject of the address he is required to present to his colleagues. He may distill the result of his recent research, if he has been doing any research or is still of an age when he can conduct research, discuss the state of the profession, usually with alarm, or offer his reflections on a segment of history, on men and movements that have been a focus of his research and reading. It is this third approach that I have chosen, largely because of a conviction that a presidential address should deal with a large and important theme.

An address of this kind must and should advance a viewpoint or viewpoints, and the deliverer of it must be permitted a further latitude—to lay out various positions, some of them speculative and intended to provoke debate, and to make his own definitions of some terms. In this address concerned with radicalism, I define it in the usual American meaning—a movement to accomplish important or substantial change within the system, change that looks to a new ordering of society rather than to a returning to the past. My thesis is that although radicalism has not appeared often in the South, when

Delivered as the presidential address to the Organization of American Historians, Chicago, Illinois, April 12, 1973.
Reprinted from *Journal of American History*, LX (September, 1973), 267–93, © 1973 by the Organization of American Historians, by permission.

it has, it has been more intense and insistent than in other sections. In support of this thesis I offer that the two greatest political radicals in recent history have been Huey Long and Lyndon B. Johnson and that the most radical mass movement in recent times has been the black civil rights movement—all three of these phenomena coming out of the South, that supposedly conservative South that would win in a landslide any contest to pick the section least likely to dissent. Two of these phenomena, Long and the civil rights masses, were so radical that they were willing to bend or even break the system. The third one, equally rooted in the South, equally committed to change, remained convinced that reform must come within the system— Lyndon Johnson.[1]

The persisting image of an undissenting South is, like most stereotypes, based partly on fact, but also on fancy, and is in need of revision. The region has actually had a tradition of dissent. Carl Degler has reminded us that during most of the nineteenth century the white South dissented from the views of the majority in the nation, and indeed at the high point of its protest, in 1860–1861, took the extreme step of withdrawing "from the consensus entirely." This deviation was, however, as Degler emphasizes in an apt phrase, a "peculiar dissent," designed not to further social change but to preserve a regional status quo.[2] In grim pursuit of this end, white southerners before the Civil War and especially after it erected a structure of conformity hitherto unknown in American life, suppressing feelings of class difference among themselves in a manner unparalleled in modern democratic societies. This straitjacketing of thought was often glossed over with constitutional or cultural justifications, but its purpose was to prevent any interference with the prevailing racial pattern, indeed, to prevent any discussion of the racial question. And for a time the restraints were unchallenged. This compliant postwar South was well described by Rebecca West: "Consider the South of that day: which like all American scenes is now altered out of recognition. Then the race issue was a huge monolith in the middle of the landscape round which black and white Southerners alike sat in silence. Nobody moved, to take a forward step or a backward step. All was as quiet as the tomb or the womb." West goes on to suggest that if, as William Faulkner and other writers allege, incest and rape and murder were being committed behind the graceful colonnades of the plantations, "it must have been by members of the Noise Abatement Society who took their membership seriously."[3]

The enveloping silence would not endure, the stifling curtain would eventually be lifted. Noises would ring out, most of them behind the colonnades but some before them; challenges would be flung and steps taken, some backward but some forward, as many white and black southerners showed an increasing concern with normal economic and social objectives. Many of the first challenges were mere gropings for a better way of life for common whites, as exemplified in the farmer uprisings within the Democratic party during the 1880s. But one was a genuine striving for important change—the Populist movement. C. Vann Woodward has contended, and I think demonstrated, that southern Populists were "consistently more radical" in demanding economic reform than the westerners. Even more remarkable was their advocacy of racial reform, of political equality for blacks, an end that they pursued against "incredible odds." Woodward rightly stresses that this commitment was unique in the white South. He might have added that with the exception of the stand of the Radical Republicans, it was unique in the North.[4]

The challenges and the clamor would continue during the twentieth century and would become more frequent and strident. As before, however, most of the efforts were gropings toward vague economic objectives and were concerned mainly with improving the lot of whites. The agrarian demagogues—to use that imprecise term—exploited the frustrations of poverty and ignorance and employed a violent rhetoric against the holders of power. But once in power themselves, most of them did remarkably little to help those they had exploited, either because they did not know what had to be done or because they were thwarted by the skilled resistance of the old rulers. Moreover, the demagogues, with rare exceptions, did not include blacks in their economic plans, operating on the unrealistic premise that poverty could be alleviated by aiding one part of the poor while ignoring the other; as for the demagogues who did not ignore the Negroes, they attacked them as being in some way responsible for the plight of the whites.

Appearing simultaneously with the demagogues were the middle-class progressive reformers, who emerged usually in urban centers and were concerned mainly with such problems as the city scene, utilities, and bossism. They employed a moderate rhetoric and accomplished some moderate reforms, but they did little to alter existing power relationships and included blacks in their benefits only incidentally. Very rarely did a biracial movement surface or was a biracial social order advocated, in fleeting moments in labor disputes or in the erratic rise of the Southern Tenant Farmers Union. Still, in the first three decades of the century the South had witnessed things it had not seen since the slavery-segregation issue had possessed the southern mind—a stirring of thought and a forced discussion of issues hitherto not deemed discussable, a growing awareness that economic and social issues mattered as much as racial shibboleths, and as a result of this ferment, a questioning of the sacredness of West's monolith, of the holy of holies itself.

Those white politicians who were beginning to question—and for a time they were few in number—did not dare to call for the overthrow of the monument. Indeed, they paid lip service to its inscriptions while chipping away at its base, extolled its ideal while eroding its reality. They were segregationists "but"—for segregation but for this right or that right for blacks. In manipulating their strategy they demonstrated what William Appleman Williams has called the white southerner's talent for working the system from the side.[5] Some of them accomplished significant successes in equalizing economic benefits, but their manipulations required time to effect change and were not directed to bringing the monolith down, a result which most of them could not admit even to themselves they wanted to realize. Its overthrow was the achievement of another group of southerners, a group who could not wait—black southerners, during the 1960s.

An adequate discussion of the civil rights movement here is prevented by considerations of space and limitations of knowledge. It can only be recorded that it was a movement of abounding vitality, employing the technique of direct action, and of stirring success. As Pat Watters has written: "A minority of the region's people had forced change of basic institutions against the will of the majority."[6]

There may be armchair strategists or cocktail circle critics who think that the objective of the movement, the ending of legal segregation, was not very radical. Such persons should ponder Vincent Harding's observation that for blacks the goal of winning assimilation into southern society, indeed, into American society, was not simplistic or moderate but radical—in fact, revolutionary.[7]

Another result of the movement deserves recording—the almost instant and astonishing crumbling of white resistance to public integration once integration was decreed, and the comfortable adaptation to new racial practices. It is not contended here that the South is the most integrated section of the country, although it may be that, or that it has become the nation's model of race relations, although there are flickering suggestions that it will become that. Nevertheless, Marshall Frady's prediction could prove accurate: that "it may be the South after all where the nation's general malaise of racial alienation first finds resolution."[8] His hope is shared by various black leaders. Father A. J. McKnight, a leader in the black cooperative movement, has said: "If the black man has a chance in this country, it's in the South; the North is hopeless as far as the black situation is concerned." And Fannie Lou Hamer, when asked if Negroes had a better chance in the South, replied simply: "I like the South better than I do the North. I would rather live here."[9]

The possibility that white and black southerners could resolve the racial malaise has intrigued writers and caused them to speculate as to the reasons this could happen. Willie Morris has suggested that members of the two races can act together more easily in the South because they have similar "rhythms and tempos." Expressing the same thought but with a different emphasis, Pat Watters argues that the races "have had a human intercourse of sorts (however crippled and cruel) lacking elsewhere." Leslie Dunbar has offered a shrewd explanation of the unexpected yielding of the whites. "I have never met a white Southerner," Dunbar wrote, "not even the most determined of segregationists, who did not betray some moral uncertainty; and in that fact he differs and is set apart from the majority of his fellow Americans." Therefore, Dunbar concluded, after the white has made and lost his fight he can forget it: "He has, after all, shared a land with his black neighbors for a long while; he can manage well enough, even if the patterns change."[10]

These formulas of a shared experience are useful in achieving an understanding of the present situation in the South. But as explanations of why it has come about, they are incomplete and inadequate. They do not account for the abrupt shift of the blacks from apparent docility to angry militance, nor for the move, almost as sudden, of the whites from savage resistance to serene cooperation. These phenomena are the result of something implanted deep in the southern psyche—an inclination to take extreme stances as a life style. W. J. Cash identifies the southerner's dominant trait as an intense individualism, perhaps "the most intense individualism the world has seen since the Italian Renaissance and its men of 'terrible fury.'"[11] Such men take extreme positions on all issues. The positions have usually been conservative but sometimes have been radical, as in the explosive dissent of the Populists and the brave defiances of some politicians. The southern style rarely allows a middle ground. As Aubrey Williams once remarked wryly: "In the South we have no liberals—only conservatives and radicals."[12]

The tendency to extremism in the whites has its roots in the southern past. They, like the blacks, have lived long as second-class citizens. Their relegation began even before the Civil War when they came under the disapproval of the majority section for their support of slavery. Since the war they have experienced suppression and poverty and frustration and an increasing sense of alienation from the outside power that held them down while mocking at their backwardness. They heard enough of the mockery, in books and journals, on radio and television, and in the question asked so frequently and always with wondering scorn: "How is it—you know—what is it really like down there?"[13] Feeling the pervasive contempt of the majority and all the other frustrations of their environment, the whites turned usually to conservative leaders who salved their egos with reassurances that they were, despite all the sneers, the best people in the country, who proclaimed that there was no need for change in a society already happy and stable, who cried up the racial issue if they saw their constituents becoming interested in other issues—in short, extremists bent on preserving the status quo. Occasionally, however, the system produced leaders who talked about the present, who called for change, who subordinated or spanned race and section—genuine radicals who had to overcome greater obstacles than radicals in other regions. Two of them were so remarkable as to deserve commemoration.

Lyndon B. Johnson on numerous occasions expounded on his admiration for Franklin D. Roosevelt, the man who had been like a father to him, who had shaped his early political thinking. He liked to think of himself as Roosevelt's heir, and as President he aspired to lead as Roosevelt had. But in introspective moments he recognized that he had a very different political ancestry. An old friend of his once remarked that if Johnson had permitted himself as a young man a fantasy dream as he drifted off to sleep, it probably had been the fantasy that he was the heir of Roosevelt—but he woke in the morning to the knowledge that he was really the heir of Huey Long.[14]

Johnson, in fact, realized his link with Huey and admitted Huey's influence upon him. In a speech in New Orleans near the close of the 1964 campaign he recalled that when he had gone to Washington as a young secretary to a Texas congressman, he had made an arrangement with the Senate page office to notify him when Senator Long was about to make a speech. He had listened to Huey's "every word," and "I never heard him make a speech that I didn't think was calculated to do some good for some people who needed some speeches made for them and couldn't make them for themselves." Thirty years ago Long had advocated goals just recently realized, Johnson went on—full employment, enlarged educational opportunities, medical care, and social security. "He was against poverty," Johnson snapped at his audience, not completely friendly to him nor to Long, ". . . and spoke [against it] until his voice was hoarse."[15]

Although Johnson acknowledged a relationship with Long, he placed it in a narrow political context—they were two men who happened to have the same objectives in government. The Texan did not seem to realize that the kinship between him and Huey was more than fortuitous or political, that it was a thing of the spirit or self, a way of looking at life and the system and a way of operating the system, an expression of the peculiar social-economic environment from which both had come. They were southern whites who had chosen to be dissenters, one early in his career, the other later, and in accomplishing their dissenting goals each developed a distinctive style, because in their society such a style was necessary to accomplishment and being products of that society they naturally assumed it. It was a style that was alien to Roosevelt and his world, or to John F. Kennedy and his.

The resemblances between Huey and Lyndon are many. They were born into families of similar economic background—average farm families, neither richer nor poorer than others in their immediate area, although, as both came to realize early, poor in comparison with many persons in their states. The Longs and the Johnsons had to work hard to make a living, and although neither family knew real poverty, each had only a secondhand knowledge of real plenty. Huey and Lyndon occasionally exaggerated the hardships of their early lives, but they had experienced some hardship and had seen other persons experience more; both recalled in later years witnessing the tragedy of farms sold under mortgage. Each had fathers and grandfathers who preached Populist philosophies to them, and each grew up in an area that had a tradition of agrarian dissent—Long in Winn Parish in the Louisiana uplands and Johnson in the Texas hill country.[16]

In exercising leadership, the two men displayed startlingly similar qualities. Each had that abnormal energy that generally characterizes the great politician and enables him to accomplish seemingly impossible tasks. Long usually worked twenty hours a day and Johnson eighteen hours. Not content to restrict their labors to face-to-face contacts, both were inveterate telephone users: Long called individuals at all hours of the day or night; Johnson on an average took one hundred calls per day. They worked hard because they were oppressed by time. "I may not live long enough to do everything I want to do," Huey said once. "I just can't afford to be slowed up." Mrs. Johnson, who tried vainly to get her husband to slow down, once exclaimed: "Lyndon acts as if there is never going to be a tomorrow."[17]

One outlet for this energy was also a technique of governing. Both men prided themselves on their knowledge of detail, of everything going on around them, but especially of people, enemies and friends. Each believed that if he knew enough, he could control the actions of other men; if he knew more about the other man than that man knew about him, he would be his superior in any encounter. Long assumed that every man had something in his past to conceal. "I can frighten or buy ninety-nine out of every hundred men," he once boasted. Johnson, in the words of one observer, sensed "that every man had his price or his breaking point."[18] This urge to dominate sometimes asserted itself to destroy even friends or associates if they would not submit to domination. Huey sometimes broke a man in his organization merely to show his power. "He liked to break people, especially the strong . . . ," one admirer recalled. "But then they knew their place." An admirer of Johnson spoke in similar wry tribute: "The trouble with Lyndon is that he is a sonofabitch. The next worse trouble is that he is a great sonofabitch. He will probably do more for the United States, destroying everybody around him, than any other President."[19]

Long and Johnson were alike finally in that they had a common style of communication, a style that was shaped in the rural South where they had been shaped. In their environment a politician, especially a dissenting one, had to reach across great distances to arouse a submerged electorate, had, in Theodore White's words, to "out-shout, out-dramatize, out-campaign, out-smile, and out-entertain" the other man.[20] He had also to out-promise him, or if not this, to express his promises in exaggerated terms. Huey was the more adept, or more realistic, in proposing goals that seemed realizable and easily adapted his stump style to the then-new medium of radio. Lyndon too often painted his large aspirations as accomplishments and could not adapt his style to television; having to operate in a time when the media were more sophisticated and snobbish, he became a victim of the "credibility gap."

In their private and sometimes in their public style of communication, both men had the southern rural politician's gift of catching up a meaning or a moral in an earthy idiom. Long ran to profanity, specializing in reflections on paternal or maternal ancestry, Johnson to four-letter words. When Hiram W. Evans, head of the Ku Klux Klan, threatened to come to Louisiana to campaign against Huey, the Kingfish authorized this statement to the press: "Quote me as saying that that Imperial bastard will never set foot in Louisiana, and that when I call him a sonofabitch I am not using profanity, but am referring to the circumstances of his birth." Asked if he saw any resemblance between himself and Hitler, Huey roared: "Don't liken me to that sonofabitch. Anybody that lets his public policies be mixed up with religious prejudices is a plain Goddamned fool." Johnson's barnyard vocabulary was a matter of wonder to reporters and shock to easterners. Explaining that he had considered firing J. Edgar Hoover but had found it too difficult, he said: "Well, it's probably better to have him inside the tent pissing out, than outside pissing in." Asked, when Senate majority leader, why he had not replied to a speech by Vice-President Richard Nixon, he said: "Boys, I may not know much but I know the difference between chicken shit and chicken salad." Huey could almost instantly pass from crudeness to lofty and poetic language, and so could Lyndon. One of Johnson's cabinet members, reflecting on this quality in his leader, said: "This was a man like a combination of Boccaccio and Machiavelli and John Keats."[21]

Although as southern politicians, Long and Johnson had many similarities, they differed in significant ways. They diverged most largely in their concept of power. Both desired it and exulted in its use. Both wanted to alter the existing system in significant degree, but in attempting to achieve their goals they resorted to very different techniques.

Long was a rare, perhaps an unexampled, politician. He was aware of his singularity as he was aware of everything else about himself. As English correspondent Anthony Howard has perceptively noted: "His whole preoccupation was with himself—a subject of study that he clearly found as fascinating as everyone else." He was not being playful or boastful when he told a group of reporters trying to classify him to say that he was "sui generis" and to let it go at that.[22]

Long differed most from other politicians in possessing an almost chilling capacity to calculate events, in being able to stand apart and view himself and his constituencies and coolly measure his political chances and plan his political future. As a youth, he had said that he would be successively a secondary state official, then governor, and

United States senator, and finally President; and at the time of his death at the age of forty-two he had achieved all but the last goal. It is possible to read too much into his predictions. This was not an expression of the kind of brooding mysticism that possessed Adolf Hitler. Long was not driven by a demonic dream to go on to a predetermined end regardless of the consequences. He intended originally to reach the top by employing the traditional methods of the American politician. Still, his sense of destiny was unusual in a politician, and because of it he was capable of altering the methods.

Huey began his climb by winning election to the Public Service Commission in 1918. Before his arrival on it the commission had been a moribund agency whose seats were usually reserved for elderly political hacks. He transformed it into an effective and modern regulatory institution and in the process made himself a statewide reputation by attacking the Standard Oil Company and other corporations. He ran for the governorship in 1924, narrowly missed victory, ran again in 1928 and was elected. It is at this point, as he assumed the office, that we encounter a problem in judging him, an enigma in his makeup that has not been resolved and probably can never be resolved.

While still a youth, Huey had developed a set of political beliefs from whose principles he never wavered. He had read a great deal about the concentration of wealth and had concluded that a more equitable distribution of it was necessary, although at this time he had no definite plan as to how the redistribution should be brought about. From his environment he had absorbed a tradition of dissent. His native Winn Parish had opposed secession in 1860–1861 and remained cool to the war for southern independence, had been a stronghold of the Populist party during the 1890s, and after the passage of Populism had nurtured a surprisingly strong Socialist party. It was the dissent of Populism that most influenced the young Long. He took from it a conviction that poverty and squalor were not inevitable and that government had an obligation to combat these evils.[23]

As governor, Long proposed a program calling for massive highway construction, increased aid to education (including free textbooks for every child regardless of religion or race and free night schools to erase adult illiteracy), improved public health facilities, and, to finance these projects, bigger corporate taxes and deficit spending. It was not a radical program but rather a traditional progressive or liberal one. But to Louisiana conservatives, unseeing and unteachable, it was radical, akin to communism, and they fought it at every turn and, driven by fear and rage, tried to remove Long from office by impeaching him.

He defeated the attempt, but after the ordeal he seemed a changed man. "It was his crossroads," one of his sisters said. "It did something to him." What it did constitutes the problem suggested earlier in this paper. Some of his associates think that until the impeachment he was a typical reformer, somewhat idealistic and inclined to use traditional methods to achieve reform, but that the experience transformed him, made him ruthless and insatiably hungry for power. Other associates insist that the impeachment did not change him, that he had always lusted for power and would have taken it if there had been no attempt on him. The question cannot be settled, but there is probably truth in both views. Huey had ideals before the impeachment and would continue to have them, but he had never had any illusion that change would be accomplished by idealistic methods alone. The impeachment made him realize the lengths to which conservatives would go to resist change, impressed on him the difficulty of effecting change within the democratic framework. He had always known that power was necessary to a politician, was what politics was really about, but from now on he was not satisfied to have "normal, circumscribed" power. He demanded "unbridled power," and after he went to the Senate in 1932, he created in Louisiana a domination not seen before or since in an American state, one-man rule of all three branches of government.[24] As he pursued his last dream, the presidency, he would have a solid base in his own state, would never have to look over his shoulder to catch the reaction at home.

Long came to the Senate with one purpose: he would use this great forum as a platform to advance his presidential candidacy. While waiting for the right time to make his bid, he would cooperate with his nominal leader, President Roosevelt, if the latter adopted the Long economic program, that is, let himself be dominated by Huey. Roosevelt would not subordinate himself to anyone, however; and the two men broke and fought out their differences before a fascinated public. This was probably the way Huey wanted it. Oppressed by time, he could not wait to be President; and he had come to have great contempt for Roosevelt as a man and as a politician and leader. Roosevelt was not combatting the Depression vigorously enough, he thought. More importantly, the President was not doing anything to solve the most pressing problem in America, the maldistribution of wealth—was not bringing about needed and drastic change.

As a national leader, Long was more radical than he had been in Louisiana. Impressed since his youth by the danger posed by concentrated wealth, he made the redistribution of it his principal issue in the Senate. In 1934 he revealed a specific plan to accomplish his aim, named, to the fright of conservatives, "Share Our Wealth." It was based on the taxing power of the federal government. The government would impose two taxes, a capital-levy tax that would prevent a family from owning a fortune of more than five million dollars and an income tax that would prohibit a family from earning more than one million dollars in a year. As Huey put it, he was going to cut the great American fortunes down to "frying size." From the revenue derived from these taxes, the government would provide every family in the country with a "homestead" of five thousand dollars, or "enough for a home, an automobile, a radio, and the ordinary conveniences." The government would also guarantee that every family receive an annual income of $2000 to $3000, provide pensions to the aged, and finance the college education of young persons of proven ability. Lastly, the government would limit the hours of labor to thirty hours a week and eleven months a year and would aid farmers in marketing their crops. In 1935 Huey added details to his plan—a vast public works program, a central bank, "absolute government control" of the railroads with the probability they would have to be nationalized, federal aid to education at all levels, and a huge public health program to ensure that for the first time the government "would care for the health of the American people."[25]

Why did Long become more radical on the national scene than he had been in Louisiana? Critics then and later charged that he did not really believe in his SOW plan, that it was a nostrum he had hastily concocted to help him win the presidency. The critics perhaps could not believe that a southerner could be a radical. Actually, Huey had not changed. He had held egalitarian or populist beliefs since his youth, and the problem of concentrated wealth had been one of his earliest interests. He had not addressed himself to the question as governor because it could not be dealt with on the state level. But as senator and would-be President he could do something about the problem, and the advent of the Depression had convinced him that action had to be taken fast. His motivation throughout his career, other than his own advancement, was a determination to help poor people. In this respect, it is significant that in his category of those who needed help he included the blacks, the poorest of the poor. He did not have to face a civil rights movement, and he could not profit from the small black vote in Louisiana; but with a realism rare in southern politicians, and for that matter in northern politicians, he realized that poverty could not be erased by aiding just one segment of the poor. The black press appreciated his concern. As one editor expressed it, Huey was for the man "farthest down," and although the Negro was seldom mentioned in Huey's speeches, the black was included in the "farthest down" program.[26] Some black men demonstrated their appreciation of the Kingfish by naming one of their sons after him. One such child was born in Monroe—Huey P. Newton.

Long's encounter with the Roosevelt administration reinforced his opinion that democratic politics was incompatible with reform politics, that important change could not be achieved in what Tom Wicker has called "the slow and manipulable workings of democracy." Fiercely attacked by the New Deal liberals for his methods in Louisiana, he concluded that these moderates were more concerned with form than with substance.[27] In Louisiana he had dispensed with the substance of democracy while retaining the form, and if he had become President he might have established a similar rule in the national government, not because he wanted to be a dictator but because he would have convinced himself that effective reform could not be accomplished unless he had dictatorial powers. Capable of subverting the system to ensure change, he stands as perhaps the supreme American radical.

In contrast to Long, Johnson came to his rendezvous with reform over troubled and tortuous paths, advancing and then retreating but inexorably moving forward. He reached it finally as President, and in that office he secured the passage of legislation that Huey had fought for vainly, in the areas of education, health, and welfare, and other measures that even Huey had not dreamed of. Forced to confront the civil rights issue, he embraced it and pushed to enactment bills that provided a basis for far-reaching changes in race relations. In the general area of reform, however, he was not as radical as Huey. Although he launched an imaginative program to alleviate poverty, he did not attempt to redistribute wealth or to alter seriously the power relationship between the government and business. More importantly, he did not give up on the system or consider subverting it. Lyndon did not want to master the system but to manipulate it, to bring conflicting persons and opinions together in compromise, his celebrated and sometimes ridiculed "consensus."

He once said that his tendency to resolve conflict derived from his southern heritage, from his memory of a land "where brother was once divided against brother." It came more probably from his experience as a majority leader of the Senate, and was also, although he did not realize this, a technique forced on him by his time. He sought to effect reform when most Americans were relatively prosperous, whereas Huey had operated in the crisis of the Depression. His task was more difficult on another score. The size of the United States is one reason that radicalism has fared badly here. Largeness is normally the enemy of change—the larger the federation, the more difficult it is to infect all its parts with the fever of discontent. Huey in the Depression could try to unite the parts with flaming class rhetoric, but Lyndon had to appeal to the reason, or self-interest, of consensus.[28]

Johnson has claimed that as a youth and young man he was influenced by the Populist ideas of his hill-country neighbors: they believed that government had an obligation to help people to a better way of life, and so did he. That he had leftist leanings is attested by his admiration for Long. He also looked up to Maury Maverick, the crusading congressman from the San Antonio district. It may be doubted, however, that his early views were as radical as he remembers, or that as a fledgling politician he even had a coherent philosophy. His third hero was Roosevelt, who stood to the right of Long and Maverick. Elected to Congress at the beginning of Roosevelt's second administration, Johnson followed generally the lead of his chief and voted with liberals on most issues, being especially ardent in support of public power. He was at this time a Texas or southern liberal. His votes were in part a reflection of his views and of the desires of his constituents, white farmers who liked the administration's agricultural policy and especially welcomed cheap electricity. But his votes resulted quite as much, possibly more, from his adoration of Roosevelt, his friend and also protector. That Roosevelt's influence may have been the greatest factor is evidenced by the fact that after the President's death Lyndon moved to the right.[29]

His main departures from the New Deal line had been on matters of oil depletion and civil rights. No Texas politician could oppose the tax favor to the oil industry and hope to survive; such an act would have been as quixotic as being against milk in Wisconsin or coal in West Virginia. Nor could Johnson support measures to breach the wall of segregation. Although his district contained few blacks—approximately one out of every seven persons in it was non-white—it was a typical southern constituency, committed to preserving white supremacy. Reflecting its prejudices, Johnson as congressman voted against six civil rights bills. He later explained that at that time he did not think these bills were the right way to handle the problem but candidly added that his position was largely dictated by political considerations: "One heroic stand and I'd be back home, defeated, unable to do any good for anyone." There was, however, another side to his record. Like other southern politicians who were secretly troubled by the region's racial stance, he often maneuvered behind the scenes to secure economic benefits for blacks and Mexican-Americans, as he had done when head of the National Youth Administration in Texas. And not once in his twelve years in the House, according to a student of this phase of his career, did he rant about civil rights on the floor or insert in the record an anti-black diatribe, that technique of southern politicians known as "talking Nigra."[30]

In Roosevelt's death Johnson had lost more than an admired leader. To many southern, and northern, liberals the President had stood as a guardian who with his friendship could bestow prestige upon a congressman and award projects to his district. But with Roosevelt gone and the reform impetus of the New Deal obviously spent, Johnson began to inch to the right. His change in direction became more pronounced after he won election to the Senate in 1949. Now he had to represent a much larger constituency and a more conservative one, the vast complex of Texas with its varied economic interests. In the Senate he often voted with the conservatives, supporting the Taft-Hartley bill and other anti-labor measures. But on some issues he continued to vote liberal. He was clearly trying to stake out for himself a viable middle position. In part, he was responding to the realities of Texas politics. The Democratic party of his state was rent by division, the most bitter being between conservatives and liberals. Lyndon had always to tread warily between these two factions, to play one against the other, to hope to satisfy both. He never had a solid base in his own state, and this fact explains some of his meanderings in national politics. Unlike Long, he had continually to look over his shoulder to measure the reaction at home. But he had an additional reason to follow a middle course. He wanted to be a national and not just a regional politician, and he even harbored the dream of being President. Thus, although he pleased conservatives in Texas with some of his votes, he displeased them with others as he tried to reach out to that constituency beyond Texas and the South, whose aspirations he wanted to understand and if possible gratify.[31]

His ambivalence was most apparent in the area of civil rights. As a senator he occasionally had to discuss the issue that he had been able to ignore as a congressman, but even now he never made a ranting or rabid speech. His strongest criticism of the liberals pressing for civil rights, voiced with greater intensity after he became the leader of his party, was that they were obsessed with a question not capable then of resolution. "I want to run the Senate," he exclaimed once. "I want to pass the bills that need to be passed. . . . But all I ever hear from the liberals is Nigra, Nigra, Nigra." Interestingly, in his New Orleans speech in the presidential campaign of 1964 he used the same refrain of "Nigra" to express his impatience with white supremacists who could think of nothing but race. That he was not obsessed with race he demonstrated in various acts. When he heard that the one funeral parlor in a small Texas town had refused to bury a Mexican lad killed in Korea, he arranged to have the youth buried at Arlington National Cemetery and accompanied the family to the funeral. He broke the segregation barrier at the Rice Hotel in Houston by refusing to attend a dinner there in his honor unless Negroes were invited. And he refused to sign the Southern Manifesto protesting the Supreme Court's desegregation decision, a defiance that caused night riders to burn a cross on the lawn of his ranch.[32]

Johnson broke finally with his racist past, and with many of his segregationist colleagues, in 1957. Using the prestige of his position as majority leader and his unequaled parliamentary skills, he secured in that year the passage of the first civil rights act since Reconstruction. It was only a partial or beginning solution of the problem, but still its mere enactment was a considerable achievement. As Theodore H. White perceptively noted, Johnson had done something that had been prevented for generations—he had made "the matter of race relations again a subject for discussion and legislation in Washington." But in order to get the bill through, he had had to accept compromises; and for this he was bitterly denounced by the liberals, who viewed him, in the words of one writer, "as the modern Machiavelli in a Stetson hat and Texas boots who had headed the civil rights forces off at the pass." They did not similarly denounce northerners with civil rights records who also accepted the compromises.[33]

He had expected the criticisms, predicting that his support of the bill would be treated "cynically in some quarters" and "misunderstood in others." His motives in sponsoring it were several. He undoubtedly hoped to further his presidential candidacy. But something more than ambition was involved. As his national interests had widened, he had acquired a broadened and deepened vision of his country, and that dream included political equality for black Americans. He would later claim that he had been concerned about the status of minorities since his days as a teacher in a small Mexican-American school in Texas, when he had observed how prejudice had scarred the children there. His recollection was probably accurate.

Johnson had never been a racist, in the sense of hating members of other races, although in his career he had hewed largely to the racist line. But he had not had to think much about the problems of minorities before he became a senator and a presidential aspirant. Now he was thinking, and because of his origins he would end up with a larger concept of the problem than would politicians in other sections. In his vision of equality he would include also that second group of looked-down-on Americans, white southerners. That he had in mind whites as well as blacks is indicated in a passage in his speech supporting the bill in which he asked his colleagues to forswear hatred and prejudice. "Political ambition which feeds off hatred of the North or hatred of the South is doomed to frustration," he declaimed. "There is a compelling need for a solution that will enable all Americans to live in dignity and in unity."[34]

Johnson continued to support civil rights legislation, but his votes and voice did his presidential candidacy no good. Beyond the borders of his own region, he garnered few supporters, was assumed to be a secret segregationist. As Louis Heren has well put it, "the curse of the South" was still upon him. He realized the handicap he carried: "I don't think anybody from the South will be nominated in my lifetime," he said in 1958. "If so, I don't think he'll be elected."[35] Although he persisted in his campaign, he was resigned to defeat by Kennedy in 1960; he knew, as Heren observed, that as a southerner "he had less chance than a Catholic of being elected president." But, to the astonishment of many of his friends, having lost the first prize, he accepted the second prize, the offer of the vice-presidential nomination from Kennedy. He perhaps hoped to be the heir apparent in 1968, but even if this reward were not achieved, he could as vice-president become a national politician and thus move more surely along the road he had now marked off to travel.[36]

His bright hopes were soon extinguished. After helping his party win the election by holding key southern states in line, he entered on the phase of his career that has been aptly called "the Johnson eclipse." As vice-president he would be a shadowy and pathetic figure, obscured by the insignificance of the office and by the dazzling luster of the man in the Oval Office, who, as I. F. Stone has observed, was the first of all the Presidents to be a Prince Charming. Johnson, who knew about power and had exulted in its use, now had none and could only watch others use it, most of them younger men, the courtiers of Camelot who ignored or patronized him and out of his hearing called him Uncle Cornpone.

Then came a blazing day in 1963, and as one correspondent has written, "suddenly, shockingly," he was President, the uncultivated southerner with his strange style that grated on the eastern opinion-molders, replacing Prince Charming, whose style had captivated the molders because it seemed like their own. There was a difference in style between Kennedy and Johnson, admitted by some of the latter's friends, one of whom summed it up as "the difference between a John Stuart Mill and a combination of John C. Calhoun and Baron Munchausen."[37] Johnson realized that his image was a handicap. He feared that he had another and greater burden, the prejudice against him because of his sectional origin. But whether he knew it or not, his origin also gave him a strength. A southerner committed now to change, he was committed more deeply than politicians from other sections were likely to be, and he would move farther and faster on the road to change than Kennedy had or probably would have.

In the space permitted here it is possible only to sketch an outline of the changes he brought about. The War on Poverty may have employed some tactics that were not fitted to the problem and that caused it to fall short of complete victory, and the vision of the Great Society may have held forth hopes that were not fully realizable. But both were grandly conceived, and in defending them Johnson uttered perhaps the most eloquent commitments to social justice ever made by a President.[38] The torrent of legislation began to roll immediately after his accession to the presidency, swelled to a tide during the hundred days following his assumption of the office in his own right, slowed somewhat during the remainder of his administration but still continued—435 acts by one estimate, many of them landmark laws dealing with education, health services and medical care, housing, welfare, urban and rural renewal, and the preservation of natural beauty.[39] One member of Johnson's cabinet, Anthony Celebrezze, in commenting on the enactment of thirty-six bills in which he was interested, has declared his belief that 70 percent of them would have failed to pass if Johnson had not intervened. Another member, Wilbur J. Cohen, has said that the legislative program was so encompassing and came so furiously that it could not be comprehended by the public. "It was too big, it was too much for them to swallow," Cohen stated, adding that it would not be appreciated until twenty years hence when the historians could get around to evaluating it. Until that time it should be possible to accept White's appraisal of what he called Johnson's "legislative architecture." Within that framework, White predicted, American life would "proceed for a generation."[40]

One of the more impressive achievements of that architecture was the enactment of the four milestone civil rights measures—the Civil Rights Act of 1964, the Voting Rights Act of 1965, the Fair Housing Act of 1966, and the Federal Jury Reform Act of 1968. Johnson was, of course, only one of the individuals and forces responsible for their passage, but he was the strongest single influence, and without his support they might not have been enacted and certainly not in the form they took. He had made his commitment to civil rights during the frustration of the vice-presidency, and whatever the combination of reasons that brought him to it, the commitment was final and complete. As one observer put it, on this issue he had decided to shove in "all his chips." Speaking at Gettysburg in 1963, he said: "The Negro today asks justice. We do not answer him—and we do not answer those who lie beneath this soil—. . . by asking 'Patience.'" With the memories of Gettysburg around him, he perhaps reflected that his progress toward civil rights had been like that of an earlier speaker there toward emancipation. He once discussed understandingly what he called Abraham Lincoln's "troubled journey towards a new concept." His decision on becoming President to move for a civil rights bill was not a sudden purpose born in the shock of Kennedy's death. He had completed his own journey before becoming President.[41]

In pleading for support of the civil rights measures, Johnson spoke in moving words and with unmistakable intention. "We have talked long enough in this country about equal rights. . . . As far as the writ of Federal law will run, we must abolish not some, but all racial discrimination. . . . It is not enough just to open the gates of opportunity. All our citizens must have the ability to walk through those gates. . . . And the time for waiting is gone."[42] His performance impressed even doubting critics. An academic observer wrote of his address to Congress asking for support of the Voting Rights Act: "He stood at the podium the first President in American history to identify himself, publicly and in words of unqualified intensity, with the cause of the Negro." Ralph Ellison, moved by the President's address at Howard University, "To Fulfill These Rights," wrote that it "spelled out the meaning of full integration for Negroes" in a way no President had before. Also moved by the address but employing a different idiom to express his feelings was CORE leader Floyd McKissick, who said that it was a speech "to make a rattlesnake cry."[43]

Johnson insisted that his civil rights bills be passed with few or no concessions to the opposition, most of which, but not all, came from his own South. It has been surmised that as a southern President he could not accept compromise, that if he did, he would be accused of wanting no more than partial success. The more probable truth is that as a southern President and now a southern reformer, he was resolved to go all the way on this issue, and for the benefit of the whites as well as the blacks. It has been insufficiently appreciated that he believed the elimination of segregation would lift an onus from his section, would enable southern whites to stand as equals with that majority that had looked down on them for their racial practices. "I know the burdens that the South has borne," he said in one address to his people. "I know the troubles that the South has seen. I know the ordeals that have tried the South through all of these years. And I want to see those burdens lifted off the South. I want the ordeals to end and the South to stand where it should stand as the full and honored part of a proud and united land." Wicker, almost the only writer to note this aspect of his strategy, has said that only a southern President could have convinced southerners that they should discard their feelings of alienation. He was assuring them that after all "they were not immoralists or degenerates or colonial subjects but men who had lost a struggle." His promise of reunion, spoken in an accent they understood, helped to reconcile southerners to the reality that the struggle was lost.[44]

That accent which fell so easily on southern ears struck black leaders at first with dismay. Whitney Young said that, if ten years before Johnson's accession they had heard a new President speaking in such a drawl, many of them would have gotten on the first boat for Ghana. "But we know where LBJ stands," Young continued, "and we realize that he is a sincere and dedicated supporter of civil rights."[45] Most other black leaders came to share Young's appreciation of Johnson, as witness the following testimonials.

Ellison: "When all of the returns are in, perhaps President Johnson will have to settle for being recognized as the greatest American President for the poor and for the Negroes, but that, as I see it, is a very great honor indeed."[46] Clarence Mitchell: "President Johnson made a greater contribution to giving a dignified and hopeful status to Negroes in the United States than any other President."[47] Roy Wilkins: "He committed the White House and the Administration to the involvement of government in getting rid of the inequalities between people solely on the basis of race. And he did this to a greater extent than any other President in our history."[48] Robert C. Weaver: "I don't know when he got religion or how he got it, but he really understood what was bugging poor people and black people."[49] And finally Charles Evers: "Johnson did one hell of a job for black folks. Lyndon did more to make civil rights a reality than any President we have had. I bite no bones about it."[50]

In view of the magnitude of his achievements it might be thought that he would have commanded admiration and respect while President and that in the preliminary estimates of his stewardship he would be ranked as a good, perhaps a great, President. But almost the contrary has been true. Most of the evaluations of him, whether made during his presidency or after it, have been highly critical. He has been awarded at the best only qualified praise, and more frequently has been subjected to scorn or obloquy. (The tributes occasioned by his death may or may not herald a more benign view.) The prevailing view is usually and easily explained as a reaction to the Vietnam war, the great simplifier of so many judgments of the 1960s. But even before the full impact of that tragic conflict began to take its toll of the nation, it was evident that Johnson was not an admired President or, despite his great victory in the election of 1964, really a popular one. He was not held in high opinion by the members of the guild who in our society have so much to do with forming opinion—the media-men, the lords of the liberal establishment, and the intellectuals. More seriously, he was not cherished by the masses of people he had helped, whom he wanted to reach out to, whose love he craved. The reasons for his failure to evoke a favorable image demand speculation in an appraisal of him.[51]

He seemed unable to express his ideals and his program to the people or to represent himself to them as a man or as a politician. Some political journalists and media commentators have suggested that he failed simply because he was a poor communicator. The critics have in mind certain technical shortcomings, and these he certainly had. Although he was overpowering in man-to-man persuasion or with small groups and was effective before rural or smalltown crowds, he was ill at ease before large formal audiences. His voice was either too low or too loud; his delivery was halting; and his syntax was often confused. On television he was likely to be a disaster. Not as adaptable a politician as Long, who readily mastered radio, Johnson was never comfortable with television. As one of his secretaries has written, he came before the cameras "too determined to make a presentation instead of a communion with his fellow Americans."[52]

Formidable as his faults of technique were, they do not explain his failure to reach people. Other Presidents have had similar faults and still been esteemed. Harry Truman had a jerky delivery and Dwight Eisenhower had notable difficulties with syntax. In fact, of the chief executives of recent times only Roosevelt was consistently successful in communicating with the masses. Kennedy was a persuasive figure on the television screen, but he too occasionally had a calamity on this medium.[53] Johnson's defects were more apparent to the intellectuals than to the voters, and his forensic style was a major factor in alienating the intellectual community, a separation that began in 1964 before his conduct of foreign affairs had aroused other emotions. A visiting British journalist was astounded and repelled by the delight intellectuals took in reviling Johnson; their only feeling toward him seemed to be "a fastidious disdain." The President might be putting through legislation the intellectuals approved, but he was not saying the right words as he did it. A member of Johnson's cabinet who had moved in academic circles, in reflecting on the importance that academics attach to language, said that a weakness of theirs is that "when they come to appraise the accomplishment, the way you do it . . . is as important to them as the end result. And to some, even more."[54]

Some observers have ascribed Johnson's inability to communicate to something more fundamental than defective speaking or writing techniques. In their view, he had a defective concept of the presidency. He did not grasp that among all the things a President has to be, he must be preeminently a preacher and a teacher. "The sacerdotal, priestly, almost mystic quality of the Presidency eluded him," one commentator has said. Another has written that a President "must have the power to persuade a majority to do something they may not want to do. This was beyond Johnson." It was impossible for him because in public discourse he could not develop a theme, because in his heart he did not believe that public debate was a legitimate or necessary part of the governing process. His experience as Senate leader had instilled in him a conviction that legislation was the product of negotiation and bargaining and that speeches were only window dressing that a leader had to put up with. "He never understood the difference between the Hill and the White House," one of his most loyal aides has admitted. And so, the critique runs, Johnson himself was responsible for the image of him that emerged— the wheeler-dealer, the master manipulator, the cunning cajoler who worked his black arts unknown to the public.[55]

In part Johnson was the man of the image. Unable or unwilling to shed the habits of Senate leader, he sometimes as President bargained and bartered when he should have preached or taught. And when he tried to preach, his utterances often came out as platitudes; he never evoked broad national support for either his domestic program or his foreign policy. He was frequently deceptive and devious, and on occasion without reason. All Presidents find that at times they have to dissemble, but his penchant for secrecy was almost abnormal. One may admit the strictures, and yet a feeling persists that something is wrong in the overall picture, that the image has been painted in strokes too broad. For example, a careful reading of Johnson's public papers will show that the criticisms of his rhetoric have been grossly exaggerated. Many of his addresses were, of course, the products of other writers, as are those of any modern President, but they still represented his ideas. In a number of them he did develop a theme, and he did attempt to engage in meaningful public discourse. The critics, most of them journalists, missed this truth, as they did many of his deeper qualities, perhaps because they were distracted by his style. This matter of style, so dominant in the judgment-patterns of our time, looms large in the writings about Johnson. Repeatedly the term used to characterize his style, in wonder or distaste, is "bigger than life." Or as one writer put it, Lyndon "lacked terminal facilities." The suspicion arises that the Johnson image was partly in the eyes of the image-makers.[56]

The opinions of the image-makers have pervaded the writings about Johnson. These writings are the first historical judgment of the man, and as such they have value. But with rare exceptions they do not attempt to relate the man to the social order in which he moved. They place too much emphasis on Johnson and not enough on his milieu. Thus it is said that Johnson failed as a communicator because he could not be frank or did not know how to say the right words. He failed to arouse love or admiration because he was not a lovable or admirable man. The personal explanation leaves too many things unexplained. Why, for example, did not the people respond to his serious and lofty appeals to support his policies? Why, knowing his vast achievements, did they not cherish him? It may be that there was something in the social environment and some interaction between him and the environment that made it impossible for him to reach the people or receive a sympathetic judgment in his time.

Johnson himself believed that it was his southern origin which had prevented him from getting a fair hearing, had subjected him to derision, and finally had driven him from office. Brooding in retirement on the Pedernales, he reflected on the "disdain for the South that seems to be woven into the fabric of Northern experience" and wondered when it would end.[57] There was perception in this—his southernism had caused distrust of him and brought scorn on him and inhibited a view of him as he really was. There was also a measure of exaggeration and self-commiseration. Johnson was a very insecure man and therefore hungry for approval and assurance from other persons. Along with this he had that sectional insecurity that afflicts many white southerners, their apparent exuberant arrogance to the contrary. Like them, he yearned for esteem from those to whom he secretly felt inferior but wanted to impress, eastern liberals, eastern intellectuals, and particularly Harvard professors, the people whom Kennedy had impressed. Not getting their approbation, he ascribed his failure to their prejudice against the South, but at the same time worried that they might be right. Consequently, he was always rearranging himself for their approval and for public approval and could rarely be himself. In this he was singularly unlike Long, who did not care at all what easterners or intellectuals thought of him and would never have entertained the thought that he was inferior to Harvard professors, or, for that matter, to any person.

Johnson gave too much weight to the affliction of his southern origin. Nevertheless, he was right in sensing that he was an alien in the America of the 1960s. His origin did have something to do with the alienation because he had been shaped in the South and carried its peculiar manner with him and because many observers persisted in seeing him through the lens of their concept of the South. But the estrangement was compounded of other factors, many of which can be caught up in the word "generational." Johnson had been shaped politically in the age of the Great Depression and the dictator-ridden years before World War II, and he carried with him into the 1960s the values of that time—and was confronted with a generation that rejected those values. It may be that a much-quoted statement of one of his intellectuals in residence should be turned around to read that Johnson was the right man from the wrong place at the wrong time under the wrong circumstances. This may have been his real tragedy.[58]

He was a stranger in his time and defied the standards and style of his time—"a great, raw man of immense girth," as one observer saw him, wandering "in the Pepsi generation," a gaudy, flamboyant man, "the Jolly Green Giant," roaming the country in "the age of muted gray." One of his more sensitive aides, musing on this aspect of him has written: "He was a manipulator of men, when the young were calling for everyone to do his own thing; a believer in institutions such as government, universities, business, and trade unions, when these were under constant attack on the campuses; a paternalist, in a time of widespread submission to youthful values and desires."[59] He overstated and overacted in an age that prized understatement and self-depreciation. He believed in heroes and extolled them in the age of the non-hero. He preached patriotism, as he understood it, equating it with an appearance of strength, to an age that understood it very differently. He believed in measured, manipulated change within the system and a consensus built on compromise in a time when many people demanded radical change or aimless change and rejected the system. Long would have been much more at home in the turbulent 1960s—Huey Long, who had no interest in America's relations with the outside world and equated patriotism with the selfish designs of bankers, who had evaded military service in the war to make the world safe for democracy and had unabashedly explained to the Senate that one of his reasons for doing so was that he "was not mad at anybody over there"; Long, who believed in radical and directed change—if necessary outside the system.[60]

It is not possible as yet to arrive at a measured evaluation of Johnson. But surely it is time to take a new look at him, to attempt to see him as he really was, this tormented man from his tormented region who had such large visions of what his country might become. Until the evaluation is made, we can accept one that he himself made in a subdued moment. He said that he was not sure what the historians would say about the achievements of his administration. "But I do believe—in fact, I know—that they will all say we tried."[61]

Lyndon Johnson and the Art of Biography

The Senior Scholars' Colloquia are now in their third year, by my reckoning, as a part of the AHA program, and the program committees are convinced that they have stimulated wide interest and have added zest to the program. Several people have asked me today, rather sneeringly I thought, what a senior scholar was. In fact, several people said, smirking, "Is it something like being a senior citizen?" My reply to that is, "No, it's more like being a golden oldie."

This year's committee has defined a colloquium very simply. It's a session at which senior scholars meet informally with whatever auditors appear, talk about their work and research activities, respond to questions, and engage in discussion with those in attendance. The committee lays no injunction on the scholar as to how he chooses to conduct his session. The speaker opens the session himself, and the only suggestion the committee makes to participants is an obviously sensible one, that they make some introductory remarks, or descriptive remarks, before beginning their session. The speaker is allowed to adjourn the meeting at his discretion, although the committee suggests an hour and a half as a good maximum.

I'm engaged now in two projects. I am writing and striving to finish a history of U.S. wars aimed at the general reader and the specialist, the scholar. I am now in World War II and getting hopeful

Paper given at the 1977 American Historical Association convention in Dallas, Texas, December 29, 1977.

that eventually I'll be able to finish it. At the same time, or in time taken from the war book, I am doing research on a life of Lyndon Johnson, and it's the Johnson project that I've chosen to talk about today. In my remarks I'll say something about the state of my research. I will venture some of my ideas concerning this remarkable man, and I'll also venture some opinions about the art of biography, a subject that interests me greatly.

First of all, I think I should explain why I decided to do a life of LBJ. The desire to work on the life of Johnson was born soon after I completed my biography of Huey Long, and I think that my attraction to LBJ was inevitable. I had written about one fascinating southern politician, and here was another one, equally fascinating, waiting to be treated.

I want at this stage to introduce some of my ideas about biography and biographers, to discuss some of the problems involved in doing good biography.

First of all, and I think this is vital, the biographer has to be attracted to his subject. That is, the biographer has to feel that this person he wants to write about is an interesting and important person and a person who needs explanation. I can think of a number of men—I'm going to say "men" because heretofore most of the politicians have been men—I can think of a number of men about whom I could not write a good biography because I'm not attracted to them. Herbert Hoover, for example—I don't think I could write a biography of Herbert Hoover. Dull. Or, as I like to irritate Frank Vandiver by saying, I couldn't possibly write a good biography of Jefferson Davis. Legalistic. You have to be interested in the person you want to write about. Some men don't draw me, some men do. I like men who move things forward, who leave their world different, men who use power. I think the achievements of such men should be recognized and their motives should be examined.

Now the fact that you're drawn to a person doesn't mean that you can't be objective about him. It does not exclude objectivity, but it does presume, I think, a kind of empathy with the subject, even if the subject is villainous. I'm sure Shakespeare was attracted to Iago. A magnificent villain, but he was drawn to him. This attraction is vital. The men I have been drawn to in history are, notably, Abraham

Lincoln, Huey Long, Lyndon Johnson—great power artists. Maybe this shows something about me, I don't know. Some of my graduate students have suggested it means maybe I want power. But these are the kind of men who attract me.

And while I'm on the subject of great political leaders I will dare some other ideas. I subscribe to a version of the great man theory of history. I think the great leader appears in response to conditions. He can't come out of the blue, but in some cases, the great leader having appeared may give history a push or a direction that it otherwise would not have taken. For example, I think the situation in Germany, and I've said this before, after World War I called for a leader to appear who would in some way relieve the frustrations of the German people. But that kind of man did not have to be an Adolf Hitler. It could have been a very different kind of leader, and in that case the history of the world would have been different. The situation in Louisiana in the 1920s called for a leader who would in some way release the ambitions of the masses of Louisiana, who would help those people. But that leader did not have to be a Huey Long. It could have been a lesser leader, a lesser reformer who would have brought less change with him.

So I subscribe to a version of the great man theory of history. Of course, that theory has been in decline in recent years, which may be one reason why biography itself has been under somewhat of a cloud. At least that is the opinion of the English historian Christopher Hill. Hill says biography has been out of favor with purist historians since the decline of great men theories. "We are all sociologists now and inclined to see rulers as products of their age, rather than as directors of them—corks, not waves."

I also subscribe to the Robert Penn Warren thesis of change, that good may come out of evil. Robert Penn Warren described a politician Willie Stark, very much like Huey Long, who wanted to do good. He found that in order to do good he had to do evil, and wanting to do more good he had to do more evil, and finally, said Warren, the evil consumed him and destroyed him. I wouldn't make it so dramatic. Huey Long wanted to do good. He found that in order to do good he had to have power. He grasped for more power, and finally he wasn't sure in the end which goal he was pursuing, the good or the power. But whatever the case, whether it's Willie Stark or Huey Long, the story reminds us, I think, that the life of a great political leader may be also a great tragedy, a personal tragedy.

When you say that good may come out of evil or that leaders may have to do evil to do good, this disturbs many people. They don't like to hear this. Many people in Louisiana were disturbed at my biography of Huey Long because I didn't pause at intervals and say, "Look, this thing that I just described that he did was evil or it was bad." They wanted me, I think, to draw morals, but I don't think this is the function of the biographer, to sit in perpetual judgment. His primary job is to try and get inside his subject's brain and to see the view of the world that person had. Now if he can do that, if he can get the world view of his subject, he may be able to explain why his subject acted as he did.

That's imperative, I think; he has to get the subject's view of the world. Thus, Huey Long had a view of his world, and it was a world that was peopled by enemies who were trying to destroy him. And in that he was partly right. They were. Of course he overdid it, and he kept believing it after he had in effect almost destroyed them. But that was his view of the world and that explains, I think, why Long erected in Louisiana that tremendous power concentration of his own. He was going to erect a power structure that not all of his enemies could ever prevail against, and he felt that he had to do it that way. Now I did draw some lessons from this. I said this power structure of Long's was the most daring and dangerous power structure in American history, in any state. But I also said that men like Huey Long, the rebels in history, are often created by an unyielding establishment that refuses to recognize demands for needed change.

Now, briefly on what I plan to do with LBJ. It will be a big book; I would estimate at this stage seven or eight hundred pages, but not an exhaustive treatment. I am mindful of Namier's warning that political biography may be history's worst enemy, that the too long biography may obscure the sweep of events, or dim the grand design, or lose the supporting cast. And it will be primarily a political biography, because LBJ was primarily if not completely a political creature, because he was in politics almost continually from young manhood to his twilight years. Politics was his life.

But a political biography has to be more than a political account. As any biographer must do, the political biographer must try to explain the inner life of his subject. He must, as Robert Towers puts it, "attempt to discover and interpret the interplay of forces, genetic, familial and cultural, that constitute the psychodynamics of the life under examination." As examples of what the biographer must search for, Towers lists the personalities and relationship of his parents, the subject's place in his family order, his developing sense of social and sexual identity, his choice of love objects, his response to adult crises, choice of a career, and other things. I agree that the political biographer has these obligations. Any biographer, in fact, is duty bound to try to discover everything that he can about his subject and to utilize every tool or approach that will help him to understand his subject and to interpret that subject to others.

I can accept the compulsions laid upon the modern biographer, but at the same time I have some reservations about psychobiography. Much of it, by my reading, is too glib or facile. Reading some of the products of today, I wonder how the psychobiographers can be so sure of the accuracy of their generalizations, particularly when these generalizations are based upon fragmentary evidence. I wonder, among other doubts, if it is not an exaggeration to attribute as much importance to the influence of a subject's parents as some writers do. Robert Novak has suggested that this tendency represents, perhaps, some complex on the part of intellectuals with respect to parents.

A good example of a biographer who is fascinated with the influence of parents is Doris Kearns in her life of Lyndon Johnson. I'll say at the beginning that in many ways I think this is a good book. It is shrewd and reveals a good deal about him, and many of her insights, I think, are given with restraint and are very accurate. But on this business of parents she thinks that a lot of LBJ's problems stemmed from the conflict between his mother and father. Johnson as a youth, according to Kearns, felt that he had to please his cultured mother without at the same time humiliating his less cultured father, and this tension produced an almost lifelong sense of near paralysis when he had to choose between irreconcilable goals. Maybe it happened that way. But it would seem to me that the psychological imperatives involved are universal. Certainly other young men have experienced similar tensions but were not affected as Kearns says Johnson was affected. Why did this conflict have this particular effect on Johnson, if it did, and not on other young men? Psychotheories, it seems to me, don't give us the answers to such questions.

Now George Reedy, who knew Johnson very well and has studied many aspects of his life, including his parents, believes that Lyndon Johnson's mother had another influence on him. Reedy said that his mother tried to inculcate in him that he must be a cultured Victorian gentleman. He tried, but he couldn't, and the result was that he always felt guilty and inferior in the presence of what he thought were cultured persons or persons that seemed to be like the ideals that his mother had held up to him. Reedy has a theory about this tendency in Johnson to be bowled over by Ivy League intellectuals. Reedy brags he went to the University of Chicago, and he said at Chicago Hutchins taught him that Harvard was a place where rich men sent their sons to learn how to be bond salesmen, and Yale was a place where rich men sent their sons to learn how to be stock salesmen, and Princeton was a place where rich men sent their sons when they couldn't discipline them, and that Chicago was a place where you went to get an education. Reedy added that he thought that the free world would have been better off if Lyndon Johnson had graduated from some other school than Southwest Texas State College.

Finally, in regard to the dangers of overdoing the psychic explanation, I quote a warning issued recently by Barry Karl. I realize that in quoting this I am being somewhat contradictory in my earlier view that the great man may have a role in history, but this is what Karl says about his tendency to find personal flaws in historical subjects. He writes,

> Periodically we are treated to a particular kind of reminiscence in journals like the *New Republic,* the theme of which is the question, 'How could I have been so thrilled with the Kennedy inaugural address when it ought to have been clear it was going to end in Vietnam?' The new study of Lyndon Johnson by Doris Kearns can be used to pose similar problems. All of them seem to me to suggest a serious fallacy, the transformation of the consequences of large historical events into

tragic flaws which can then be imposed upon individuals as personality defects which ought to have been correctable by better upbringing, presumably in another place at another time. The complexities of this kind of suprahistorical moralizing are enormous. History becomes a form of punishment intended to teach us lessons. Like all brutal methods of training, it is limited to the good it can do, the compassion it can generate, the respectful understanding of the past it can elicit. The past is everybody's fault and nobody's fault. Any other point of view makes history easier and more intelligible than it is. However gratifying this may be, it is a gratifying fantasy. History had better be something else.

As to the state of my research, I'm well into it, I think, but still in a preliminary stage. I am using and am terribly impressed by the resources of the LBJ Library. It has, in fact, so many resources that sometimes the researcher must be appalled by them. A number of people have asked me if I will use the technique I relied on in doing the Huey Long—oral history interviews. Yes I will. But the people at the library have been doing an awful lot of interviewing on their own. I think they have some four hundred interviews. However, I will do some interviewing, or maybe reapproach some people that they have talked with to find out something that interests me particularly. I'm a great believer in oral history as a research technique, particularly in political history. I think it's reliable in many areas. In fact, in some cases the only way you get the inside story, I think, is in the oral interview.

Now, lastly, I have some tentative or preliminary thoughts or ideas about this man Lyndon Johnson. As I see him now, he was a liberal with a real compassion for poor people and a great believer in using the power of government to solve problems. But he was not, in my opinion, a radical, as Huey Long was. I see Huey Long as a radical. Huey Long, I think, would have subverted the system if he had to. Lyndon Johnson never questioned the capitalistic system, never questioned the bases of capitalism.

One of the best of the several interviews I have read in the LBJ Library is by a very interesting woman by the name of Virginia Foster Durr from Alabama, longtime southern liberal, sister-in-law of Hugo Black. She knew Lyndon Johnson from the thirties on through his presidency, had respect for him, and yet is very objective about him. She had this to say about Johnson's belief in capitalism, and she compared him with Roosevelt, whom she had known, too, of course. "Now Roosevelt and Lyndon," she said, "both believed in the capitalistic system and in democracy. Roosevelt fought fascism when Hitler came up on the grounds of dictatorship. Lyndon fought communism on the grounds of dictatorship. In other words, they both believed in political democracy, but neither one of them, I think, ever questioned the capitalist system's being a beneficent system. Even Roosevelt, when it had fallen flat on its face in 1933, just completely done for, picked it up and revived it. Of course a lot of criticism of the left wingers at that time was that he had revived the capitalist system, that he could have at that time just taken over the banks and taken over everything. Lyndon had exactly the same attitude. He used to say, 'Business is what makes the mail run.' People say he was impressed by big business, or owned by big business," Durr said. "I never thought he was impressed or owned by it. I just think he believed in it."

He believed in it, but he did not have really, one may suspect, a philosophy of government or of economics. He did not have a philosophy. That's another thing that Virginia Durr emphasizes, and probably accurately. He did not have philosophies about a lot of things, or if he did he wouldn't discuss them. Now, of course, he was noted for not discussing. One man remembered that he had a sign on his desk when he was senator that said, "If you're talking, you're not learning." So he preferred to do, rather than to talk. But Virginia Durr said you couldn't get him to discuss philosophies of issues in the 1930s. She wanted him to fight for repeal of the poll tax and she wanted to talk to him about the philosophy behind the poll tax, and she couldn't get him to do it. She said, "Lyndon never discussed things like that. You couldn't get Lyndon to sit down and discuss the philosophy of government or the philosophy of the poll tax or the philosophy of oil depletion allowance. Lyndon acted." Once when she reproached him for not supporting a move to repeal the poll tax, he said, "We can't do it yet. We haven't got the votes. When we get the votes, then we'll try and do it."

This was a thing that was always present in his mind, I think, that he always talked about. If you're going to do anything, and this of course was born out of his Senate years, you have to have the votes. One of his great criticisms of the liberals, in the Senate particularly, was that they never knew where the votes were. He knew; they didn't. One of his famous statements was "The conservatives can't speak, and the liberals can't count." Which may be right. He believed in the democratic system, and I think partly because he could manage the democratic system. But it was hard for him to explain it, because he did not have this philosophical mind. And of course this was both a strength, I think, and a weakness, that he knew how to work the system and work it for what he thought were good ends, and yet he had difficulty in explaining maybe why he was doing these things.

However, one man who was very close to him would disagree somewhat with that, and that is Douglass Cater. Cater said, "The cliché was that he was the master consensus builder who really didn't care much about issues. But," said Cater, "I found that that cliché was, like all clichés, quite inadequate—that Johnson did not in those Senate years stress the substance of issues in his speeches on the floor of the Senate or in his dealing with other senators because that would have negated his purpose, which was to reach a rolling consensus. But seeking a consensus was not a negative act for him," said Cater. "It wasn't the lowest common denominator, or what just any old body would agree on. It was trying to find out what was the maximum that you could get a majority to support. Generally his idea of what constituted good public policy corresponded with my own idea that he was not on the vanguard of liberalism, but he was certainly liberally inclined. And he was not for preserving the status quo. So, although he didn't talk about substance a great deal in his public rhetoric, I felt he understood the substance. He was by no means ignorant of what were the subtleties of the issues he was dealing with."

One last thing in conclusion here about some of my preliminary judgments or findings. I've been very much interested in this reputation that Johnson had for deviousness or misrepresentation, and last summer when we—I say "we," Mrs. Williams who is my research associate and I—interviewed George Reedy, I asked him about it. Reedy is a very interesting man to talk to about Lyndon Johnson because he's ambivalent about him. On the one hand, he's tremen-dously impressed by him. On the other hand, he's resentful of him in many ways. And he has some very interesting and very fixed ideas about the office of the presidency. But I asked Reedy, who was press secretary and was himself concerned with this, "What about the so-called credibility gap?" And Reedy made this interesting statement. He said, "Lyndon Johnson never lied." But he said this, and he used this phrase several times in his conversation with me, "He had an uncertain perception of reality." An uncertain perception of reality. Reedy said, "What he wanted to be real, he would assume to be real, and very often he could make it become real." He was determined to shape his environment, and he thought he had shaped it when he said he had. Of course, in some cases he hadn't and couldn't do it, but in other cases he did. Reedy said—and again coming back to this fact that he could make some things become real—"In all my years in politics, I never met such an elemental force."

Notes

The Committee on the Conduct of the War

1 Grimes to Mrs. Grimes, November 6, 1861, William Salter, *Life of James W. Grimes* (New York, 1876), p. 153.

2 New York *Tribune*, October 28, 30, 1861; Thaddeus Stevens to his nephew, November 6, Thaddeus Stevens MSS. (in Library of Congress); *Congressional Globe*, 37 Cong., 2 Sess., pt. 1, p. 78, speech of Representative Eliot; General David Hunter to Lyman Trumbull, December 9, Lyman Trumbull MSS. (in Library of Congress).

3 New York *Tribune*, December 4, 5, 10, editorial and Washington correspondence; *National Anti-Slavery Standard*, December 14; J. H. Bryant to Lyman Trumbull, December 5, Trumbull MSS. For the report, see *Senate Documents*, 37 Cong., 2 Sess., II, no. 1.

4 John G. Nicolay and John Hay, *Complete Works of Abraham Lincoln* (New York, 1905), VII, 28–60, Radical comments are given in New York *Tribune*, December 4; *National Anti-Slavery Standard*, December 4; Grant Goodrich to Lyman Trumbull, December 6, Trumbull MSS.; C. H. Ray to Trumbull, December 6, *ibid.*

5 Senator Henry Wilson, *Cong. Globe*, 37 Cong., 2 Sess., pt. 1, p. 164; Representative Conway, *ibid.*, p. 83; George W. Julian, *Speeches on Political Questions* (New York, 1872), pp. 202–204; J. W. Schaffer to Trumbull, December 24, Trumbull MSS.; S. Sawyer to Trumbull, December 18, *ibid.*

6 For Radical denunciation of this procedure, see *Cong. Globe*, 37 Cong., 2 Sess., pt. 1, pp. 33–34; for Representative Shellabarger's resolution condemning the offending generals, see *ibid.*, p. 8; Edward L. Pierce, *Memoir and Letters of Charles Sumner* (Boston, 1894), IV, 166; New York *Tribune*, December 20; James Terrel to Trumbull, December 4, Trumbull MSS.; Emerson Etheridge to Andrew Johnson, December 19, Andrew Johnson MSS. (in Library of Congress).

7 Detroit *Post and Tribune, Life of Zachariah Chandler* (Detroit, 1880), pp. 253–54, hereafter cited as *Life of Chandler;* Charles Sumner to Francis Lieber, September 17, 1861, Pierce, *Sumner*, IV, 42; Benjamin F. Wade to Zachariah Chandler, September 23, Zachariah Chandler MSS. (in Library of Congress); James W. Grimes to William P. Fessenden, September 19, Salter, *Grimes*, pp. 152–53; New York *Tribune*, September 16, 18, contain the Radical reactions to Lincoln's revocation of Frémont's proclamation. For Radical denunciation of the removal of Frémont, see Thaddeus Ste-

vens, letter of November 5, Stevens MSS.; Gustave Koerner to Trumbull, November 18, Trumbull MSS.; Grimes to Mrs. Grimes, November 13, Salter, *Grimes*, pp. 154–55; O. J. Hollister, *Schuyler Colfax* (New York, 1886), p. 181. The Frémont-Radical connection is treated in T. Harry Williams, "Frémont and the Politicians," *Journal* of the American Military History Foundation, II (1938), 179–91.

8 R. H. Kettler to Trumbull, December 22, Trumbull MSS.; J. W. Schaffer to Trumbull, December 24, *ibid.*; B. W. Reynolds to Trumbull, December 16, *ibid.*; Joseph Medill to Edwin M. Stanton, January 21, 1862, Edwin M. Stanton MSS. (in Library of Congress); speech of Senator Lane of Kansas, *Cong. Globe*, 37 Cong., 2 Sess., pt. 1, pp. 110–11; New York *Tribune*, December 14, 1861. Fears of a military dictatorship were intensified by injudicious remarks in the New York *Herald*, a McClellan organ, December 11.

9 Grimes to W. P. Fessenden, November 13, Salter, *Grimes*, pp. 156–57.

10 At the battle of Ball's Bluff, Colonel Edward Baker, United States Senator from Oregon and a Republican, was killed while leading the Federal forces. Radical critics blamed General Charles Stone, Baker's superior and McClellan's intimate, for Baker's death and the defeat. New York *Tribune*, October 26; J. W. Grimes to Mrs. Grimes, November 10, Salter, *Grimes*, pp. 153–54; Thaddeus Stevens to his nephew, November 5, Stevens MSS.; Sumner's eulogy of Baker, Pierce, *Sumner*, IV, 67. Representative Roscoe Conkling was the author of a House resolution requesting the Secretary of War to furnish information regarding Ball's Bluff, *Cong. Globe*, 37 Cong., 2 Sess., pt. 1, p. 6.

11 *Cong. Globe*, 37 Cong., 2 Sess., pt. 1, pp. 16–17.

12 The resolution was adopted unanimously and without debate in the House. Two precedents for the Committee on the Conduct of the war existed. In 1791 a Congressional committee investigated the failure of General St. Clair's western expedition and presented a report exonerating him. *Annals of Congress*, 2 Cong., 1792, pp. 490–93, 602, 877, 895. The reverses of the American arms during the War of 1812 provoked a House investigative committee, but this body seems to have been inactive. *Ibid.*, 13 Cong., 1 Sess., pp. 413–21. Grimes described these earlier agencies in his speech defending the creation of an investigative committee. *Cong. Globe*, 37 Cong., 2 Sess., pt. 1, pp. 29–30.

13 *Cong. Globe*, 37 Cong., 2 Sess., pt. 1, p. 110; *Life of Chandler*, p. 216.

14 With the beginning of a new Congress in December, 1863, the Committee was given a renewal of existence and more specific powers. Resolution of Thaddeus Stevens, *Cong. Globe*, 38 Cong., 1 Sess., pt. 1, p. 260.

15 Benjamin F. Wade, *Traitors and their Sympathizers* (Washington, 1863), p. 2.

16 Wade to General Patterson during the Bull Run inquiry, *Reports of the Committee on the Conduct of the War*, 1863, II, 78, hereafter cited as C. C. W. In its first report the Committee defined itself as an agency to "advise what mistakes had been made in the past and the proper course to pursue in the future." *Ibid.*, I, 4.

17 Wade, *Traitors and their Sympathizers*, p. 2. Sometimes the information was selected. See Chandler's speech, July 16, 1862, *Cong. Globe*, 37 Cong., 2 Sess., pt. 4, p. 3386. "The committee has been in constant, almost daily, communication with the administration, and has from time to time submitted such information as in their opinion should be furnished to the executive." For an account of a conference with Lincoln and the Cabinet, see *ibid.*, p. 3390.

18 The 1863 report censured Lincoln for failing to maintain intercourse with the Committee. C. C. W., 1863, I, 4.

19 R. B. Warden, *An Account of the Private Life and Public Services of Salmon Portland Chase* (Cincinnati, 1874), pp. 400–401; Francis Fessenden, *Life and Public Services of William Pitt Fessenden* (Boston, 1907), pp. 230–31; John Cochrane, *War for the Union* (New York, 1875), p. 19; George W. Julian, *Political Recollections*,

1840−1872 (Chicago, 1884), p. 204; Pierce, *Sumner*, IV, 63; *Life of Chandler*, p. 187; A. G. Riddle, *Benjamin F. Wade* (Cleveland, 1886), p. 316.

20 *Journal* of the Committee, *C. C. W.*, 1863, I, 83, 85; Julian, *Recollections*, p. 204.

21 *Life of Chandler*, pp. 218−19; F. A. Flower, *Edwin McMasters Stanton* (Akron, 1905), pp. 137, 345.

22 Wade's speech, *Cong. Globe*, 38 Cong., 2 Sess., pt. 2, p. 826.

23 *Ibid.*, 37 Cong., 2 Sess., pt. 1, pp. 164−65.

24 *Ibid.*, 37 Cong., 3 Sess., pt. 1, p. 326.

25 See Benjamin F. Wade, *Facts for the People* (Cincinnati, 1864), p. 3; *Journal* of the Committee, *C. C. W.*, 1863, I, 86−88. For example of the Committee setting its opinion on the feasibility of organizing the army into corps against the opinion of McClellan, see Julian, *Recollections*, pp. 204−205.

26 *C. C. W.*, 1863, I, 62−63.

27 *Ibid.*, 1863, II, 262, "Ball's Bluff."

28 *Ibid.*, 1863, I, 700; Wade, *Facts for the People*, p. 2; *Life of Chandler*, pp. 225−26.

29 *C. C. W.*, 1863, I, 68; III, 3. The summons usually went to the officer concerned through the medium of the War Department. New York *Tribune*, March 29, 1865. In 1865 Generals Sherman and Weitzel resisted a summons on the ground that they could not leave their command. The Committee transmitted a resolution to Stanton asking him to issue "peremptory orders" to the two officers to appear before the committee. *Journal*, *C. C. W.*, 1865, I, xxxviii. The Committee did not gather all its testimony in Washington. The Committee or delegated sub-committees often traveled to the scene of operations and took evidence on the spot. In the course of their work, they went to Alexandria, City Point, Fortress Monroe, Centreville, Falmouth, and Petersburg in Virginia; New York City; Baltimore; Annapolis; Boston; Mound City and Cairo, Illinois; Columbus, Kentucky; and Memphis and Ft. Pillow, Tennessee. At Falmouth and Petersburg they appeared in the Union camp immediately after a battle.

30 The desire of the radicals to make McClellan reveal his plans was one of the reasons for the creation of the Committee. Julian, *Recollections*, p. 201.

31 *C. C. W.*, 1863, I, 122, 129−30, 179.

32 *Ibid.*, 1863, I, 171−72; II, 266−67, "Ball's Bluff."

33 *Ibid.*, 1863, II, 313, 316−17, "Ball's Bluff"; *ibid.*, II, 76, 150, "Bull Run"; *ibid.*, 1865, II, 31, 65, "Red River."

34 *Ibid.*, 1863, II, 275, "Ball's Bluff."

35 Heintzelman's testimony, *ibid.*, 1863, I, 118−21, 346−59; Keyes, *ibid.*, I, 600−14; Hooker, *ibid.*, I, 575−80; Diary of Samuel P. Heintzelman, MS. (in Library of Congress), entries of December 24, 28, 1861; Joseph Hooker to Chandler, December 19, 1864, Chandler MSS.; E. D. Keyes to Stanton, October 27, 1862, Stanton MSS.; John Barnard to Stanton, January 15, 1863, *ibid.*

36 Benjamin F. Butler, *C. C. W.*, 1863, 285−87; Lew Wallace, *ibid.*, III, 349−52.

37 S. M. Allen to Benjamin F. Butler, May 26, 1890, *Private and Official Correspondence of Benjamin F. Butler During the Period of the Civil War* (privately issued, 1917), II, 595. Allen claimed to have been an investigator or "scout" working without pay for the Committee. See also New York *Tribune*, December 24, 1862, p. 1, Army of Potomac correspondence.

38 Colonel W. B. Hazen to John Sherman, December 10, 1862, John Sherman MSS. (in Library of Congress); New York *Tribune*, January 26, 1863, Army of Potomac correspondence; George Meade, *Life and Letters of George Gordon Meade* (New York, 1913), I, 324; Detroit *Free Press*, April 7, 1863; New York *World*, September 5, 1864.

39 Peter Michie, *George B. McClellan* (New York, 1901), p. 165; William Swinton,

Campaigns of the Army of the Potomac (New York, 1882), p. 89; Sir Frederick Maurice, *Statesmen and Soldiers of the Civil War* (Boston, 1926), p. 68; Colonel G. F. R. Henderson, *The Science of War* (London, 1906), pp. 13–14, 18, 212; W. H. Hurlburt, *General McClellan and the Conduct of the War* (New York, 1846), p. 160; James Joy, "The Committee on the Conduct of the War," Detroit *Free Press*, January 10, 1863.

40 *Journal, C. C. W.*, 1863, I, 68. It was expected that the witness would maintain the same silence. *Ibid.*, 1863, II, 78, "Bull Run." The Committee reserved the right to lay vital testimony before the President and the Cabinet. *Ibid.*, 1863, II, 431, "Ball's Bluff."

41 Detroit *Free Press*, January 10, 1863; New York *World*, April 13, 1863.

42 Wade, *Traitors and their Sympathizers*, p. 2; *C. C. W.*, 1863, II, 431, "Ball's Bluff"; *ibid.*, 1865, I, 99.

43 Wade to Charles A. Dana, February 3, 1862, Charles A. Dana MSS. (in Library of Congress).

44 *Journal, C. C. W.*, 1863, I, 100–102; *Cong. Globe*, 37 Cong., 2 Sess., pt. 4, pp. 3386–92; *Life of Chandler*, pp. 228–38; Chandler to Mrs. Chandler, July 6, 11, 1862, Chandler MSS.

45 *C. C. W.*, 1863, II, 426–33, "Ball's Bluff." Stone testified again in February, 1863. This time he had read the previous testimony and could answer specifically the charges of hostile witnesses. The astonished Wade asked, "Why did you not give us these explanations when you were here before?" Stone replied, "Because the Committee did not state to me the particular cases. . . . I gave general answers to general allegations." *Ibid.*, II, 492–96.

46 The Committee had ruled that for the purpose of taking testimony a quorum was not necessary. This enabled one or two Republican members to examine witnesses at any time. People answering a summons would frequently find only Wade and Chandler present. *Journal, C. C. W.*, 1863, I, 71.

47 George G. Meade to Mrs. Meade, March 6, 1864, Meade, *Meade*, II, 169; *C. C. W.*, 1865, I, 329–51.

48 *C. C. W.*, 1863, II, 426–33, "Ball's Bluff."

49 *Journal, C. C. W.*, 1865, I, xix.

50 *Ibid.*, 1863, I, 74, 79; II, 17–18, 504–505, 509–10, "Ball's Bluff." Wade's speech on the Committee's part in the arrest of Stone, *Cong. Globe*, 37 Cong., 2 Sess., pt. 2, pp. 1666–68, 1735–37. Wade, *Traitors and their Sympathizers*; the title of this pamphlet refers to Stone and his Congressional supporters.

51 *C. C. W.*, 1865, I, 111.

52 *Ibid.*, 1863, I, 113–16, 122–30, 165–68.

53 *Ibid.*, I, 128, 142, 159.

54 Wade, *Facts for the People*, pp. 2, 6; Julian, *Recollections*, pp. 203–204.

55 *Journal, C. C. W.*, 1863, I, 72–73; Julian, *Recollections*, pp. 201–203; Chandler's account, *Cong. Globe*, 37 Cong., 2 Sess., pt. 4; *Life of Chandler*, p. 225.

56 *Journal, C. C. W.*, 1863, I, 75; *Harper's Weekly*, February 1, 1862; Joy in Detroit *Free Press*, January 10, 1863; *Life of Chandler*, pp. 225–26; Wade, *Facts for the People*, p. 2. The conference was held January 15.

57 *Journal, C. C. W.*, 1863, I, 85; Julian, *Recollections*, p. 204. See also Stanton to Dana, January 24, 1862, Dana MSS., promising that the eastern army would be forced to move.

58 *The War of the Rebellion: A Compilation of the Official Records of the Union and Confederate Armies*, ser. I, vol. V, p. 41, hereafter cited as *O. R.*; Stanton to Wade, January 27, Stanton MSS.; Maurice, *Statesmen and Soldiers*, pp. 68–69; Flower, *Stanton*, pp. 138–39; H. J. Raymond, *Life and Public Services of Abraham Lincoln* (New York, 1866), p. 265.

59 *Journal, C. C. W.,* 1863, I, 84–86.

60 *Life of Chandler,* pp. 227–28.

61 See General E. D. Keyes to Stanton, May 13, 1862, Stanton MSS., for an analysis by a Radical officer of the political differences of the two factions and the effect upon promotions; Governor William Sprague before the Committee, *C. C. W.,* 1863, I, 536; Chase diary, October 6, 1862, Warden, *Chase,* pp. 498–99; New York *Independent,* May 26, 1864.

62 General McDowell, a Committee favorite who would be one of the corps commanders, told Heintzelman that this was the Committee's purpose. Heintzelman diary, February 21, 1862.

63 *O. R.,* ser. I, vol. V, p. 18; *C. C. W.,* 1863, I, 86–88; Julian, *Recollections,* pp. 204–205.

64 Wadsworth's report, April 2, Stanton MSS.; H. G. Pearson, *James A. Wadsworth of Geneseo* (New York, 1913), pp. 118–20.

65 *C. C. W.,* 1863, I, 251–53.

66 *O. R.,* ser. I, vol. XIV, p. 66; New York *World,* May 3, 1862, January 19, 1863; New York *Herald,* April 27, 1862, January 19, 1863; Joy in Detroit *Free Press,* January 10, 1863; speech of Senator Harris, April 14, 1862, *Cong. Globe,* 37 Cong., 2 Sess., pt. 1, p. 1653.

67 Chase to T. M. Key, April 18, 1862, J. W. Schuckers, *Life and Public Services of Salmon Portland Chase* (New York, 1874), p. 434; Grimes to Mrs. Grimes, May 22, Salter, *Grimes,* p. 197; P. C. Watson, Assistant Secretary of War, to Stanton, May 8, 9, Stanton MSS.

68 Chase to McDowell, May 14, 1862, Schuckers, *Chase,* p. 495; Stanton to H. Dyer, May 18, Stanton MSS.; McDowell to Stanton, May 9, *ibid.*

69 *C. C. W.,* 1863, I, 276; Wade, *Facts for the People,* pp. 5–6.

70 *Journal, C. C. W.,* 1863, I, 102; *Cong. Globe,* 37 Cong., 2 Sess., pt. 4, pp. 3386–92; *Life of Chandler,* pp. 229–38; Zachariah Chandler, *The Conduct of the War* (Washington, 1862).

71 Chandler to Trumbull, September 10, 1862, Trumbull MSS.

72 *C. C. W.,* 1863, I, 643.

73 Julian, *Recollections,* p. 225; Julian, *Select Speeches* (Cincinnati, 1867), p. 33.

74 *C. C. W.,* 1863, I, 655, 661, 670; Cochrane, *War for the Union,* p. 40; Meade to Mrs. Meade, December 20, 1862, Meade, *Meade,* I, 340.

75 *Senate Reports,* 37 Cong., 3 Sess., no. 71; New York *Tribune,* December 14; *Frank Leslie's Newspaper,* January 10, 1863; *Harper's Weekly,* January 10. An aftereffect of the Committee's visit was to lessen the confidence of the beaten army in Burnside and to inspire camp-fire debate as to his competence. Cochrane, *War for the Union,* pp. 47–48; "Excerpts from the Journal of Henry Raymond," *Scribner's Monthly,* XIX (1879–80).

76 *C. C. W.,* 1863, I, 687–746.

77 *Ibid.,* I, 56–57; Franklin to McClellan, April 6, 1863, W. S. Myers, *General George Brinton McClellan* (New York, 1934), p. 408; Franklin, *A Reply of Major-General William B. Franklin to . . . the Committee on the Conduct of the War* (New York, 1863).

78 Wade, *Facts for the People,* p. 4.

79 Julian, *Speeches on Political Questions,* p. 204; Detroit *Advertiser and Tribune* (Chandler's organ), April 24, 1863.

80 Meade to Mrs. Meade, May 20, 1863, Meade, *Meade,* I, 379; Chandler to Mrs. Chandler, May 29, Chandler MSS.; New York *Independent,* May 28, Washington correspondence.

81 Hooker's testimony, *C. C. W.,* 1865, I, 111–18, 142; see also *ibid.,* 14–15, 15–16, 83.

82 *Ibid.*, I, iv.

83 *Ibid.*, I, 311, 321, 325.

84 New York *Independent*, October 22, 29, 1863. Washington correspondence; *Wilkes' Spirit of the Times*, August 29.

85 New York *Independent*, December 10, Washington correspondence.

86 General W. T. Sherman to his wife, October 4, 1863, M. A. DeWolfe Howe, ed., *Home Letters of General Sherman* (New York, 1909), pp. 278, 227–28; Colonel S. Noble to Trumbull, January 6, 1863, Trumbull MSS.; *C. C. W.*, 1863, III, 337–43.

87 General David Hunter to Stanton, December 15, 1863, Stanton MSS.; General John Palmer to Trumbull, January, 1864, Trumbull MSS.; Pierce, *Sumner*, IV, 172.

88 *Life of Chandler*, p. 240.

89 *C. C. W.*, 1865, I, i, iv, lvi–lvii, lxxv, 311, 375; Meade to Mrs. Meade, March 6, 9, 14, 1864, Meade, *Meade*, II, 169, 176–78; New York *Tribune*, March 7, 8, 1864.

90 *Journal, C. C. W.*, 1865, I, xix.

91 N. W. Stephenson, ed., *An Autobiography of Abraham Lincoln* (Indianapolis, 1926), pp. 416–17.

92 *C. C. W.*, 1865, I, i, 11–12; Julian, *Recollections*, 249; Meade to Mrs. Meade, December 20, 1864, Meade, *Meade*, II, 253–54; Grant to Meade, February 9, 1865, *ibid.*, p. 344.

93 *C. C. W.*, 1865, II, 1.

94 *Ibid.*, pp. 10–49.

95 Butler to Wade, February 7, 1865, *Butler Correspondence*, V, 540–42; General Godfrey Weitzel to Butler, January 30 (after Weitzel testified), *ibid.*, pp. 512–13.

96 *C. C. W.*, 1865, II, i–viii. It will be noted that the Committee devoted most of its attention to the Army of the Potomac. This was because that army was often near Washington and its officers could come to the capital in a short time. The Committee members could repair to the camp of the army with the same ease.

Lincoln and the Radicals:
An Essay in Civil War History and Historiography

1 Joshua F. Speed to Joseph Holt, November 28, December 8, 1861, in Joseph Holt Papers (Library of Congress).

2 Howard K. Beale, ed., *The Diary of Edward Bates* (Washington, 1933), 333, entry of February 13, 1864.

3 Thaddeus Stevens to ———, November 17, 1862, in Thaddeus Stevens Papers (Library of Congress).

4 *Wilkes' Spirit of the Times* (New York), June 18, 1864.

5 *Congressional Globe*, 38 Cong., 2 Sess., 165.

6 David Donald, *Lincoln Reconsidered* (Vintage Edition; New York, 1961), 103–27.

7 Eric McKitrick, *Andrew Johnson and Reconstruction* (Chicago, 1960), *passim*.

8 *Congressional Globe*, 37 Cong., 1 Sess., 119, 142–43, 189; New York *Evening Post*, December 5, 1861; New York *Times*, December 5, 1861.

9 Roy P. Basler, ed., *The Collected Works of Abraham Lincoln* (Rutgers, 1953), V, 48–49; George W. Julian, *Select Speeches of George W. Julian* (Cincinnati, 1867), 33.

10 The economic beliefs and program of the Radicals are subject to all kinds of semantic analyses. It can be argued, for example, that the Radicals were really radical in that they proposed to overthrow or destroy one of the largest aggregations of property in the country, to execute a gigantic confiscation of private property. The paradox here was, as some of them came to realize, that confiscation would be employed by men who believed in *laissez faire* to strengthen a system that glorified private ownership. Or, to take another approach, while the Radicals customarily cast their attacks on

slavery in moral terms, it can be said that to them slavery was a symbol of many things and that within the context of the symbol there were economic facets of which they were perhaps unaware. That is, a Radical may have denounced slavery as a sin without realizing all his motives, one being that the sinners, the slaveholders, prevented an industry in his state from getting tariff protection.

We know a great deal about what the Radicals were against economically and something about what specific measures they were for. But we do not know enough about their image of the economy as a whole. Did they agree or differ as to its structure? Ben Wade once made a speech in Kansas in which he was reported to have advocated some kind of equal division of property. If he said it—Wade denied he had phrased it exactly that way—why did he say it? Do his remarks reveal the zeal of a revolutionary or a radical? Did he have sincere equalitarian instincts? Or was he merely indulging in an oratorical flight that might aid his political ambitions? The entire subject of the Radical concept of economics needs more research before we can generalize broadly.

11 *Congressional Globe*, 38 Cong., 2 Sess., 165.

12 John G. Nicolay and John Hay, *Abraham Lincoln: A History* (New York, 1914), IX, 100.

13 Wendell Phillips to George W. Julian, March 27, 1864, in Giddings-Julian Correspondence (Library of Congress); Theodore C. Smith, *Life and Letters of James A. Garfield* (New Haven, 1925), I, 375; *Wilkes' Spirit of the Times*, January 30, 1864.

14 Joshua R. Giddings to George W. Julian, March 22, 1863, in Giddings-Julian Correspondence; L. Maria Child to Julian, April 8, 1865, *ibid.*

15 *Congressional Globe*, 38 Cong., 2 Sess., 161.

16 New York *Tribune*, May 12, 1863.

17 Edward L. Pierce, *Memoir and Letters of Charles Sumner* (Boston, 1887–93), IV, 142–43. For other similar Radical expressions, see Congressman Charles Sedgwick, in Sarah F. Hughes, ed., *Letters and Recollections of John Murray Forbes* (Boston, 1899), I, 96–97, 321; Horace Greeley to Mrs. Margaret Allen, June 17, 1861, in Horace Greeley Papers (Library of Congress); J. H. Walker to Thaddeus Stevens, February 27, 1864, in Stevens Papers; C. A. Preston to John Sherman, December 1, 1863, in John Sherman Papers (Library of Congress); J. H. Jordan to Lyman Trumbull, February 20, 1862, in Lyman Trumbull Papers (Library of Congress); David Prince to Trumbull, September 16, 1862, *ibid.*

18 New York *Tribune*, January 24, 1863, Stevens to ——, in Stevens Papers, September 5, 1862.

19 *Congressional Globe*, 37 Cong., 1 Sess., 75; *ibid.*, 37 Cong., 3 Sess., 1338.

20 New York *Tribune*, September 11, 1862; *Congressional Globe*, 37 Cong., 2 Sess., 1896.

21 T. Harry Williams, *Lincoln and the Radicals* (Madison, 1941), 14–17.

22 *Wilkes' Spirit of the Times*, January 30, 1864.

23 The election of 1864 is treated in Williams, *Lincoln and the Radicals*, Chapter 12.

24 New York *Herald*, August 24, 1864.

25 *Frank Leslie's Illustrated Newspaper* (New York), October 31, 1863.

26 For the organization and work of the Committee, see Williams, *Lincoln and the Radicals*, Chapter 3.

27 Washington *National Intelligencer*, December 6, 1861.

28 *Congressional Globe*, 37 Cong., 2 Sess., 1918.

29 London *Times*, quoted in Detroit *Free Press*, January 23, 1863.

30 Williams, *Lincoln and the Radicals*, 208–11; Allan Nevins, *The War for the Union, II, War Becomes Revolution* (New York, 1960), 352–62.

31 Francis Fessenden, *Life and Public Services of William Pitt Fessenden* (Boston,

1901), I, 231–51; Theodore C. Pease and James G. Randall, eds., *The Diary of Orville Hickman Browning* (Springfield, 1925), I, 596–604.

32 Fessenden, *Fessenden*, I, 233–34, 253; *Harper's Weekly* (New York), January 3, 1863.

33 *Harper's Weekly*, August 29, 1863, "Lounger's" column.

34 Springfield *Illinois State Register*, January 13, 1863, quoted in A. C. Cole, "President Lincoln and the Illinois Radical Republicans," *Mississippi Valley Historical Review*, IV (March, 1918), 427.

35 New York *Tribune*, June 13, 1862.

36 Tyler Dennett, ed., *Lincoln and the Civil War in the Diaries of John Hay* (New York, 1939), 108.

The Louisiana Unification Movement of 1873

1 Deciding the victor in the election of 1872 would have puzzled even a Solomon. Both parties were guilty of fraud and falsification of the vote, but the federal government, controlled by the Republican party, accepted the verdict of the election furnished by the Louisiana Republicans.

2 This summary of political events is based upon an examination of New Orleans papers for 1872 and 1873. For an account of the election of 1872 and Kellogg's governorship, see John E. Gonzales, "William Pitt Kellogg: Reconstruction Governor of Louisiana" (M.A. thesis, Louisiana State University, 1945).

3 The New Orleans *Times*, May 8, 1873, contains six columns of reports of such assorted violent events throughout the state.

4 New Orleans *Daily Crescent City*, quoted in Opelousas *Journal*, June 7, 1873. See also New Orleans *Republican*, May 18, 1873.

5 The only mention of the unification movement to be found in the secondary works dealing with Louisiana and Reconstruction is a slighting reference of one sentence in Alcée Fortier, *A History of Louisiana*, 4 vols. (New York, 1904), IV, part 2, pp. 134–35.

6 *Appleton's American Annual Cyclopedia* (New York, 1862–1903), XII (1872), 474; Ella Lonn, *Reconstruction in Louisiana after 1868* (New York, 1918), 140–41, 154; Henry C. Warmoth, *War, Politics, and Reconstruction: Stormy Days in Louisiana* (New York, 1930), 178; New Orleans *Daily Picayune*, December 2, 1871, February 18, 1872, May 23, 1873 (letter by "Conservative"); New Orleans *Times*, February 18, June 5, 6, 7, 1872.

7 New Orleans *Republican*, January 12, 15 (letter by J. Henri Burch), July 24, 1873; New Orleans *Times*, May 28 (interview with a Negro leader), May 29 (interview with a Reform leader). It is to be noted that in 1872 the Democrats also accepted in general terms the legal equality of the Negro. Lonn, *Reconstruction in Louisiana*, 153.

8 New Orleans *Times*, April 1, 1873. *Ibid.*, April 8, contains a similar letter by "Juvenus."

9 *Ibid.*, April 22, 1873.

10 *Ibid.*, April 29, 1873. See issue of May 3 for an approving reply to Mr. Chucks by "Truth," a Negro.

11 *Ibid.*, May 1, 1873.

12 *Ibid.*, May 4, 1873.

13 *Ibid.*, May 16, 1873 (letter by "Progress"); *ibid.*, May 29 (letters by "Progress" and "Last-Ditcher").

14 *Ibid.*, June 7, 1873 (a young social leader quoted in "Round About Town"); *ibid.*, June 13 (letter by "Sigma"); New Orleans *Picayune*, June 6 (letter by "S").

15 New Orleans *Times*, May 29, 1873.

16 *Ibid.*, May 18, 1873; *ibid.*, May 23 ("Round About Town"); *ibid.*, June 2, edi-

torial: "We are at the dawn of a new dispensation. Politically, old things are passing away and all things are becoming new."

17 *Ibid.*, June 2, 1873.

18 *Ibid.*, May 30, 1873.

19 *Ibid.*, June 6, 1873.

20 *Ibid.*, June 23, 1873.

21 New Orleans *Herald*, quoted in New Orleans *Republican*, May 31, 1873.

22 *L'Abeille de la Nouvelle Orleans*, quoted in Opelousas *Courier*, June 7, 1873.

23 New Orleans *Picayune*, June 6, 1873.

24 *Ibid.*, June 8, 1873.

25 New Orleans *Republican*, May 28, June 1, 3, 4, 7, 1873.

26 New Orleans *Deutsche Zeitung*, May 30, quoted in *ibid.*, June 1, 3, 1873.

27 New Orleans *Times*, June 3, 1873.

28 *Ibid.*, May 28, 1873. The interview is with an anonymous Negro leader, but the description of him identifies him as Dr. Roudanez.

29 *Ibid.*, June 1, 1873. Again the interview is with an anonymous leader and again the description affords an identification.

30 *Ibid.*, June 3, 1873. See also *ibid.*, June 2, for letters from Negroes supporting unification.

31 New Orleans *Republican*, June 1, 1873.

32 New Orleans *Times*, May 26, 30, 1873.

33 New Orleans *Republican*, June 13, 1873. The *Republican*, at this point, began to swing over to support unification.

34 New Orleans *Times*, June 16, 1873.

35 Obviously fifty men cannot be identified in an article of this space. The author is thoroughly familiar with the names of the New Orleans leaders of the period. Most of them appear on the list of the Committee. The presidents of practically every corporation and bank in the city were members. It should be noted that most of the leading business men of New Orleans were not natives of Louisiana. They had come to the city from the North or from other southern states to seek their fortunes as young men. Those from outside the state who were leaders in the 1870s had lived in Louisiana during the decades before the Civil War and had thoroughly identified themselves with the life of the state. See New Orleans *Republican*, June 5, 1873.

36 R. L. Desdunes, *Nos Homes et Notre Histoire* (Montreal, 1911), 181–82.

37 There is a sketch of Day in Edwin L. Jewell (ed.), *Jewell's Crescent City Illustrated* (New Orleans, 1873), 129. Some of the above information about his business connections was obtained from business notices in the New Orleans *Picayune*, April 15, May 3, September 5, 1873. Day was a native of Connecticut who had come to New Orleans in 1832.

38 *Jewell's Crescent City Illustrated*, 122; *Edwards' Annual Directory to the . . . City of New Orleans for 1873* (New Orleans, 1873), 291; New Orleans *Times*, March 5, 1874, p. 2; Thomas O'Connor (ed.), *History of the Fire Department of New Orleans* (New Orleans, 1895), 532–36; business notices in New Orleans *Picayune*, March 4, 6, 1866, April 8, 15, 1873, and New Orleans *Times*, August 13, 1873. Marks was born in Charleston, South Carolina, of Jewish parentage, and came to New Orleans about 1836. Before 1860 he was a prominent Whig.

39 Business notices in New Orleans *Picayune*, April 14, May 25, 1873; New Orleans *Republican*, July 18, August 17, 1873; New Orleans *Times*, January 30, 1874.

40 *Jewell's Crescent City Illustrated*, 100; *Proceedings of the Louisiana Bar Association, 1898–1899* (New Orleans, 1899), 93.

41 See the sketch of Antoine in *Journal of Negro History* (Washington, 1916–), VIII (1923), 85–87; Charles B. Roussève, *The Negro in Louisiana: Aspects of His History and His Literature* (New Orleans, 1937), 105, 129.

42 Rousséve, *Negro in Louisiana*, 129, 156; A. E. Perkins, *Who's Who in Colored Louisiana* (Baton Rouge, 1930), 58.

43 Perkins, *Who's Who in Colored Louisiana*, 49; Warmoth, *War, Politics, and Reconstruction*, 147; Charles Nordhoff, *The Cotton States in the Spring and Summer of 1875* (New York, 1876), 61.

44 Rousséve, *Negro in Louisiana*, 51, 118–20; Perkins, *Who's Who in Colored Louisiana*, 57–58; Warmoth, *War, Politics, and Reconstruction*, 51–54; W. E. Burghardt Du Bois, *Black Reconstruction* (New York, 1938), 456–58.

45 New Orleans *Republican*, February 23, April 13, 1873. There were two other Charles H. Thompsons in New Orleans. One was collector of customs and the other a teacher at the Negro school, Straight University. *Edwards' Annual Directory*, 430. The newspaper evidence seems to make it clear that the one on the resolutions committee was the preacher.

46 New Orleans *Times*, New Orleans *Picayune*, New Orleans *L'Abeille*, June 17, 1873.

47 So far as can be discovered, this is the first time that this document has been published in complete form in any secondary study. Governor Warmoth published approximately the first half of it in his *War, Politics, and Reconstruction*, 240–41, but he erroneously called it the Reform party platform of 1872. Du Bois, *Black Reconstruction*, 481, reprinted this partial version from Warmoth. The document appears in full in *House Reports*, 43 Cong., 2 Sess., No. 261, Part 3, "Louisiana Affairs," pp. 1037–38. The original manuscript, complete with the signatures of the members of the resolutions committee, is in the Department of Archives, Louisiana State University, Baton Rouge. The document was published in the *Times* and the *Picayune* of June 17, 1873, and in succeeding issues for almost a month. The version reproduced here is the one that appeared in the newspapers. This is done because the manuscript document is in rough form, lacking such things as proper punctuation, and because it is believed that the document should be presented as it was given to the public. All differences between the two versions have been indicated, however, by including in brackets all material from the manuscript that did not appear in the newspapers. It is to be noted that the differences are few and involve for the most part questions of diction.

48 It is probable that this clause was omitted from the report because of the repugnance of the whites for the Republican-made constitution and many Republican laws.

49 This stronger statement was doubtless deleted out of deference to the sensibilities of the press.

50 John R. Ficklen, *History of Reconstruction in Louisiana through 1868* (Baltimore, 1910), 185, quotes Beauregard's views on Negro suffrage in 1867.

51 New Orleans *Picayune*, July 1, 1873; New Orleans *L'Abeille*, July 1; New Orleans *Republican*, July 2. For comments on Beauregard's statement, see New Orleans *Times*, July 1, pp. 1, 2. See also a letter from Beauregard to Jubal A. Early, quoted in *Times*, August 8, p. 3.

52 New Orleans *Times*, July 23, 1873, p. 2. See also *ibid.*, July 25, p. 3.

53 *Ibid.*, June 18, 1873, editorial and "Round About Town"; June 27 (letter by "C. B.").

54 New Orleans *Picayune*, June 25, 1873. See also issues of June 18 and July 9.

55 New Orleans *Republican*, June 16, 19, July 12, 1873. The issue of June 20, however, carried letters by readers questioning the sincerity of the whites and the success of the movement.

56 Archbishop Perche, writing in *Le Propagateur Catholique*, official journal of the Diocese of New Orleans, quoted in *Picayune*, June 22, 1873. Unification was denounced, however, by another Catholic journal of the city, *The Morning Star and*

Catholic Messenger, which said that Beauregard was violating his principles as a southern gentleman and a Catholic by accepting unification. See *Morning Star,* quoted in New Orleans *Republican,* July 1.

57 Hebert, quoted in New Orleans *Times,* July 11, 1873; Mouton, in *ibid.,* July 12.

58 *L'Abeille,* June 18, 1873. See also *Picayune,* June 18, p. 2, where prominent supporters of unification raised the same question.

59 New Orleans *Times,* June 19, 21, 1873; *Picayune,* July 12, 1873.

60 New Orleans *Republican,* July 1, 3, 1873; Alexandria *Rapides Gazette,* July 26, 1873.

61 Monroe *Ouachita Telegraph,* June 21, 1873.

62 Shreveport *Times,* quoted in *ibid.,* July 19, 1873.

63 Clinton *Patriot-Democrat,* June 28, 1873, quoted in St. Francisville *Dunn Leader,* July 12. Strong white opposition to unification in Plaquemines Parish was noted in *L'Abeille,* July 16, and in Catahoula Parish in Monroe *Ouachita Telegraph,* July 19.

64 New Orleans *Times,* June 24, 1873 (letter from a citizen of Plaquemines); *ibid.* July 13 (dispatch from Franklin); *Picayune,* June 26 (letter from a citizen of Marksville).

65 Brashear *News,* quoted in Donaldsonville *Chief,* June 28, and *Picayune,* June 26, 1873. See also Opelousas *Courier,* June 21, and Convent *Le Louisianais,* July 12.

66 For Republican approval, see Opelousas *Journal,* June 21, 1873; Alexandria *Rapides Gazette,* July 19, 26; Baton Rouge *Grand Era* (Negro), quoted in New Orleans *Republican,* June 24; Franklin *Attakapas Register,* quoted in Opelousas *Courier,* June 21. For Republican disapproval, see St. Francisville *Dunn Leader,* July 19; Natchitoches *Times,* quoted in New Orleans *Picayune,* July 13; West Baton Rouge *Sugar Planter,* quoted in New Orleans *Republican,* July 29; Lake Providence *Lake Republican,* August 2.

67 New Orleans *Times,* July 11, 1873; New Orleans *Picayune,* July 11, 13, 15; New Orleans *Republican,* July 11. These issues carry the unification platform, with the signatures of approximately one thousand approving citizens.

68 For a sketch of Allain, see Alice Dunbar-Nelson, "People of Color in Louisiana," in *Journal of Negro History,* II (1917), 75. See also Perkins, *Who's Who in Colored Louisiana,* 49, 52.

69 For sketches of Burch, see A. E. Perkins, "James Henri Burch and Oscar James Dunn in Louisiana," in *Journal of Negro History,* XXII (1937), 321–25; Perkins, *Who's Who in Colored Louisiana,* 49-50; Harrisburg *National Progress,* quoted in New Orleans *Republican,* April 13, 1873; New Haven *Palladium,* quoted in *ibid.,* September 10, 1873. See also Warmoth, *War, Politics, and Reconstruction,* 191, 193. For white opinion of Burch, see New Orleans *Times,* May 28, 29, 1873; Clinton *Patriot-Democrat,* quoted in St. Francisville *Dunn Leader,* July 12.

70 On Lewis, see Perkins, *Who's Who in Colored Louisiana,* 56, 58; New Orleans *Picayune,* May 13, 1873; New Orleans *Republican,* February 20.

71 The signers were Lewis, Mary, Roudanez, Antoine, who have been identified; and Paul Boseigneur, a Negro labor leader; William Moody, a preacher; William Rodolph, a Republican ward leader; and a D. or C. Rillieux, who cannot be identified. His initial is given differently in the newspapers. There were several prominent Negroes of this name but none with either of the above initials. The original manuscript of the Negro pledge is in the Department of Archives, Louisiana State University.

72 This summary of the meeting is drawn from the *Times, Picayune, Republican,* and *L'Abeille* of July 16, 1873.

73 New Orleans *Times,* July 17, 1873.

74 New Orleans *Republican,* July 17, 19, 1873.

75 New Orleans *Picayune*, July 18, 1873.

76 New Orleans *Herald*, quoted in Monroe *Ouachita Telegraph*, July 26, 1873 in Opelousas *Courier*, July 26, and in Alexandria *Rapides Gazette*, July 26. The Opelousas *Courier*, July 26, a Democratic paper which had approved unification, said that unfortunately some "wolves in sheep's clothing" had been allowed to slip in among the Negro supporters of the movement.

77 Shreveport *Times*, August 20, 1873.

78 Thibodaux *Sentinel*, August 2, 1873; Alexandria *Rapides Gazette*, August 2, 9; Opelousas *Courier*, September 6. There seems to have been no formal abandonment of the movement by its sponsors. It disappeared in silence.

79 New Orleans *Times*, July 22, 1873.

80 *Ibid.*, June 30, July 1, 3, 7, 1873; *Picayune*, July 18 (letter by "B").

81 New Orleans *Times*, June 2, 1873 (letter by "Tendis"); *ibid.*, July 13 ("Round About Town").

82 For the attitude of the Democratic politicians, see Roundabout in *Times*, July 22, 1873. For the Republican politicians, see Governor Kellogg, quoted in *Republican*, November 4; Pinckney B. S. Pinchback, *ibid.*, September 19; and James R. West, *ibid.*, June 28.

83 Alexandria *Rapides Gazette*, July 26, 1873. See also Brashear *News*, quoted in *Picayune*, July 26.

84 David H. Donald, "The Scalawag in Mississippi Reconstruction," in *Journal of Southern History* (Baton Rouge, 1935–), X (1944), 447–60.

85 It is not known whether "unification" movements appeared in all the southern states. There were co-operation organizations formed in South Carolina and Mississippi. See Francis B. Simkins and Robert H. Woody, *South Carolina during Reconstruction* (Chapel Hill, 1932), 447–54; Alrutheus A. Taylor, *The Negro in South Carolina during the Reconstruction* (Washington, 1924), 195–97; John S. Reynolds, *Reconstruction in South Carolina, 1865–1877* (Columbia, 1905), 139–43; James W. Garner, *Reconstruction in Mississippi* (New York, 1901), 238-43. The South Carolina and Mississippi movements seem to have been narrower in the scope of their platform than the one in Louisiana, being restricted largely to political issues. Both, it is significant to note, were led by planters and business men.

An Analysis of Some Reconstruction Attitudes

1 Francis B. Simkins, "New Viewpoints of Southern Reconstruction," in *Journal of Southern History* (Baton Rouge, 1935–), V (1939), 49–61; Howard K. Beale, "On Rewriting Reconstruction History," in *American Historical Review* (New York, 1895–), XLV (1940), 807–27; Horace Mann Bond, "Social and Economic Forces in Alabama Reconstruction," in *Journal of Negro History* (Washington, 1916–), XXIII (1938), 290–348. These writers do two things that so many writers on the subject have not done: they treat Reconstruction as a national development rather than as something happening in an insulated South, and they relate it to southern forces before and after Reconstruction.

2 Howard K. Beale, *The Critical Year: A Study of Andrew Johnson and Reconstruction* (New York, 1930), 1, 8, 115, 143–45; Beale, "On Rewriting Reconstruction History," *loc. cit.*, 813.

3 William B. Hesseltine, "Economic Factors in the Abandonment of Reconstruction," in *Mississippi Valley Historical Review* (Cedar Rapids, 1914–), XXII (1935), 191–210. See also, Hesseltine, *The South in American History* (New York, 1943). 488–89.

4 W. E. Burghardt Du Bois, *Black Reconstruction: An Essay toward a History of the Part which Black Folk Played in the Attempt to Reconstruct Democracy in*

America, 1860–1880 (New York, 1938), 182, 185–87. Beale, in his article, "On Rewriting Reconstruction History," *loc. cit.*, 818–19, admitted that there were minority elements of democratic idealism in the Republican party and that Stevens and Charles Sumner were representatives of these elements. For the contrary view that Stevens thought solely in terms of power for his class and party, see Richard N. Current, *Old Thad Stevens: A Story of Ambition* (Madison, 1942).

5 The term Marxist is here applied to those writers who frankly state that they are interpreting history according to the laws and predictions of Karl Marx and to those who without acknowledging Marx write history that conforms to the Marxian pattern.

6 James S. Allen, *Reconstruction: The Battle for Democracy, 1865–1867* (New York, 1937).

7 *Ibid.*, 18, 22, 81, 89.

8 Howard Fast, *Freedom Road* (New York, 1944), 71.

9 It is significant that those Negroes who envisioned Reconstruction as a real social revolution for their people saw little idealism in the Republican party. Thus the New Orleans *Tribune*, a Negro newspaper, said: "The Republican party of the North was not formed upon the true basis of justice and equality, as the history of abolition and slavery plainly shows; and it has only the right to claim credit for having abolished slavery as a political necessity and of having given the ballot to the black men as an arm of defence to the loyal white men. Emergency, nay necessity, had more to do with the abolition of slavery and the passage of the Military Bill than had philanthropy and love for the negro." Quoted in New Orleans *Times*, July 4, 1873.

10 Helen J. and T. Harry Williams, "Wisconsin Republicans and Reconstruction, 1865–1870," in *Wisconsin Magazine of History* (Madison, 1917–   ), XXIII (1939), 17–39.

11 The views of the Dunning school are in William A. Dunning, *Reconstruction: Political and Economic, 1865–1877* (New York, 1907), especially pp. 116–17, 213; Walter L. Fleming, *The Sequel of Appomattox: A Chronicle of the Reunion of the States* (New Haven, 1921), especially pp. 47–48, 50–52, 87–88. These criticisms of Dunning and Fleming are not made in any carping spirit. It is recognized that they and other members of the Dunning school were pioneers in the study of Reconstruction and made important factual contributions to its history. It should also be noted that Fleming was aware that many planters were for Negro suffrage and that most farmers were against it. See his *Civil War and Reconstruction in Alabama* (New York, 1905), 387–88. But he ascribed the planters' attitude merely to a desire to control the Negro vote in order to maintain their power in the legislature.

12 Du Bois, *Black Reconstruction*, 346–47, 350.

13 *Ibid.*, 130–31. These criticisms of Du Bois do not detract from the fact that his book was a valuable contribution to Reconstruction history. In some respects he got closer to the truth of Reconstruction than any other writer.

14 Allen, *Reconstruction*, 111–15, 126, 183–84, 193. On different pages Allen states that a significant portion of the common whites joined the Republican party and again that practically all of them did. The book as a whole gives the impression that the poorer whites as a class became Republicans.

15 Fast, *Freedom Road*, 263.

16 Paul Lewinson, *Race, Class, and Party: A History of Negro Suffrage in the South* (New York, 1932), 23, 37, 52; Roger W. Shugg, *Origins of Class Struggle in Louisiana: A Social History of White Farmers and Laborers during Slavery and After, 1840–1875* (Baton Rouge, 1939), 230; Hesseltine, *South in American History*, 485; Dunning, *Reconstruction*, 213; Fleming, *Sequel of Appomattox*, 47–48, 50, 87–88; Fleming, *Civil War and Reconstruction in Alabama*, 387–88.

17 Bond, "Social and Economic Factors in Alabama Reconstruction," *loc. cit.*,

294–95. Bond finds that at the beginning of Reconstruction there was some political co-operation between poor whites and Negroes.

18 Kimball Young, *Social Psychology* (New York, 1944), 262–63, 269.

19 There was logic in this position. Many of the Negro leaders were exponents of radical agrarianism. Said the New Orleans *Tribune:* "There is no more room in the organization of our society, for an oligarchy of slaveholders, or property holders"; and again, "There is in fact, no true republican government, unless the land, and wealth in general, are distributed among the great mass of the inhabitants." Quoted in Du Bois, *Black Reconstruction,* 458–59. This agrarianism never secured any significant victories because the carpetbaggers, scalawags, and professional Negro politicians, interested mainly in corruption and power, choked it off. See Shugg, *Origins of Class Struggle in Louisiana,* 243–44.

20 New Orleans *Times,* August 13, 1865.

21 *Ibid.,* December 24, 1866.

22 *Ibid.,* February 2, 1868. There are similar statements in the issues of November 26, 30, 1866, January 26, 1867.

23 Hampton, Alexander H. Stephens, Benjamin F. Perry, and other leaders had suggested a limited Negro suffrage based on property and education, thus permitting only those Negroes to vote who were conscious of property rights. Hampton believed the planters could easily control such voters. Lewinson, *Race, Class, and Party,* 37–39; Fleming, *Sequel of Appomattox,* 50–52.

24 New Orleans *Crescent,* October 23, 1867.

25 *Ibid.,* May 14, 1868.

26 New Orleans *Daily Picayune,* May 10, 1868.

27 *Ibid.,* May 23, 1868.

28 *Ibid.,* May 24, 1868.

29 J. W. Robb, in Jackson *Clarion,* March 19, 1868, quoted in New Orleans *Times,* March 22.

30 *House Reports,* 43 Cong., 2 Sess., No. 261, Part 3, pp. 646–47.

31 Du Bois, *Black Reconstruction,* 590–91.

32 Letter of Archibald Mitchell, in New Orleans *Picayune,* June 18, 1873.

33 New Orleans *Times,* May 29, 1873.

34 *Ibid.,* May 30, 1873.

35 *Ibid.,* June 6, 1873.

36 *Ibid.,* June 23, 1873.

37 *Ibid.,* June 9, 1873.

38 *Ibid.,* August 13, 1867. "On 'Change" column. The business columns of the newspapers contain much information about the activities of business men in Reconstruction. Historians have overlooked this important source.

39 *Ibid.,* August 17, 1867. See also issue of September 5.

40 David H. Donald, "The Scalawag in Mississippi Reconstruction," in *Journal of Southern History,* X (1944), 447–60.

41 *Ibid.,* 449–50.

42 *Ibid.,* 453–55.

43 Francis B. Simkins and Robert H. Woody, *South Carolina during Reconstruction* (Chapel Hill, 1932), 447–54; Alrutheus A. Taylor, *The Negro in South Carolina during the Reconstruction* (Washington, 1924), 195–97; John S. Reynolds, *Reconstruction in South Carolina, 1865–1877* (Columbia, 1905), 139–43; James W. Garner, *Reconstruction in Mississippi* (New York, 1901), 238–43.

44 T. Harry Williams, "The Louisiana Unification Movement of 1873," in *Journal of Southern History,* XI (1945), 349–69.

45 Beauregard believed that in the long run Negro suffrage would increase the political power of the South. The whites could control the Negroes "with a little educa-

tion and some property qualifications" and "defeat our adversaries with their own weapon." Quoted in New York *Tribune*, April 1, 1867. For other expressions of a similar view, see *ibid.*, April 4, 1867, quoting Mobile *Tribune* and Wilmington (N.C.) *Dispatch*.

46 Williams, "Louisiana Unification Movement," *loc. cit.*, 359–61. It is to be noted that rich whites could ask for the destruction of segregation without having to encounter many of the results of non-segregation. This was particularly true in education. As a North Louisiana newspaper pointed out, the rich sent their children to private white schools; the poorer whites had to send theirs to public schools which the rich proposed to make biracial. Shreveport *Times*, quoted in Monroe *Ouachita Telegraph*, June 28, 1873.

47 Du Bois, *Black Reconstruction*, 611.

48 New Orleans *Times*, May 28, 1873.

49 This point is well developed in Du Bois, *Black Reconstruction*, 611–12.

50 C. Vann Woodward, *Tom Watson: Agrarian Rebel* (New York, 1938), 58–72. For similar developments in other states, see Francis B. Simkins, *Pitchfork Ben Tillman, South Carolinian* (Baton Rouge, 1944), 79–80; Willie D. Halsell, "The Bourbon Period in Mississippi Politics, 1875–1890," in *Journal of Southern History*, XI (1945), 519–37.

51 Woodward, *Tom Watson*, 80–81; Judson C. Ward, "The Republican Party in Bourbon Georgia, 1872–1890," in *Journal of Southern History*, IX (1943), 200. See, also, Simkins, *Pitchfork Ben Tillman*, 164, 167. The planters also employed the Negro vote against the Republicans. In 1884 Edward Gay, Democrat, was running for Congress from a South Louisiana district against Republican William P. Kellogg. Edward N. Pugh, Democratic leader of Ascension Parish, outlined for the sugar planters methods of swinging the colored vote behind Gay. Let owners and managers tell the Negro workers to vote for Gay, he advised: "They naturally receive with deference the expression of opinion by their employers on all subjects. . . . Nearly all the leading colored men are with us and they need only the offer of substantial moral support from the employers to swell the number of the supporters of Mr. Gay from the ranks of the colored employees." Edward N. Pugh to William Porcher Miles, October 30, 1884, in W. P. Miles Papers (Southern Historical Collection, University of North Carolina).

52 Although the impetus for disfranchisement generally came from farmer leaders, the rich whites acquiesced in the movement. They did so partly out of a desire to placate the white masses and partly because the farmers, particularly during the agrarian unrest of the 1890s, sometimes tried to vote the Negroes on their side. The competition for the colored vote frightened many whites and forced the wealthy whites to pay out large monetary sums to retain their Negro supporters. Undoubtedly the planter-business class saw in disfranchisement a chance to eliminate a purchasable vote that was steadily becoming more expensive. See George M. Reynolds, *Machine Politics in New Orleans, 1897–1926* (New York, 1936), 21, 26–27, 29–30, 35. "As the situation had developed," writes Reynolds, "it seemed best to take the Negro vote off the market and leave only the white electorate with its comparatively small venal vote to be traded in on election day" (p. 26). For an itemized account of how much it cost the planters in one Louisiana parish to buy Negro votes in the election of 1892, and a complaint about the price, see Henry McCall to William Porcher Miles, May 4, 1892, in Miles Papers.

Interlude: 1918–1939

1 Other lesser naval powers having Pacific interests, Belgium, the Netherlands, Portugal, and China, were invited later. Soviet Russia, which was not recognized dip-

lomatically by the United States and most other governments, was not asked to attend.

2 The function of industrial procurement was assigned specifically to the Assistant Secretary of War.

3 Pershing as Chief of Staff apparently viewed the office in a more benign light than he had during the war.

World War II: The American Involvement

1 The United States and twenty-five other nations signed in January 1942 at Washington the United Nations Declaration committing the members to fight "Hitlerism."

2 Women for the first time served in support capacities in the armed forces. However, their number was small in relation to the total, and it is accurate to speak of the World War II force as a male force.

3 As in World War I, administration of the draft was placed in the hands of local boards of citizens, and the names of individuals called up were drawn by lot.

The Military Systems of North and South

1 The North's objectives could be obtained only by a total military victory. The South, on the other hand, could attain its objectives by preventing the North from winning such a victory. But the South's policy objectives were total; it could accept no result except independence.

2 The several statements in these essays calling attention to the absence of plans at the beginning of wars are not to be taken as a belief in the necessity or feasibility of having a previously drawn up and detailed scheme of operations. Indeed, the possession of a rigid design may handicap a nation, as the experience of Germany with the Schlieffen plan attests. Especially today, when the nature of war is so fluid, it may be advantageous to be able to choose among a number of plans after war begins. What I am saying here is that in some of our wars *no thinking* about what might happen had been done before the advent of hostilities.

3 It is recognized, of course, that on occasion the Confederacy did go over to the offensive, as in Bragg's invasion of Kentucky in 1862 and, most notably, in Lee's thrusts into the North in 1862 and 1863. But these operations were exceptions to the rule. Also, in every case where an offensive was attempted, the size of the Confederate army could have been significantly augmented by adding to it forces that were guarding places at home.

4 The best treatment of Confederate command arrangements is Frank E. Vandiver, *Rebel Brass: The Confederate Command System* (Baton Rouge, 1956).

5 It may be said that this criticism of Scott, especially in view of his age and former services, is too harsh. In defense of Scott one may argue that such a move as he proposed, and particularly the blockade, was the only operation immediately feasible for the North and that few people in 1861 foresaw the frightful length and extent to which the war would go. On the other hand Scott, before the shooting started, had busied himself devising political plans to avert war, and it is evident that his mind was working in the direction of diplomatic or economic action instead of war.

6 Because of the several critical references to Jomini in this essay, it is necessary, to avoid being unfair to him, to qualify some of my statements. At no point have I meant to imply that there is any contradiction between Jomini's concept of concentration and offensive action. He realized fully the advantage of the offensive. Although at times he advocated the destruction of enemy armies, at others he recommended the occupation of places, and it was the latter objective which his American admirers

adopted. Nor have I meant to argue that there may not be times in war when massive concentration at one point may not be decisive. It may be, especially in relatively small countries like those in Europe to which Jomini applied his doctrines. It may be doubted, however, that one big breakthrough by the North would have collapsed the South. The point made here is that several simultaneous attacks, which the North was well able to mount, constituted the best strategy for the side with the superior resources. But the Northern generals tended to insist, using Jomini's principle of concentration, that only one big effort should be made at a time, meaning, of course, by one army—their particular army. It can be argued that Jomini's concepts were not intrinsically faulty but that his American followers were misinterpreting them.

Freeman, Historian of the Civil War: An Appraisal

1 This essay is based upon a paper given at the joint meeting of the Mississippi Valley Historical Association with the American Historical Association in Chicago, December 28, 1953. I wish to record my thanks to Mr. Bruce Catton, editor of *American Heritage*, and Professor Robert H. Woody, Duke University, for providing me with stimulating suggestions about the subject. They are not, however, to be charged with the opinions here expressed. Both of them, and particularly Professor Woody, would disagree with much that I have written.

2 *R. E. Lee* (4 vols., New York, 1934–1935), III, 524.
3 *Ibid.*, I, 459, 552–53.
4 *Ibid.*, I, ix.
5 *Ibid.*, II, 428.
6 *Ibid.*, II, 446.
7 *Ibid.*, II, 343.
8 *Ibid.*, III, 52.
9 *Ibid.*, I, 404, 416.

The Gentleman from Louisiana: Demagogue or Democrat

1 Much of the information in this paper was obtained from interviews, many of them tape-recorded, with dozens of Huey P. Long and anti-Long leaders. Some of these men have no objection to being quoted by name, while others do object. Because of the difficulty of segregating such sources, no documentation of the interviews has been attempted. The writer is firmly convinced that the scientifically conducted interview is a valid source for the history of the recent past. Indeed, it may be the only source in a technological age when few people write letters or diaries.

2 It may be contended that there is some exaggeration in the above statements. Of course, any generalizations concerning the whole people of a state are subject to qualification. What I have described as the Louisiana attitude toward corruption is especially prevalent in south Louisiana, which contains, however, a substantial majority of the state's population. Some observers would argue that tolerance of corruption has been replaced in the last decade or so by a stricter view, and this may be true. Certainly today most people would say that elections have been conducted honestly—and point to voting machines as the reason.

3 Pendleton Herring, *The Politics of Democracy* (New York, 1940), 146–47.
4 Ralph Waldo Emerson, *Complete Works*, Concord Edition (12 vols., Cambridge, Mass., 1903–1904), VI, 258.
5 Roger W. Shugg, *Origins of Class Struggle in Louisiana* (University, La., 1939), 150–51.
6 W. J. Cash, *The Mind of the South* (Garden City, N.Y., 1954), 252–53, 255–56.
7 Cash, *Mind of the South*, 287–88.

8 The size of the debt is differently computed, depending on what items are included. Long claimed that he was not responsible for over $42,000,000 in bonds issued against the Port of New Orleans under previous governors and sold as state obligations. The maturities fell due in his administration.

9 Cash, *Mind of the South*, 289.

10 Allan P. Sindler, *Huey Long's Louisiana* (Baltimore, 1956), 105.

11 Eric Hoffer, *The True Believer* (New York, 1951), 111-14, 153.

12 Hoffer, *True Believer*, 147-48.

13 Jacques Maritain, *Man and the State* (Chicago, 1951), 141.

14 Gerald W. Johnson, "Live Demagogue, or Dead Gentleman," *Virginia Quarterly Review*, XII (January 1936), 9.

Huey, Lyndon, and Southern Radicalism

1 In studying the problem of change in the South, I have profited from the research of my seminar on this subject at Louisiana State University in 1972. The members of the seminar were Nixon G. Dalrymple, William J. Boyles, Joe C. Mason, Terry Miller, Maria M. Pyles, Stanley J. Smith, John L. Tucker, Stephen P. Vidrine, Elmiria B. Wicker, and Elizabeth Williams. I am indebted to another of my graduate students, Michael Gillett, for providing me with items secured in his own research on Lyndon B. Johnson.

2 Carl N. Degler, "The Peculiar Dissent of the Nineteenth Century South," Alfred F. Young, ed., *Dissent: Explorations in the History of American Radicalism* (DeKalb, Ill., 1968), 111-12.

3 Rebecca West, "When Silent Was the South," London *Sunday Telegraph*, June 18, 1972.

4 C. Vann Woodward, *The Burden of Southern History* (Baton Rouge, 1968), 150, 151, 156-57.

5 William Appleman Williams, "Ol Lyndon," *New York Review of Books*, XVII (Dec. 16, 1971), 3.

6 Pat Watters, *The South and the Nation* (New York, 1969), 4.

7 Vincent Harding, "Black Radicalism: The Road from Montgomery," Alfred F. Young, ed., *Dissent: Explorations in the History of American Radicalism* (De Kalb, Ill., 1968), 322, 324.

8 Quoted in Willie Morris, *Yazoo: Integration in a Deep-Southern Town* (New York, 1971), 86n.

9 The statements from Father A. J. McKnight and Mrs. Fannie Lou Hamer were obtained by my students Joe C. Mason, Terry Miller, and Maria M. Pyles.

10 Morris, *Yazoo*, 85-86; Watters, *South and the Nation*, 63; Leslie W. Dunbar, "The Annealing of the South," *Virginia Quarterly Review*, 37 (Autumn 1961), 499.

11 W. J. Cash, *The Mind of the South* (New York, 1941), 31.

12 As quoted to the author by H. L. Mitchell.

13 Williams, "Ol Lyndon," 3; Reg Murphy and Hal Gulliver, *The Southern Strategy* (New York, 1971), 253. The wording of the question is somewhat changed from how it is stated in Murphy and Gulliver.

14 Theodore H. White, *The Making of the President 1964* (New York, 1965), 357.

15 *Public Papers of the Presidents of the United States: Lyndon B. Johnson: Containing the Public Messages, Speeches, and Statements of the President 1963-64* (2 vols., Washington, 1965), II, 1285; *Public Papers of the Presidents of the United States: Lyndon B. Johnson: Containing the Public Messages, Speeches, and Statements of the President 1965* (2 vols., Washington, 1966), I, 195; *Public Papers of the Presidents of the United States: Lyndon B. Johnson: Containing the Public Mes-*

sages, Speeches, and Statements of the President 1966 (2 vols., Washington, 1967), II, 1145.

16 T. Harry Williams, *Huey Long* (New York, 1969), 17–24, 45; William C. Pool, Emmie Craddock, and David E. Conrad, *Lyndon Baines Johnson: The Formative Years* (San Marcos, Texas, 1965), 48, 176; Rowland Evans and Robert Novak, *Lyndon B. Johnson: The Exercise of Power* (New York, 1966), 6–7; Philip Geyelin, *Lyndon B. Johnson and the World* (New York, 1966), 29; Brenham (Texas) *Banner-Press*, Sept. 23, 1937; *Public Papers of . . . Lyndon B. Johnson . . . 1966*, II, 922.

17 Williams, *Huey Long*, 320–21, 749; Joseph Kraft, *Profiles in Power* (New York, 1966), 9; *Public Papers of . . . Lyndon B. Johnson . . . 1963–64*, I, 368–69; Eric F. Goldman, *The Tragedy of Lyndon Johnson* (New York, 1969), 20–21.

18 Williams, *Huey Long*, 751; David Halberstam, "Lyndon," *Esquire*, LXXVIII (Aug. 1972), 74–76; Hugh Sidey, *A Very Personal Presidency: Lyndon Johnson in the White House* (New York, 1968), 247; Wilbur J. Cohen, interview (Lyndon Baines Johnson Library, Austin, Texas).

19 Williams, *Huey Long*, 751–52; Goldman, *Tragedy of Lyndon Johnson*, 127.

20 White, *Making of the President 1964*, 357.

21 Williams, *Huey Long*, 703, 761; Halberstam, "Lyndon," 76; Cohen interview.

22 Anthony Howard, "Tom Sawyer in a Toga," *New Statesman*, LXXIX (April 3, 1970), 477; Williams, *Huey Long*, 414.

23 Williams, *Huey Long*, 13–14, 23–24, 44.

24 *Ibid.*, 409–10; Howard, "Tom Sawyer in a Toga," 477; Otis L. Graham, Jr., "Man of the Left," *Progressive*, 34 (March 1970), 45.

25 Williams, *Huey Long*, 693, 846.

26 *Ibid.*, 703–05; Shreveport *Sun*, April 22, 1933.

27 *New York Times Book Review*, Nov. 2, 1969.

28 *Public Papers of the Presidents of the United States: Lyndon B. Johnson: Containing the Public Messages, Speeches, and Statements of the President 1968–69* (2 vols., Washington, 1970), I, 482. For the suggestion as to the difficulty of change in a large country, the author is indebted to an essay by Peregrine Worsethorne, "Some Sense in Labour's Sulks," London *Sunday Telegraph*, Dec. 17, 1972.

29 Michael C. Janeway, "Lyndon Johnson and the Rise of Conservatism in Texas" (senior thesis, Harvard University, 1962), 59. The author is indebted to Michael Gillette for a copy of this valuable study and to the author for permission to cite it.

30 Leonard Baker, *The Johnson Eclipse: A President's Vice Presidency* (New York, 1966), 199–201; Evans and Novak, *Lyndon B. Johnson*, 121; White, *Making of the President 1964*, 252–53; Lyndon Baines Johnson, *The Vantage Point* (New York, 1971), 155.

31 Evans and Novak, *Lyndon B. Johnson*, 31, 241, 242, 250.

32 *Ibid.*, 32, 119; Baker, *Johnson Eclipse*, 204; Janeway, "Johnson and the Rise of Conservatism in Texas," 63n.

33 Theodore H. White, *The Making of the President 1960* (New York, 1961), 133; Baker, *Johnson Eclipse*, 216.

34 Evans and Novak, *Lyndon B. Johnson*, 139; *Public Papers of . . . Lyndon B. Johnson . . . 1965*, I, 286. For a discussion of Johnson's evolving views on racial matters, see Harry McPherson, *A Political Education* (Boston, 1972), 126–55.

35 Louis Heren, *No Hail, No Farewell* (New York, 1970), 19; White, *Making of the President 1964*, 253; Tom Wicker, *JFK and LBJ: The Influence of Personality upon Politics* (New York, 1968), 152; Johnson, *Vantage Point*, 89.

36 Heren, *No Hail, No Farewell*, 15; Evans and Novak, *Lyndon B. Johnson*, 287.

37 I. F. Stone, *In a Time of Torment: Our most distinguished independent journalist, on the most urgent issues and key personalities of our time: LBJ, the war in Viet-*

nam, Fulbright, the Negro Revolution, the Kennedys, Malcolm X, the Left, the Right, and Where Do We Go From Here? (New York, 1967), 12; Halberstam, "Lyndon," 86; Geyelin, Johnson and the World, 7, 18.

38 Public Papers of . . . Lyndon B. Johnson . . . 1963–64, I, 114, 822; Public Papers of . . . Lyndon B. Johnson . . . 1965, II, 797; Johnson, Vantage Point, 72–73, 87. For an evaluation of the Great Society's programs in the ghettos, see Frances Fox Piven and Richard A. Cloward, Regulating the Poor: The Functions of Public Welfare (New York, 1971), 261–62, 276, 281.

39 Evans and Novak, Lyndon B. Johnson, 492–93; White, Making of the President 1964, 396–97, 400–01; Heren, No Hail, No Farewell, 229; Anthony Celebrezze, interview (Lyndon B. Johnson Library, Austin, Texas).

40 Celebrezze interview; Cohen interview; Theodore H. White, The Making of the President 1968 (New York, 1969), 101.

41 Baker, Johnson Eclipse, 219, 229; Johnson, Vantage Point, 156–57; Public Papers of the Presidents of the United States: Lyndon B. Johnson: Containing the Public Messages, Speeches, and Statements of the President 1967 (2 vols., Washington, 1968), I, 177–78.

42 Public Papers of . . . Lyndon B. Johnson . . . 1963–64, I, 9, 116, 482; Public Papers of . . . Lyndon B. Johnson . . . 1965, I, 284, 285; ibid., II, 635–40, 841, 899.

43 Goldman, Tragedy of Lyndon Johnson, 320; Ralph Ellison, quoted in James MacGregor Burns, ed., To Heal and to Build: The Programs of President Lyndon B. Johnson (New York, 1968), 207–08; Robert Sherrill, The Accidental President (New York, 1967), 197.

44 Public Papers of . . . Lyndon B. Johnson . . . 1963–64, II, 1450; Public Papers of . . . Lyndon B. Johnson . . . 1965, I, 284; Wicker, JFK and LBJ, 170, 171, 175.

45 J. Evetts Haley, A Texan Looks at Lyndon: A Study in Illegitimate Power (Canyon, Texas, 1964), 226.

46 Quoted in Burns, ed., To Heal and to Build, 216.

47 Clarence Mitchell, interview (Lyndon B. Johnson Library, Austin, Texas).

48 Roy Wilkins, interview, ibid.

49 Ebony, XXVII (April 1972), 182.

50 Charles Evers interview with John Tucker.

51 For Johnson's desire to be loved, see Evans and Novak, Lyndon B. Johnson, 294; White, Making of the President 1964, 33–34.

52 George E. Reddy, The Twilight of the Presidency (New York, 1970), 157–60; McPherson, Political Education, 172; Douglass Cater interview (Lyndon B. Johnson Library, Austin, Texas).

53 For sensible comments on the communication problem, see Cater interview.

54 Goldman, Tragedy of Lyndon Johnson, 162, 336–37, 439; Baker, Johnson Eclipse, 195–96; Cohen interview.

55 White, Making of the President 1968, 100; Heren, No Hail, No Farewell, 261–62; Sidey, Personal Presidency, 100, 107–08, 169–70; Halberstam, "Lyndon," 86; Geyelin, Johnson and the World, 245–46; McPherson, Political Education, 51–52.

56 Burns, ed., To Heal and to Build, 3; Kraft, Profiles in Power, 18; Evans and Novak, Lyndon B. Johnson, 3, 508; Sidey, Personal Presidency, 42–43.

57 Johnson, Vantage Point, 95.

58 The reference is to Eric Goldman's dictum that Johnson was the wrong man. Goldman, Tragedy of Lyndon Johnson, 531.

59 Sidey, Personal Presidency, 99–100; McPherson, Political Education, 445.

60 Williams, Huey Long, 116.

61 Public Papers of . . . Lyndon B. Johnson . . . 1968–69, II, 1260.

Books and Articles by T. Harry Williams

Books

Lincoln and the Radicals. Madison: University of Wisconsin Press, 1941.

Editor, *Selected Writings and Speeches of Abraham Lincoln*. Chicago: Packard and Company, 1943.

Lincoln and His Generals. New York: A. A. Knopf, 1952.

P. G. T. Beauregard, Napoleon in Gray. Baton Rouge: Louisiana State University Press, 1955.

Editor, *With Beauregard in Mexico*. Baton Rouge: Louisiana State University Press, 1956.

A History of the United States, with R. N. Current and Frank Freidel. 2 vols. New York: A. A. Knopf, 1959.

Americans at War: The Development of the American Military System. Baton Rouge: Louisiana State University Press, 1960.

Romance and Realism in Southern Politics. Athens: University of Georgia Press, 1961.

Editor, *Military Memoirs of a Confederate*, by E. Porter Alexander. Bloomington: Indiana University Press, 1962.

McClellan, Sherman and Grant. Brunswick, N.J.: Rutgers University Press, 1962.

The Union Sundered. New York: Time, Inc., 1963.

The Union Restored. New York: Time, Inc., 1963.

Hayes: The Diary of a President. New York: David McKay Press, 1964.

Hayes of the Twenty-third: Civil War Volunteer. New York: A. A. Knopf, 1965.

Huey Long. New York: A. A. Knopf, 1969.

The History of American Wars, from 1745 to 1918. New York: A. A. Knopf, 1981.

Chapters in Other Works

"Abraham Lincoln: Pragmatic Democrat." In *The Enduring Lincoln*, edited by Norman A. Graebner. Urbana: University of Illinois Press, 1959.

Introduction to V. L. Bedsole and Oscar Richard, *Louisiana State University: A Pictorial Record*. Baton Rouge: Louisiana State University Press, 1959.

"Lincoln: The Military Strategist." In *Abraham Lincoln: A New Portrait*, edited by Henry B. Krantz. New York: Putnam's, 1959.

"Lincoln and the Causes of the Civil War." In *Lincoln Images*, edited by O. Fritiof Ander. Rock Island, Ill.: Augustana College Library, 1960.

"Lincoln and the Committee on the Conduct of the War." In *Lincoln for the Ages*, edited by Ralph G. Newman. Garden City, N.Y.: Doubleday, 1960.

"The American Civil War." In *The Zenith of European Power*, edited by J. B. Bury. Vol. X of *The New Cambridge Modern History*. Cambridge: Cambridge University Press, 1960.

"The Military Leadership of North and South." In *Why the North Won the Civil War*, edited by David Donald. Baton Rouge: Louisiana State University Press, 1960.

"P. G. T. Beauregard: The South's First Hero." In *The Unforgettable Americans*, edited by John A. Garraty. New York: Channel Press, 1960.

"Disruption of the Union: The Secession Crisis, 1860–1861." In *Major Crises in American History*, Vol. I, edited by L. W. Levy and M. D. Peterson. New York: Harcourt, Brace and World, 1962.

"Lincoln and the Radicals: An Essay in Civil War History and Historiography." In *Grant, Lee, Lincoln, and the Radicals*, edited by Grady McWhiney. Evanston: Northwestern University Press, 1964.

"The Gentleman from Louisiana: Demagogue or Democrat." In *The Pursuit of Southern History*, edited by George Brown Tindall. Baton Rouge: Louisiana State University Press, 1964.

Introduction to *Every Man a King: The Autobiography of Huey P. Long*. New York: Quadrangle Books, 1964.

"Trends in Southern Politics." In *The Idea of the South*, edited by Frank E. Vandiver. Chicago: The University of Chicago Press, 1964.

"The Military Leadership of North and South." In *American Defense Policy in Perspective*, edited by Raymond G. O'Connor. New York: John Wiley and Sons, 1965.

"The Military Systems of North and South." In *Patterns in American History*, Vol. I, edited by Alexander De Conde *et al.* Belmont, Calif.: Wadsworth Publishing Company, 1965.

Foreword to A. J. Liebling, *The Earl of Louisiana*. Baton Rouge: Louisiana State University Press, 1970.

"The Politics of the Longs." In *Huey Long*, edited by Hugh Davis Graham. Englewood Cliffs, N.J.: Prentice-Hall, 1970.

"Huey Long and the Politics of Realism." In *Essays on Recent Southern Pol-*

itics, edited by H. M. Hollingsworth. Austin: University of Texas Press, 1970.

"The Civil War." In *Interpreting American History*, edited by John A. Garraty. New York: Macmillan, 1970.

THW with others. *The Meanings of American History*, Vol. II. Glenview, Ill.: Scott, Foresman, 1972.

"The Coming of the War." In *Shadows of the Storm*, Vol. I, edited by William C. Davis. Garden City, N.Y.: Doubleday, 1981.

Articles

"General John C. Frémont and the Politicians." *Journal of the American Military History Foundation*, II, No. 4 (Winter, 1938), 179–91.

"Benjamin F. Wade and the Atrocity Propaganda of the Civil War." *Ohio Archaeological and Historical Quarterly* (January, 1939), 33–43.

"The Attack upon West Point During the Civil War." *Mississippi Valley Historical Review*, XXV, No. 4 (March, 1939), 491–504.

"General Banks and the Radical Republicans During the Civil War." *New England Quarterly*, XII, No. 2 (June, 1939), 268–80.

"The Committee on the Conduct of the War." *Journal of the American Military Institute*, III, No. 3 (Fall, 1939), 139–56.

with Helen J. Williams. "Wisconsin Republicans and Reconstruction." *Wisconsin Magazine of History*, XXIII, No. 1 (September, 1939), 17–39.

"The Navy and the Committee on the Conduct of the War." *United States Naval Institute Proceedings*, LXV, No. 12 (December, 1939), 1751–55.

"Andrew Johnson as a Member of the Committee on the Conduct of the War." *Proceedings of the East Tennessee Historical Society*, No. 12 (1940), 70–83.

with James Ferguson. "*The Life of Jefferson Davis* by M'Arone." *Journal of Mississippi History*, V (October, 1943), 197–203.

"Precedent Exists for Congressional War Committee." New York *Times*, January 10, 1943.

"Civil War Papers Spilled Secrets." *The Quill*, January–February, 1944, pp. 5–12.

"Free State Government for Louisiana." *Journal of the Illinois State Historical Society*, XXXVII (March, 1944), 85–86.

"Voters in Blue: The Citizen Soldiers of the Civil War." *Mississippi Valley Historical Review*, XXXI (September, 1944), 187–204.

"The Louisiana Unification Movement of 1873." *Journal of Southern History*, XI (August, 1945), 349–69.

"General Ewell to the High Private in the Rear." *Virginia Magazine of History and Genealogy* (April, 1946), 157–60.

"An Analysis of Some Reconstruction Attitudes." *Journal of Southern History*, XII (November, 1946), 469–86.

"The Macs and the Ikes." *American Mercury*, LXXV (October, 1952), 32–39.

"Abraham Lincoln: Principle and Pragmatism in Politics." *Mississippi Valley Historical Review*, XL (June, 1953), 89–106.

"Robert E. Lee." *Compton's Encyclopedia*, 1954.

"The Changing History of Our Civil War." *Commentary*, XVIII (August, 1954), 161–65.

"Investigation: 1862." *American Heritage*, VI (December, 1954), 16–21.

"Freeman, Historian of the Civil War: An Appraisal." *Journal of Southern History*, XXI (February, 1955), 91–100.

"Beauregard at Shiloh." *Civil War History*, I (March, 1955), 17–34.

"Thaddeus Stevens: An American Radical." *Commentary*, XXI (June, 1956), 578–83.

"The Civil War Letters of William L. Cage." *Louisiana Historical Quarterly*, XXXIX (January, 1956), 113–30.

"The Reluctant Warrior: The Diary of N. K. Nichols." *Civil War History*, III (March, 1957), 17–39.

Eighteen essays on Union generals for *World Book*.

"George B. McClellan." *Encyclopedia Americana*.

"The Civil War." *World Book*, 1960, pp. 472–93.

"Reconstruction." *World Book*, 1960, pp. 166–71.

"Abraham Lincoln: The Military Strategist." *Civil War Times*, October, 1959.

Lectures in Military History, No. 2, U.S. Air Force Academy, 1960.

"The Hard School of Experience." Louisville *Courier-Journal*, November 20, 1960, pp. 53–54.

"Grant Moves In." Louisville *Courier-Journal*, November 20, 1960, pp. 73–74.

"A Real Good Hearty War Dies Hard." *New York Times Book Review*, March 12, 1961.

"Impact of Leadership on Planning and Strategy." *The Official Army Information Digest* (August, 1961), 15–21.

"The Politics of the Longs." *Georgia Review*, XV (Spring, 1961), 20–33.

with Stephen Ambros. "The 23d Ohio—Regiment of Presidents." *Civil War Times Illustrated*, III, No. 3 (May, 1964), 22–25.

"Badger Colonels and the Civil War Officer." *Wisconsin Magazine of History*, XLVII, No. 1 (Autumn, 1963), 35–46.

"The Gentleman from Louisiana: Demagogue or Democrat." *Journal of Southern History*, XXVI, No. 1 (February, 1960), 3–21.

"Huey, Lyndon, and Southern Radicalism." *Journal of American History*, LX, No. 2 (September, 1973), 267–93.

"Now, Maybe, We Can Begin to Appreciate Lyndon Johnson." *Southern Voices* (May, 1974), 66–71.